Water is the Animal

Water is the Animal

Fin De Millénaire Reflections Of Planet Earth

James Burrill Angell

Writer's Showcase

San Jose New York Lincoln Shanghai

Water is the Animal
Fin De Millénaire Reflections Of Planet Earth

Writer's Showcase
an imprint of iUniverse.com, Inc.

For information address:
iUniverse.com, Inc.
5220 S 16th, Ste. 200
Lincoln, NE 68512
www.iuniverse.com

ISBN: 0-595-15423-9

Printed in the United States of America

To our mother.

*"Wanderers allow themselves to be
bowled along by the beauty and variety
of the world."*

Bruce Chatwin

January '93: "A starship ride has been promised to you by the galactic wizard." Fortune cookie at the Red Crane Restaurant, Clement Street, San Francisco.

March '93: On the way to Quito, forest of towering tropical cumulus from Cuba southward. First sliver of Ramadan ending moon appears from spectral remnants of lingering Pinatubo glow. Then waning crystalline Venus peeks from dark orange horizon on its journey to an underworld from which it will reappear as the morning Mayan deity months hence. A month ago sickle and planet were paired. Now the drift toward reconciliation same time next year.

Altitude-clean Quito, a refreshing change from lowland Latin America. Qechua Indians roam the 9,000' high colonial streets and fill the cathedral squares in this compact ville surrounded by towering volcanic peaks; the most famous of which, Cotapaxi, looms to the south, a gargantuan glaciated bulge reminiscent of Mt. Ranier, but almost five thousand feet higher!

The first oddity noticed on the Cessna descent into Havana is the lack of traffic. The only ribbon of highway leaving the city (to the southeast), is completely deserted except for one or two cars. The city streets are more like Beijing in that they're full of bicycles, one industry communism promotes.

1

Most of the classic old Chevys that used to ply the *calles* are parked for lack of gas. Beautiful colonial city though, waiting patiently to be revived. It's going to be an ugly land grab when Castro falls. I've got my eyes on a deserted coastal range along the south coast north of Jamaica, the Sierra Maestra. Just a dusty little road winds along the base of these huge green mountains plunging into Caribbean surf: unexploited, like most of that verdant isle.

April '93: These flights are trips down memory lane. Last week, flying along the length of the Keys, it was old snorkeling grounds and coral-dry campsites perched beside banyan tree shallows viewed from a Cessna trip to Havana. Today it's the rich memories of Isla Mujeres, Vallodolid, Chichen Itza and Tulum as we sweep along the dry Quintana Roo coast of the Yucatan toward Guatemala City. The northern tip of Isla Mujeres, first visited after road-tripping down from New York between archaeology jobs, is where I first strung a hammock between palms and snorkeled the days away. A colleague was so culture shocked she didn't speak once we crossed into Mexico until we crossed back over the border. Then returning months later after blowing off lab work in Denver, hitchhiking across country, down the Baja, through heartland Mexico to Palenque, then to Colonial Merida and back across to the Isla before sharing sacred mushrooms with crazy Quebecois. All these thoughts embodied in a glance out a window jetting over the water planet. Tulum: Mayan ruins perched on cliffs dropping into turquoise churning white.

Flying over Andros Island in the Bahamas, one realizes that nature is the greatest abstract expressionist. Deep-blue tidal cuts between convoluted land forms tailing off into capillary-like rivulets that dissipate into lighter blue bordering on white shallows. Offshore, puffs of stationary white sand, underwater clouds, float in the azure shallows, while dark cumulus shadows race along the smooth surface. Eying the sea floor for galleons.

May '93: "Roses red and poppies filled with gentle rain…" After staring at the Earth's surface from above, day after day, one understands that the fragile surface exploited by *Homo sapiens* will rapidly return to nature with a potent virus. It is indeed a thin veneer. What was it Ian Anderson wrote and sang with Jethro Tull? "Will freeways and power lines keep us apart? No, I don't think so, I saw some grass growing through the pavement today!"

The interstate clover-leaf configuration as ceremonial center!

What generation after generation of humanity would have given to skim across the top of sunlit clouds the way we do, yawning, nonchalantly checking our watches.

The Museo Nacional's yellow colonial fortress, pock-marked with bullet holes, has the most wonderful views of downtown San Jose and its volcano encircled locale. The archaeology of Costa Rica! The 1500 year old anthropomorphic, bichrome red ceramics of individuals in cross legged sitting positions are contemporaneous with Moche and Viju pottery from the coastal deserts of Peru. And the flying metates! Toucans and monkeys carved from basalt cling to legs supporting beautifully carved table-like surfaces. The full size funereal beds, also carved from basalt, with bas-relief human and monkey heads encircling the smooth surface meant for the corpse: larger alternating monkeys and toucans top one, while another has somersaulting monkeys gleefully sending the deceased into a playful afterlife. Then there are the three-legged curved basalt metates with surreal animal faces snarling from the tapered end. Or the aesthetically simple round basalt metates with carved monkeys holding up the working table surface with their arms, while their tails blend to form the circular base of the piece. The head cult: statuary with head in one hand and hatchet in another! The basalt balls of all sizes found strewn around the Costa Rican countryside reminiscent of Olmec heads—the same roundness, just no facial features! A culture in the land of fire based on the carving of basalt.

Also the meeting place of ancient technologies, as Clovis points from North America meet "fish tail" points from South America: the only place these projectile points are found side by side. The spectacular carved jade collection, so reminiscent of prehistoric Asian pieces the influence is obvious, and sources for so few pieces identified that the possibility of jade trade between Asian and Central American civilizations has to be considered.

And the peculiar burial packets found in the mangrove swamps of the Caribbean coast. When the corpse's flesh had rotted from the bone, the indigenous people would gather up the cleansed bone, arrange them neatly in a square packet, then bury the skeletal remains in the swamps which cover the eastern portion of the isthmus.

From space, extraterrestrials wouldn't be able to see much evidence of human civilization on the bright side of the planet. But on the dark side, electric lights might be mistaken for some sort of growth, much like the fungi that glow in the deep dark of Earth's forests. The U.S. as successful fungi!

Human cities as a form of lichen. You can almost imagine yourself bending over downtown La Plata, Argentina in its autumnal light, and moving a palm over the rough texture of this primitive yet complex life form.

How about a book with abstract landscapes interspersed with photos of human civilization from on high: reinforcing the primitive nature of *Homo sapiens* settlement, a creature who builds hard shells for protection the same way coral does.

Autumn in Buenos Aires: maples red, sky dark blue and multicolored parrots rooting amongst freshly fallen yellow ginkgo leaves. The geographical and cultural transition one takes in stride, but the seasonal change strikes one intensely. The fresh pungent odor of decaying leaves under a clear southern hemisphere sky brought on flashbacks of cross-country running in high school, and contrasts markedly with the encroaching summer humidity and burgeoning greenery of the Mid-Atlantic states.

Snow-deep soaring foothills of the Andes rise like the Rockies from the Great Plain-like Pampas, then descend into a condensed version of the dry American basin and range found from the western slope of the Rockies to the Sierra and Cascades. Then the central range of the Andes leaps from the desert, its snow clad peaks reaching the blue-black fringes of Earth's atmosphere in a tectonic lurch that thrusts Aconcagua 23,000' above sea-level, before the sharp drop to a foggy California-like coast and polluted Santiago.

Rivers are arteries and feeder streams capillaries. It's the same water-based pattern repeated over and over again on the surface of this and other planets where water once flowed. Whether it's the thigh of a human leg, or the Andean borne, blood-red, silt-laden waters of the Rio Paraguay flowing across the Pampas of South America, water is the animal!

June '93: Streaking above tan Saharan nothingness: its hazy skies and quarter waning moon hanging in contrasting deep blue depths of space, one is reminded more of the surface of Mars with face pyramids and dry riverbeds, than the water planet. Amidst the bleak, alien topography, a rounded area of towering pink sand mountains appears, surrounded by a landscape of intensely black lava. A little later, further to the north, the sand begins again, more yellow this time, and goes on and on and on and on. I think of the camel trading networks that still link Fez to Ouagadougou across a terrain as inhospitable as anything found on our neighboring planets, with the sole exceptions of oxygen and deep well water.

Light-blue horizon, the transition between atmospheric-yellow sand haze and dark blue of the abyss. The void, both finite and infinite, here in its naturalistic rendering.

Turquoise French braid sand bank surfaces from deep blue-black, pointing towards the dry outer islands of Cuba's north shore darkened by towering thunderheads soaring thousands of feet above our cruising altitude to Quito. Looking back to the northwest, the calm Caribbean is a sheet of gold as the sun begins to set; tufts of cotton cumulus close to the surface cast dark shadows, flecking the smooth shimmering surface with transient impurities.

On the return, somewhere north of Ecuador, there is only grey out the window: no Earth, no black of space, just grey with a faint, hazy rising sun encircled by a rainbow ring. The light of consciousness, thus suspended, finds definition in the craft created by the hands of *Homo sapiens:* a solipsistic machine.

July '93: Lake Titicaca's dark depths speared by golden brown knife edge of Isla del Sol ridge—mythic birthplace of Incan people—with snow-capped Nevado Sajama volcano dominating the southwest, and jagged Royal Range covered in myriad glaciers rising high above the 13,000' lake's eastern shore. Illimani, the monster, looms thick in glacial ice behind La Paz's adobe streets lined with bustling markets full of bowler-hatted women in full skirts with dried llama fetuses for sale. The highest capital in the world. The cradle of Aimara civilization at Tihuanaco dating back 4,000 years is here in the dry, light air that makes one dizzy; enhancing the alien nature of a terrain where one can jump up and kiss the abyss.

September '93: Leaving Abidjan, Cote D'Ivoire and its coastal heat and cloudbursts, on the way to Ouagadougou, Burkina Faso with its dry flat desert and adobe dwellings; then up over the Sahara, becoming drier and drier until just south of the Niger River the landscape becomes inhospitable, with the only sign of possible life the arroyos left by intermittent rains. The Niger appears incredulously, its green banks hugging close to the wide shallow waters that cut through the barren landscape, born in Sierra Leone mountains a thousand miles to the west, traveling across baking yellow sand until entering the moist coastal forests north of the Bight of Benin. Then over black mountains of Algerian coast and out over the

Mediterranean headed for the architectural and gastronomical wonder of autumnal Paris after ten days in the African bush. Transition of a lifetime.

From a grungy hotel room in Abidjan that happens to be one of the finest in town, to a charming one in The City of Light down from the Place Vendome toward Tulieres. Breathing the cool, delicate leaf-scented air after the crushing humidity of tropical Africa is a treasure. Walks past cafes bright with light and full of chattering French, along the Seine flowing fast, to Marais with its medieval character and brilliant Picasso Museum, revives the spirit after the pervasive, anxiety inducing smell of death found throughout West Africa.

October '93: A line of pink cumulus dinosaurs trudging toward the delicate necklace of the Florida Keys, their shadows muddy footprints marring the gilded surface of the sunset Caribbean.

On the journey to La Paz, Venus and Jupiter side-by-side in the predawn glow, giving the solar system depth perspective. Then deep orange builds, twinned planets slowly fade in the increasing starlight and huge, snake-like rivers of the Amazon Basin are lit as they slither through endless black rain forest.

North of Santa Cruz de la Sierra, Bolivia: oxbow country. Big muddy rios slicing through forest and marshland bordered by oxbows on either side. Incredible abstract patterns of sickle-shaped brown necklaces carving up the solid greenery with occasional circular ponds of light brown adding to the mosaic. Then farms and roads appear, but only for a short while before an unbroken, impenetrable green-ocean of trees with myriad fat rivers snaking through from the Andes. This goes on for hour after hour at five-hundred-miles-an-hour! If the Amazon Basin is the Earth's lungs, we're in fine shape! Not a sign of *Homo sapiens* until southern Columbia. Environmentalist hype?

November '93: The ancient Shenandoah mountains of the U.S.: they've been eroded for so long that there is a uniformity of pattern to their drainage systems. Mountain valleys are interspersed by descending ridges of equal width, each culminating in a broad snaking river valley that siphons the entire range; which joins with another snaking river and on into exponentially larger and larger systems, all very structured, and organized. Order in age. Compare with the capricious Rockies.

It began as a routine diplomatic courier trip. They all begin that way. The early morning flight originating in Dakar with some twenty-one diplomatic pouches was with one of the region's most notorious carriers: Ghana Airways. After an airport exchange in Banjul, the flight was scheduled to continue on for exchanges in Conakry and Freetown before terminating in Abidjan later that afternoon.

The 737 we flew was a standing joke amongst couriers in Washington who serviced West Africa. Ghana Air only had three planes. Their other 737 could be seen parted-out on the tarmac back in Accra to keep this one aloft, while the DC-10 they owned was recently forbidden by the FAA to continue flights to JFK due to lack of airport security, let alone maintenance. This particular 737 had to be one of the oldest in operation. But it wasn't the engines that were scary, they sounded all right on previous trips, rather it was the tattered state of the plane's interior that gave one an immediate sinking feeling upon boarding: the ripped aisle carpet typically tripped me as I fought for a torn seat, stained and broken into a state of recline, near the front, while the overhead bins dangled precariously, cracked, punctured and unable to close. And seat belts? There weren't any.

The pilots in their rumpled and faded uniforms roamed the galley and aisle during boarding, seemingly unembarrassed by the state of their aircraft. They were as close to gods as you could get in this part of the world without being military, so no one dared comment. All that mattered was it flew. Needless to say, there was no safety demonstration from the dispirited flight attendant as we began to taxi through dry shrubland out to the runway.

Even though I'd taken this plane on two previous trips, it was still a miracle when the entire contraption began thundering along at a speed quick enough for takeoff. When wheels-up came over pirogue-crowded beaches framing the peninsula jutting from the continent like a crooked finger, I found my disbelieving heart and mind maintain anxiety levels typically reached in fight or flight scenarios until the plane gained decent altitude.

The noise of busted overhead bins rattling, coupled with the banter of various languages, made it hard to concentrate on the status of the engines as they propelled us out over the blue Atlantic and the slow turn south past the skyscrapers of downtown rising impressively from the finger's rocky tip. It was better that way. Besides, if anything happened it was never too far to a landing strip. The trip to Banjul was only forty minutes, and likewise the stops downline made for short air time except for the Abidjan leg. By that time, if past was prologue, I'd actually acquire a sliver of faith in the decrepit old craft after several takeoffs and landings.

We got to Banjul just fine. In fact, we were given one of the finest views ever of the city on a sandspit from our sea approach heading upriver. The Gambia River could be seen in its entirety as we eventually banked in to land: from its wide estuary to its rapid diminution in the direction of its mysterious desert origin. Once on the ground I could see the mission contact and expediter waiting with outgoing pouches as we taxied toward the tiny terminal. Before exiting the aircraft, I politely asked the flight attendant if she could save my seat for me, explaining that I was the courier and I'd be flying on to Conakry. She nodded unconvincingly as I went off down the steps.

The escort and I exchanged pleasantries planeside before signing over our respective pieces. After exchanging paperwork we continued to talk shop while keeping an eye on the outgoing pouches that were to be loaded in the rear hold. My pouches for Conakry and Freetown were in the unopened front compartment, so everything seemed fine.......except for when I got back on the plane after all my pieces were loaded and the hatch closed, to discover my second row seat had been taken. The flight was oversold.

I brought this to the attention of the attendant, who looked vacantly down the length of the aircraft and shrugged. I offered to sit in the cockpit jumpseat, which, if I'd been able to, would have solved all sorts of problems later. But no, on this plane the seat had been "removed." After a few awkward moments of staring at each other the attendant showed some initiative by beginning a slow walk along the torn carpet, glancing slowly at each occupied row. I followed obsequiously, when at row twenty-seven, eight rows from the back, she spoke rudely to a woman seated with a young boy. They argued for awhile before the woman looked angrily at me, then motioned for the boy to sit on her lap. She had the aisle seat and made no effort to let me pass. That, coupled with the fact the seat ahead of her was fully reclined, forced me to crunch the two of them into their seat as I passed. It took some doing, and my reward was my very own tattered, reclined seat with a window so yellowed with age I couldn't even see the escort for a reaffirming thumbs-up before departure.

When we eventually rattled down the runway, I frankly couldn't have cared less if we lifted off or not. A crash in such a claustrophobic, suffocating situation would actually have been liberating. But no, the old bird lifted into the sky like an eager fledgling, leaving the opaque, arid Gambian countryside under blossoming cumulus as we headed south along the estuary-carved coast. As I completed paperwork in the cramped space, the woman next to me shot nasty glances and muttered to no one in particular. I just hoped that in Guinea there would be someone planeside pronto, because tactically speaking, I was in no position to be first off the aircraft. Conakry was one of those airports where things could disappear, and quickly.

The irony of the seating problem, as it turned out, is that it didn't matter. About halfway to Conakry, at twenty-five thousand feet, refreshments were served (the lone attendant with a tray of orange drink in plastic cups). The captain came back to chat and have some orange drink himself. No big deal, right? But about five minutes later the co-pilot came back to join his colleague in conversation and enjoy some refreshment as well. The aircraft was obviously on autopilot, but it was still a little disturbing. No one else seemed to pay it the least attention, so I shrugged it off and returned to my trip report. A short time later, as I meditatively sipped the last of my mystery orange and gazed at the absurdity of the situation—bins dangling, woman mumbling, seats broken, two pilots chatting and laughing—we hit a bad patch of turbulence.

The plane dropped precipitously for a few seconds, the pilots actually catching air mid-chuckle before being dashed against the fuselage. A few passengers ended up on their neighbors' laps, but the auto-pilot recovered control and righted the aircraft fairly quickly, so damage was slight. Everyone seemed to shrug the episode off with nervous laughter as the pilots gingerly picked themselves up off the galley floor. But as they rose there was a look of panic on the face of the co-pilot. He stepped toward the cockpit and began tugging frantically on the door. It was locked. The bump had jarred it loose and slammed it shut. The key, if there was one, was apparently in one of their coat pockets, inside.

So there we were, flying south over Guinea Bissau at 500mph with a pair of pilots locked out of the cockpit and twenty-seven diplomatic pouches in the hold. They pulled on the door, they picked at the lock, they kicked it, they hit it, all to no avail. It was obvious to everyone on board what the situation was, but they were remarkably calm. The woman next to me even stopped mumbling. Scrunched in my little corner, I too, took it in stride, initially anyway, sighing it off as typical.

It was rather comical to see the two uniformed men who earlier held themselves so confidently, struggling to remedy the bizarre situation. After about twenty minutes the seriousness of our predicament began to sink in, as the door meant to protect pilots from hijackers refused to budge. Passengers began to shout advice from their seats, but the pilots rudely waved them off. Then a huge, burly man in a dashiki got up from mid-plane to offer his help. The pilots visibly respected his size and concurred to let him try. Lowering his shoulder, the man got momentum in the aisle before hitting the door hard. Refrigerator Perry had nothing on this guy.

The door shuddered, and even buckled a little. The crowd roared and shouted words of encouragement for him to try again. He held up one hand like a savior, reassuring the crowd that on his second try the impediment would collapse and all would be right in the universe again.

On the second attempt he took a longer run down the aisle, but before he got to the bulkhead he tripped on the ragged carpet and went down hard at the feet of the two pilots. He was hurt, and took a while to get up. There was a moan from the gallery. He held his right shoulder and shook his head dejectedly as the flight attendant helped him to his seat. Even the pilots looked at a loss. I glanced out the window, and despite the yellowish tinge, saw the distinctive shape of the Conakry peninsula with its teeming masses jutting out to sea far below.

There was obviously only one solution all along, but the captain hadn't wanted to take it. He sternly marched to the back of the plane, his semi-stoic face revealing the vaguest tinge of anger or embarrassment, it was hard to tell which. This was the only plane that made this run and was half the nation's fleet. Having to replace the door might cost him his job.

After rustling noisily back near the toilets, he reappeared carrying an axe with an unusually long handle. As he strode back up the aisle the sight of the axe startled the passengers into a vocal frenzy. The captain was oblivious, his mind on the long-range ramifications. The co-pilot offered to do the dirty deed, but the pilot would have none of it. He waved his colleague aside, hefted the ungainly instrument over his right shoulder, and with the entire plane in anxious silence, swung down at the locked door handle. The dull edge of the axe caught just a bit of the door before glancing off and narrowly missing his leg. I slumped back in my seat of perpetual recline and muttered "come what will!"

About an hour later, mainly due to the fear-fueled slashings of the co-pilot, there was little left of the door. Never able to bust the lock to pop the door, they opted to slice a hole through the middle of it. Even then it was barely large enough, with jagged metal ripping their clothes as they squeezed through. Problem was, by the time they were back behind the controls, we had passed over not only potentially gorgeous Freetown, with its beaches and high green mountains plunging dramatically into azure seas, but also strife-torn Monrovia, and were headed into the abyss of the South Atlantic, some three degrees from the Equator.

After a sharp turn back to the northeast, the pilot eventually came over the radio and apologized for the inconvenience. He said that due to low fuel there was no way we could make it back to our scheduled destinations. We were flying on to Abidjan. Half the plane was understandably enraged, given the fact that flights to the missed stops were a rarity. Yet it's always interesting how soon people revert to their old habits after escaping tragedy. I was content to be alive. The pouches would only be delayed a week, and as far as I knew there were no priority pieces. Flying in over the pounding surf and palm-fringed lagoons of Cote d'Ivoire, then past the soaring skyscrapers of the harbor city, Abidjan had never looked so good.

When we landed I found my trusty mission escort planeside with all pouches efficiently loaded onto carts ready to go, but perplexed at the Conakry and Freetown pieces still in the mix. I raised my hand reassuringly as she began to ask the obvious and said, "You're not going to believe this one!"

Dec. '93: Just ahead of a grey cold front sweeping into D.C. from the northwest, we lift off from Andrews into twilight and head out over the Chesapeake filled with freighters in the dying light. Back to the west a thin orange glow suggests Pinatubo fallout still lingers in the upper atmosphere. Then over the Delmarva peninsula and the faint beaches of Rehobeth, before the dark abyss below and above make the glowing instrument panel the center of the universe. Not a star to be seen.

The early morning light several hours later reveals the rocky Azores scattered across the eastern Atlantic like pebbles cast from the hand of a giant. The strange sound of Portuguese fills the mild morning air as we wait for refueling. A few hours later it's off again over the vast expanse of dark-blue Atlantic until the sandy shores of North Africa fill the cockpit window.

Rabat, western outpost of Islam, surrounded by a massive red wall as it sits atop a defensive bluff. A two-walled city, with the medina surrounded by a smaller, more ancient wall: separating modern structures from ancient minarets, mosques and labyrinthian streets lined with ancient wooden doors carved in that most beautiful of written languages. Men wander the narrow streets like monks of some ancient order in hooded gowns of dark colors called *jalabas*, while women of the faith wear billowing multi-colored cloths that hide everything except the face.

The heat and dust of the city, the dry expanse of desert and the snow-capped Atlas mountains of Morocco and Algiers give way to extreme wet weather and winter darkness of Europe. Germany's rigidity is in cold contrast to rich Islamic culture, and to the warm light and stark mountains of Homer's wine dark sea the following day.

Athens, after ten years. Memories come flooding back with the sight of ships leaving Piraeus for the islands. The clarity of the city in mid-winter is refreshing, having only experienced its polluted summer. Then up off the tarmac with a perfect view of glistening Parthenon and Agora out the window, then Sounion and Poseidon's temple before seeing the Cyclades laid out to the south like orange jewels in a sea of mercury. Ios slips by, and with it the memories of a decade before: dolphins riding the prow of a Greek ferry, hiking the pine mountains of Crete, exploring the ancient ruins of Knossos and meeting my wife on that very isle passing below…which led to Cairo and the memories of nine years ago that will soon be revisited, and Giza and Aswan and Israel and back to London and kids and San Francisco…

Giza is the perfect expression of a civilization obsessed with death, burial and the afterlife: each pyramid a beautifully arranged city of the dead, for priests and high officials were entombed en masse around the bases of the three elaborate royal burial mounds. Closer to the pyramids, dismantled funeral barges used to transport the royal mummy to its final resting place were found. Like present day felucahs, they were an integral part of life on the Nile, and were essential in the afterlife, for Egyptians believed a pharaoh sailed across the sky with the sun god at death. Seeing the slow yet graceful felucahs with their lateen rigged sails moving timelessly through the contemporary metropolis, makes one wonder if the pharaohs *aren't* living in eternity, and eternity is right here.

We roar down the green line of the Nile as it's guided through baking desert sands by towering rocky cliffs. At a sharp bend below is Thebes, capital of the New Egyptian Empire that stretched from northern Syria to southern Nubia. The Valley of the Kings, founded to make their burial sites less conspicuous than the older pyramids to the north, is seen clearly in all its dry, craggy, royal splendor in the desert cliffs behind the gigantic Colossi of Memnon, alertly seated in the green floodplain for 3500 years. Memories of the great hall of papyrus pillars and entrance way lined with sculptured lions at the Temple of Amun in Karnak north of town, mix with visions of Napoleon wresting the obelisk from its ancient site at the Temple of Luxor to raise in the Place de la Concorde, and Tutankhamun's rich chamber from that barren valley below traveling the world. The distinctive shape and steps of Queen Hatshepsut's funerary temple can be made out flush against the steep cliffs even from this height. Then it's off over Nubian Desert streaked with wadis and camel trails toward the Red Sea and down to Yemen, leaving the ancient Nile in our wake.

The approach to Sanaa, Yemen brings us skimming over rough, Grand Canyon-like mountain mesas with ancient stone villages perched on steep cliffs with terraced fields filling what little tillable terrain there is. Towers rise from each village like watch towers in Tolkien. If primitive humanity exists anywhere, it is down there; or if primitive is too politically incorrect, then time capsule of the distant past. The buildings of Sanaa are one of the great architectural sights, and only slightly more advanced than the mountain settlements. This must be what Jericho looked like before the earthquake; sure proof that after 9,000 years nothing really has changed. Adobe skyscrapers, incredibly unstable, soar six to eight stories high with delicate whitewash patterns around their tops and midsections. All men have decorative knives dangling from their leather belts, one of the prime reasons why the Black Rhino of East Africa are endangered: the handles are made from their horns.

Leaving Yemen heading north, the Saudi side of the Red Sea is filled with atolls: turquoise necklaces ringed by white surf in a sea of dark blue depths, bordered by sand-storm yellow desert bleak in the east. Then we turn over Mecca, headed across the great sandy expanse of the Arabian peninsula, destination: Dhahran, jewel of the Persian Gulf.

Riyadh, isolated below in the heart of a vast desert wilderness, safe from foreign ideas, and safe from itself. Too bad the glory days of endless cash are over. In Dhahran the Saudis treat us like shit (The Khobar Barracks we stay in are bombed two years later killing seventeen American servicemen and women). So much for our military help in the Gulf War. We were mercenaries after all. They deserve their isolation.

Seven days ago with the family on the Monterey Peninsula, it was Robinson Jeffers' bouldered Thor House ("Lean on the silent rock until you feel its divinity") overlooking sea otters cracking shellfish on their tummies as they sway atop kelp forests tall in the cold, nutrient rich waters. Now, a week later, cruising down the Persian Gulf over the Straight of Hormuz at 30,000' after leaving the mean sands of Saudi: we're headed to Delhi.

From the glistening granite of Carmel to the sparkling marble of the Taj Mahal exquisitely inlaid with gemstone floral patterns. The bus trip from Delhi to Agra cuts to the heart of the Indian subcontinent's timeless poverty. Third World decrepit adobe commercial strips line village roads, while in the country prehistoric looking grass shelters with towers of dung for heating and cooking are stacked in intricately woven patterns. Bicycles clog the streets, camels pull carriages stacked with a variety of goods and cattle roam at will, stopping traffic as they saunter obliviously to one wonders where. That is the Zen of them. Healthy too, better off than most Indians.

The Taj Mahal and its surrounding red sandstone temples surpass all expectations. One of the most beautiful complexes on the planet: the blinding white dome and towers perched above the sandy banks of the sleepy Yamuna, with wading water buffalo, men casting nets, and women and children doing the washing in the heat of the day, speaks of eternity.

Then up out of smoggy, congested Delhi and what shines there perched on the northern horizon making the spirit soar? The Himalayas! In the direction of our destination of Islamabad, soars Nanga Parbat at 8200 m., while further around to the east Nanda Devi juts above the flat sub-continent. What a lurch!

Pakistan, arid and flat, Indus like the Nile as it cuts through the Thar desert piled high with sand dunes on the way down to Karachi. But, truthfully, the only word that sums up the uninspiring terrain is bleak. Drab adobe huts clustered together in one of the driest areas on earth, interrupted only by torrential flooding during the monsoon, makes for a hell of an existence. It must have been a different ecosystem when the great Harappan Civilization, contemporaneous with the Mesopotameans, flourished along the banks of the now barren Indus. I would believe in God or Mohammed too under such circumstances. Then we turn west over Karachi and follow the path of Alexander's victorious army along the rugged beauty of the Makron coast. Dry, jagged mountains plummet sharply into deep blue Arabian sea waters. Alexander lost half his victorious troops here on their return journey to Iran. Amazing they didn't all die traveling through such a fierce land. Their collective agony laid the groundwork for his own end, as well.

Flying into Fujiera on the United Arab Emirate's coast, ships loading oil, and ships moored en masse in the harbor under naked desert peaks. Minarets rise above the few trees and between the barren hills in this otherwise sleepy coastal village. Then on into Kuwait City with its mansions and expensive cars filling newly repaved roads and five star hotels: oil money what the war was all about. No sign of any Iraqi attempt to destroy the city itself, but the desert outside of town is blotched black with oil fire stains, cut up into bunkers and littered with burned out hulks of vehicles and tanks across the vast expanse. We divert a little to view the highway of death, and even from on high it still exudes the stench of a killing field.

The Saudi sand, an extension of the Sahara, is as alien as any other planet surface, except when it rises spectacularly into rugged coastal peaks and plunges into the dark-blue Red Sea. Across the water Egyptian mountains do the same, thus pinching the waters north to the Suez and Aqaba with the help of that barren triangle tipped by Mount Sinai, the center of the world. Why not? In a glance is some of the most influential terrain in human history: the green limned Nile lined with Pyramids and temples cuts through desert sands off over the mountains to the west, while below are the craggy mountains in which Moses and his people wandered and spoke to God. Up the Gulf of Aqaba (this has to be one of the clearest days in history, as the view extends to the Dead Sea) and beyond is Jerusalem, while Petra hides herself in the dry Jordanian mountains between the Dead and Red Seas, perched over the Negev desert. Just a little behind us along the Red Sea coast to the south is Mecca. If you could pinpoint a center for most of human history's major religious events, they would all be within a short distance of the southern triangular tip of the Sinai. And on a map of the world there is certainly something navel-like about it. The omphalos!

Passing directly over gnarly Mt. Sinai, where contact with the deity was made and below which the Monastery of St. Catherine stands in remembrance of that event, the Suez canal can be seen clearly to the north slicing through the desert sands. The huge metropolis descended from the pharaohs appears in the polluted distance as we cross just south of the canal and head northwest over uninhabited desert. After climbing the pyramids of Giza a week ago we are back, and there they are, lining the desert bluffs above the narrow green floodplain of the Nile just south of Cairo. Some six pyramids from Saqqara to Giza sit stoically overlooking the river and the contemporary insanity with ancient resolve. Van Daniken just might have been on to something after all. They look remarkably alien staggered above the river valley, their grey color defining the triangular shapes against the backdrop of desert sand. The mind flashes on when the city was smaller, and this series of huge pyramids sat staring out over green fields and trees and a wide, clean flowing river filled with white-winged felucahs…

Leaving Cairo and the ancient pyramids we head across the verdant Nile delta and then over ancient Alexandria. I stare to the west, into the hazy desert past toward Siwah, and wonder if it really was the final resting place of Alexander. Then along the length of Crete from east to west with the 4,000 year old ruins of Knossos, the seat of Classical Greek civilization, plainly in view. The southwestern end of the island with its spectacular mountains and pine forests and Samaria gorge dropping into the sea triggers halcyon memories of time fully lived on that very earth below; scent of orange blossom blends with the piney taste of ouzo in the mind's eye. Souda harbor, on the north side of the island, where the British barely escaped Nazi paratroopers and I met a slew of friends on the ferry from Piraeus, reminds me of the fleeting nature of one's personal history and that of the world.

Hitting the Italian coast, then flying over Rome and its faded glory and on into gloomy Frankfurt, ugly after the destruction of W.W. II. It is said in Germany that the reason Frankfurt is so stark is because it was the home of Jewish banking before the war. After the old city was leveled, its former reputation lived on, so it remained unreconstructed. When it was finally rebuilt, it was in devil-may-care-fashion. One can almost trace the path of Western Civilization in a day of flying (*the center* (Sinai) *cannot hold*).

The extremes of the last month: Carmel to Himalayas to Mid-Eastern desert to snow-capped peaks of southern Greenland with sun low on the southern horizon six days from the shortest day of the year.

January '94: Sauntering through Buenos Aires' Recoleta cemetery in a dream-like state. Mausoleums of marble grandeur crowded together: a congested city of death with high, white adobe walls vainly keeping time and the city of fury at bay. Recoleta, resting place of Evita Peron and the remains of elite Buenos Aires families. Wealth built this tightly packed necropolis, the gold plaques decorating vault walls tell of the important lives within. As one gazes into the cobweb clogged depths, the family through time is seen stacked on shelves that disappear into a subterranean abyss. Above, angels and sculpted turrets rise to the heavens, the brightness of black marble blinding in its intensity. But a second look into this particular vault reveals the topmost coffin's lid at one end has rotted away. There, lying exposed to the elements by the steady drip of time, is the noble Doctor Gonzalez's bleached skull and upper torso for all the world to see, despite the contrivance of a marble structure built for eternal preservation.

Buenos Aires waterfront strewn with trash and fearless rats with the mange. The fetid stench of the big muddy (Rio de la Plata) sloshes past freighters from around the world off-loading where the Pampas meet the estuary. Just up the hill European sophistication: Plaza San Martin, Calle Florida and the wonderful Hotel Claridge. Always amazing how closely juxtaposed the real and fantasy worlds are, the latter of course created to avoid the former.

Then the night flight from B.A. to Miami. To the east and down about twenty-thousand feet, lightning leaps in brilliant flashes from cloud to cloud, lighting up huge thunderheads rising monstrously over the Amazon Basin. Above the rain forest fireworks, a sparkling Big Dipper lies on its side in a crystal clear universe; then a flaming shooting star slashes downward just past the bucket end, leaving a lingering exclamation point in the upper atmosphere of a water planet, spinning, existing somewhere.

March '94: Due to a large load going into Yaounde, Cameroon, a truck trip overland from the port city of Douala through thick, mountainous jungle past rain-swollen rivers, is required. Checkpoints along the road every twenty kilometers are set-up by armed individuals of unknown affiliation. With only myself and a driver in a vehicle that had EMBASSY emblazoned alongside, each barricade became a potential life threatening experience. The driver had some sort of gift-for-the-gab, because after lengthy talks at each post, with heart beating wildly, their guns remained slung and they would motion us on. Yaounde was paradise after a grueling, scary ride, even though it looks as if it was just hacked from the forest: freshly turned bright red soil contrasting with dark green trees and shrubs.

Africa in microcosm: Douala: glistening black man with loin cloth and spear chasing something large thrashing through tall grass between the runway and thick jungle. He sets and throws as the Air Afrique Airbus fires its engines for takeoff, leaps joyfully, then bends to jerk his weapon out of an unseen carcass.

Woman in Cotonou, Benin squatting in colorful garb, taking a piss just off the wingtip as we prepare for takeoff. She looks at us nonplussed as she does her thing, while we stare back with equivalent disinterest.

April '94: Leaving D.C. in exquisite springtime: white marble of the monuments contrasted by soft green buds, cherry blossoms and billowy cloud in deep blue.

Rabat, Jerusalem of the west, clear light bathing fortress walls of red sandstone. Good to be back. The Alhambra perched above a river mouth sea harbor with its rose gardens and flocks of songbirds chattering away in recollection of when the Arabic world *was* civilization. Still as good as it gets in moments like this. Medina shops full of old muskets sheathed in camel bone, musty hookah, ancient Berber carpets of the tightest weave and wildest abstract designs, and the bustle of the crowd: some dressed western, most in *jalabas*, interspersed with the red towering hats and dangling tassels of the occasional water seller.

Nouackchott, Mauritania: The Starlifter has to abort a landing because of camels on the runway, then when we're finally on the ground a couple of palm trees have to be chopped down so our wings can make it into the arrival area. Some of the most desolate country on the planet, then this smallish shanty town with ramshackle housing stretching out into a vast wasteland. What planet is this? Why is this city here? The road north is the beach at low tide, but keep an eye out for the beached freighter!

Bangui, Central African Republic. The dry heat from the sub-Sahara is a wonderful change after the heat and humidity of the west. Slender wooden crafts ply the brown Ubangi. Zaire anarchy only two hundred yards across the crowded waterway. People at night lounge under the few street lights to read: there is no other electricity. Flame trees burning red on a rocky promontory jutting into the water, with wooden canoes drawn up on the sandy beaches below. Then, jetting down the length of the behemoth as it merges with the Congo, the deep jungle slowly gives way to a savannah that becomes sparser the closer to Luanda one gets.

Luanda, Angola: This nation's strife torn countryside can't be viewed from above, but once on the ground the airport is the focal point for all the absurdities of contemporary Africa. U.N. relief planes crowd the runway disgorging food for the innocents caught in the civil war, while nearby Russian cargo planes unload arms for government troops fighting Savimbi's rebels, who apparently crave democracy. Amongst the mayhem, several private Lear jets sneak out, spiriting the diamond wealth from a country that cannot feed itself. The rape is complete. Luanda, though, is a beautifully situated coastal city with red-tiled roofs, a fine harbor and beautiful beaches. There is definitely a Mediterranean feel, evidence of its Portuguese past. The dry, light-green savannahs on the way further south, mingled with scattered trees and dark green growth crowding myriad arroyos, give the landscape toward Namibia a geometrically abstract beauty.

Then the incredible emptiness of the brush terrain of southern Angola and Northern Namibia; only becomes drier and bleaker the further south we blast. Total nothingness reveals itself, the Kalahari, scrub-covered, erosion scarred nothing. Makes the red and yellow drifting sands of northwest Africa seem downright lively. Into Botswana where the landscape becomes more interesting: mesas and sage-like plants fill the vistas, much like New Mexico. Venus emerges from the rose red of a stunning sunset, only to be outdone by a full moon resting in the east paired with Jupiter. Dry, perfect temperature after the oppressive humidity of West Africa. English speaking, too, and a general friendliness and even cleanliness that doesn't exist in the west of the continent. History making as well: the first democratic elections in the three hundred year history of South Africa occurs the next morning. Gaborone is twenty miles from the border, Pretoria seventy, so feel a part of history watching the early returns on South African news. Oh, Mandela!

Harare, Zimbabwe: The British definitely got the best parts of Africa. This place is more like Europe—big deciduous trees, open fields, some even planted with corn. Salisbury, the former colonial name of the capital, fits it well in that English way, for the city is small, clean and civilized. Of course, being at about four thousand feet, with dry air and big sky reaching from horizon to horizon, feels great after the lowland humidity of our previous stops. There are low, unhealthy regions of Zimbabwe, and on the flight out we trace the path of one of them: the Zambesi valley and its namesake river. Talked with a woman who caught cerebral malaria there. She beat the long odds, and treats every day now as a miracle. We follow the brown beast draining the interior all the way to the deserted beaches framing Mozambique.

Then its over the Madagascar Channel, deep, deep blue in its break from the mainland, before atolls ringed with white foam closer to the far shore. Then Madagascar with its Northern California terrain of barren round grass hills broken by arroyos filled with trees. Into the central mountain range the same barren hills increase in size along with the villages, always with two churches side by side, one pagan, one Christian. Antananarivo nestled in a valley around a lake is about as far removed from civilization as one can get, distance-wise, but it has a charm and civility found few other places in this area of the globe. Up off the end of the island the same topography continues to be reminiscent of California wine country, until it drops into the sea on the way to the tropical Comoros. On into Dar es Salaam, yet another malarial African outpost on a harbor that has seen better days. Zanzibar off the coast looks intriguing, but I want to get back into the high country and dry air and that's just where we're heading tomorrow.

Kenya very similar to the Black Hills of North America, except there is an 18,000' volcano by the name of Kilimanjaro to the south, and herd upon herd of wild, wild life roaming the high plains. Instead of elk, deer, buffalo and antelope found in its topographical equivalent in the States, there are gazelles by the thousands, antelope of all varieties, lion of course, giraffe, warthog etc., etc. Big sky country half way round the globe. I feel right at home here. Fleecy clouds with a menacing tinge streak across an altitude sky of lengthy vistas of light and shadowy mountains of green. To the east, Nairobi's few tall buildings mark *Homo sapiens* territory in the cool high plains. Just another animal.

Then up past Mt. Kenya's 18,000' brilliance before heading out over the bleak Great Rift Valley, home of Olduvai Gorge and the earliest human ancestors: *Australiopithicus.* It's as if the earth opened up here in great cataclysm and disgorged the species that would eventually threaten the globe: *Homo habilis* to *Homo sapiens,* and reinforces the middle earth origin myths of many indigenous peoples. Lake Rudolph, a catchment for runoff from Ethiopian highlands that go no further: waters settle here to evaporate. The long narrow lake traces the line of the valley, dry, barren mountains hemming it in. Greenery soon returns after the lifeless stretches of the Chalbi desert, and continues with the gain in altitude up over the mountains surrounding Addis Ababa. But the fecund ground disappears quickly as the mountains drop dramatically into an erosion scarred desert speckled with ancient volcanoes and their black rivers of lava winding through endless maize colored sand all the way to the turquoise waters of the Red Sea at Djibouti.

Set on the tip of a tree-covered sand bar, Djibouti juts into the ocean between a finger of water slicing into the desert, and the Red Sea's mouth across from Aden. The finger is lined by sharp, bone dry peaks, ending in an untouched inland desert beach of bleach white sand two miles long. Up out of sleepy Djibouti, Mt. Jabal Sabir looms from the tip of the Saudi peninsula as it thrusts into the Indian Ocean at the Gulf of Aden. Immediately across the teal finger, a sharply eroded rise tops out on a plateau of primordial topography. Circular holes litter the ground, cracked rust-colored soils circling each with black lava flows winding off like frozen river styxs. Then sickly green lakes appear with frosted saline borders in a flat valley before the entire plateau breaks up into Monument Valley-like mesas and massive escarpments with remote villages scattered sparsely through the dessicated land. Each village in Eritrea has at its center a circular yurt-looking building: Coptic Christianity via Egypt. Asmara, the new capital after twenty-years of civil war, sits at 8,000' on the lip of high desert that plunges dramatically into the Red Sea. It must have been founded as an escape from the intense desert heat of the coast, which at Massawa, the sea-level port a stone's throw from Asmara, is the hottest place on the planet. Obviously, the only reason why the Ethiopians fought so hard and long was to keep from being landlocked. This country is barren, there can't be much of worth here.

But Asmara is a time capsule of the most wonderful sort. Italian architecture from the thirties, pastel colored houses, bougainvillea draping adobe walls, mosques, minarets, Christian churches with a European look, palm trees lining the major thoroughfare. The language, Tegrene, is cousin to Arabic and the people are a mix between that race and black Africa. It would be the perfect place to disappear. The escarpment that drops so dramatically to the east, is contrasted to the west by long deep valleys running down to an empty, unbroken expanse of dirty-sand desert, that becomes beautifully yellow at Khartoum, that grand meeting place of both Blue and White Niles.

The Blue Nile is the smaller of the two as they weave out of the desert haze from the south. They join in the heart of what is now a desert shanty town, where General Gordon and his men were slaughtered by the Mahdi a little over one hundred years ago. The city itself dates from that time—there was little before, and looking about one has to wonder maybe there was a reason for that. General Gordon's end, in fact, might be the ultimate example of dying for some abstract notion. One 360 degree gaze would have told any soldier or general all he needed to know. The shanty towns peter out into the desert, then stop, as if they too are terrified of it: only the greater fear of fighting in the south keeps these sprawling camps growing. Not even the banks of the Nile north of Khartoum are populated, just empty desert sand coming down to the waters' edge. Imagine in your mind traveling from the Nile in Sudan, all the way across the continent to Mauritania: bleak nothingness for three thousand miles, but one hell of a continent.

The combined Nile makes huge sweeping turns through the desert above Khartoum, past the ancient ruins of Meroe, before being stopped at the Aswan Dam and Lake Nasser. Its blue waters pooling back to the relocated ancient site of Abu Simbel makes one wonder how many other sites lay under the calm waters in the valley of the sixth cataract. Then, Abu Simbel's reconstruction on higher ground having passed, all there exists on this planet's surface is the steady march of sand for one thousand miles to the shores of the Mediterranean. Siwah again lost in a sandstorm.

Then the boot of Italy and its villages clinging to precipitous hillsides boggles the mind after the flat, endless desert of North Africa. But dead ahead, even more outrageous, is the profusely smoking, snow-clad summit of Mt. Etna, soaring 12,000' over the orange-scented island of Sicily. To the north, just off the island's coast, three more volcanoes jut towards the heavens from the seafloor, forming three small islands. Catania sits below in Etna's shadow, awaiting the time when she smokes quietly no more. After a soft spring evening sipping red wine on her lava hardened shores, it's up past Etna's flanks toward Palermo. Dramatic headlands carved by the sea sharply delineate terra firma from the world of Poseidon. Sardinia's unspectacular terrain passes to the west, followed by the beckoning crazy grey mountains of Corsica. The Alps deep in snow crowd the north-eastern horizon, their peaks towering over the dry beauty of Provence. A little further north Mt. Blanc dominates the crowded field to the east, while the Rhone drains the Massif Central to the west. Then Lake Geneva sparkles, cutting a dynamic glacially carved swath well into the Alps toward Sion, and a distant, spindly Matterhorn. European civility at its extreme found in Helsinki's cooly refreshing spring: cafes, nightclubs, pastel architecture, huge ferries, pine forests that stretch as far as the eye can see, everything that a place like Khartoum is not.

May '94: If you took satellite images of Virginia 200 years ago and compared them to today's, you would see the same kind of "development" that is taking place in very limited parts of the Amazon basin. Are we telling Third World countries crushed by mammoth debt loads that it was O.K. for us to do it over three hundred years, building strong countries in the process, but they can't do the same, because *they* are destroying the environment? We've already transformed ours. Having flown over both the Amazon Basin and the Pacific Northwest many times, the latter is far more devastated.

June '94: The summer of '94 will go down as some sort of record of travel. Coming up from Costa Rica's fecundity as May moved toward June, from toucans, scarlet macaws and sloths of the pastel colored, impatiens-laden jungle floors and waterfalls absorbed while rafting the Pacuare River, to the record setting heat of Washington, only to find later relief in Rio and Buenos Aires: perfect seventy-degree weather in the former and downright dreary winter in the latter, with lingering autumn leaves clinging tenaciously past their time. Flying into Santiago on the clearest day ever: Aconcagua soaring to record height from sea level and the rest of the snow-deep range as spectacular as any as the Air France Airbus descends from the heavens into the continually smog-obscured capital. In sharp contrast a few days later is the languid backwater of Asuncion, Paraguay, melting in the heat of its own irrelevance. Buenos Aires' dreary winter blues interrupted only by the passion for Maradona and the World Cup: the city coming to a complete standstill during game time. The life brought by the games is halted when their star tests positive for drugs, and returns to normal grey patterns when the national team subsequently loses to Italy. Then its back to D.C. and more intense tropical heat.

The 4th brings the Palisades Parade colorfully heading up MacArthur Boulevard. The candidates for Mayor are all there, foraying bravely into the teeth of white Washington. The most illustrious of the bunch is the former Mayor busted for crack abuse on live cameras a few years earlier. After he and the boos fade, the local gay marching band and the neighborhood kids in a flotilla of bikes with patriotic streamers, crawl past behind the local fire engine on their way to free hot dogs and coke on the sports field. The memories of such an all-American afternoon linger as I board a plane for London later that evening.

In the morning, after dropping off material with the Secretary of State, I'm at Grosvenor House overlooking Hyde Park. Take a walk down memory lane through Hyde and Kensington Parks via paths angling through forests of horse chestnut that blew my mind when they were flowering ten years earlier. To Green Lake, then up past the Orangery and the Palace to bustling Queensway and Bayswater and the dump of a Bed and Breakfast where we holed up for that winter and spring after the Negev. Then to the greatest Indian food ever at Khan's down on Westbourne Grove and the spiciness of the food making the mind hallucinate and ten years becomes the present or close to it, and all those memories that were once reality take on the immediacy of the chicken jalfreze. The intensity of the meal multiplied by the fact that less than twenty-four hours ago Marion Barry was unctuously parading though Northwest D.C., waving off his past as if it were irrelevant. Which of course it is in the long run. Later, hanging in pubs, walking through Green and St. James parks to Whitehall, meditating on pick-up football matches played amidst ancient trees with the intensity of the World Cup. Then on past Bodicea and across Westminster Bridge to gaze back on the sunset view of Parliament Monet caught so masterfully: the setting sun bathing the bridge and houses in a reddish orange glow. Then twenty-four hours later it is home to D.C., flying over spectacular Ring of Kerry cliffs and Skerry Island outpost of monks, ice bergs, the snow clad emptiness of Greenland and the bookend cliffs of Newfoundland.

Four days later it's off on the same route, watching the sun glow fade and the twilight illuminate the rugged Maine coastline and the Bay of Fundy until darkness comes with the ocean crossing. Paris in the morning, the heart of the city and its wealth of stunning architecture lit in first light. Transferring to Air France for the long run to the slave coast of Africa, the transition from the First World to the Fourth. The topography of the North African coastline exudes a shift in human perspectives: where the vast Saharan desert surrenders to the sea a psychological shift takes place in the humans separated north and south by the Mediterranean sea. You can sense this even from 30,000'. A desert of such magnitude, of such desolation, forged the Islamic mentality by continually reminding the inhabitants along thin strips of land between it and the sea of their ultimate meaninglessness. This holds true in Islam's birthplace along the shores of the Red Sea. The constant presence of the void embodied by topography does not exist north of the Mediterranean. The Sahara is so empty on its southern edge that the first hint of green south of the northern bulge of the Niger is a relief to eyes strained from staring at the subtle variations of yellow and orange sand for hour after hour. Imagine setting out from Fez for a three month crossing on camel back. The lagoons and crashing surf of Abidjan are downright refreshing. Even its shanty towns bustling with life are a welcome contrast with that primal land of sand and rock to the north.

From the relative stability of Abidjan it is off to the war zone of Liberia. Coming into Monrovia the plane cannot find the runway due to low cloud. The cockpit door is ajar, and being seated in the first row of a decrepit Fokker 100, I can hear every nerve-wracking word gazing out the window at a swamp coming up fast. At the last moment, heart in mouth, and questions of why I'm doing this job with kids at home racing through my mind, the harried tribal tongue in the cockpit intensifies, the engines are gunned and we abort a swampy landing and climb through greyness that finally dissipates over crashing surf and beach as we glide out over the ocean to regroup. Sure enough, from two miles offshore we can see the runway clearly just off the beach, and make a skimming turn back toward land. Nervous relief gives way to the horrific, pot-holed runway and shanty terminal and bullet-riddled planes on the ground. The international airport, Robert's Field, is a battle ground, so this airfield built for Cessnas in the heart of Monrovia is the only way into the country. The Fokker almost runs out of runway, so we nearly end up in the swamp anyway. The air traffic control tower is two floors high but is as much of a shack as the shanty terminal. Uniformed soldiers of unknown affiliation wander around fully armed. Locals in rags, some clothed only in ripped underwear, walk with plastic bowls on their heads across the runway toward a slum paralleling the airport and bordering the swamp. Obviously no instrument landings in a land that CNN forgot. The mission staff in Liberia get a 25% pay increase and are not allowed to bring family. With a few partially clothed skeletons at the end of the runway, and Kaplan's "Coming Anarchy" fresh in mind, it's good to get back to Abidjan's relative prosperity alive.

The following day it is on to Niamey, the capital and only city of substance in Niger. It consists of several tall buildings and shanty towns along a thin green strip bordering the great desert river of Africa. Talk about a human outpost stranded in a most inhospitable land. The only reason for its existence surely was as a center for the desert caravans trading with the black tribes of the coast. Slavery was part of the trade, whether bought by Arabs or Tuaregs or Berbers. But what goes on here now? Slave trade is ongoing, but what else? Not much, given the size of the place. The next stop, Ouagadougou, isn't even on a good sized river, yet in the middle of nowhere is a city of great activity. Scooters buzz noisily along city streets, stalls crowd the sidewalks selling everything imaginable, while colorful placards filled with heads advertise haircuts of differing styles. Its adobe housing and dirt streets in a desert setting interspersed by occasional stunted trees reminds one of West Texas. The desert-dry air feels good after the heat and humidity of Abidjan. South of the northern bulge of the Niger, one wonders where water comes from.

Into Bamako late at night with heat lightning giving shutter-like glimpses of the desert terrain. A hazy moon reflected in the Niger at a twenty-year flood high. In the morning, after a night in a hotel room with decade old bug corpses still clinging to the walls, a snake skin framed mirror with matching headboard and no T.V. or radio, a dismal face cloth my only towel, I take petite dejeuner on the balcony overlooking the wide Niger moving swiftly between high bluffs crowded with slender pirogues. The swollen waters flow in a northeasterly direction toward Timboktou and Mopti, before turning back south towards Niamey. A muezzin from a minaret near the hotel beckons the faithful to prayer in another desert outpost built by desert caravans through the centuries.

Dakar, situated on the westernmost point in Africa, is a breath of fresh sea air, surrounded as it is on three sides by the Atlantic. Its downtown marche is a fantastic blend of color, from batik to coppersmithing to fruit and vegetable and meat stands. The beaches are nestled in coves between the sheer rock cliffs, but the pollution and undertows make swimming precarious. Goree island, off the peninsula's skyscraper crowded tip, was settled by the Dutch in the late 1400's, and is perfectly situated for its infamous slave trade. The claustrophobic dungeons where thousands of slaves from the interior were crammed awaiting shipment, can still be experienced. The pastel colonial architecture belies the horror of the place; which segues nicely into the next destination, The Gambia, another former slave embarkation point.

An English speaking colony on a sand spit where the Gambia River widens to join the eastern Atlantic, Banjul is the capital of a fecund slice of terra firma that quickly dries out as the river narrows upstream towards its mysterious head waters in the Sahara. The land bordering the river is flat and well forested, with marshy lagoons and islands. To the south, southern Senegal wraps around this tiny country, completing what was to become the nation of Senegambia. Two days after I left, the first coup in the history of the country took place. The democratically elected president escaped death by hopping on board an American amphibious vessel that happened to be on a tour of African ports. Many Gambians thought the whole thing was staged by the Americans since they were there to spirit the president away. Impossible to believe given the inconsequential nature of this area of the world.

Then comes Bissau, perched in a classic African backwater, hidden on the northern edge of an estuary emptying into a brackish sea island mix. Then the mountains begin, and spectacular they are, with huge cliffs dropping off sea-facing plateaus. Fetid Conakry sits on an impressive promontory that points toward a forested circular reef. On further examination from the air, the reef must be a volcanic cone. This feature coupled with the mountains and cliffs looming behind Conakry, make for prehistoric terrain: their dark presence shielding terra incognita and the inland head waters of the Niger from view.

Freetown, Sierra Leone is down the coast a bit, perched in what could be one of the great settings for a city. At the foot of high forested mountains that plunge onto white Atlantic beaches, this could be a stunning place, but no. It is a scary disappointment. To get into town from the airport and back is a decrepit ferry ride that only makes the crossing twice a day, making an airport run an all day affair. The best hotel in town is seedy, with thugs in combat gear prowling the premises. Monrovia is just a little ways down the coast, so in the end of my West African travels, is my beginning. And word has it that Liberian guerrillas, after decimating their own country, are heading north to set up bases in Sierra Leone to further rape and pillage, thus ensuring the continuation of the primal anarchy our species is known for. The next day, after returning to Abidjan, Air France whisks me back to the First World: Paris, uncomfortable in mid-summer heat, but light years from what has to be one of the worst corners of the globe.

In the coolness of early evening, a walk through the gorgeous Parc Monceau filled with odd ruins scattered amidst brilliant foliage and flowers, excises the long flight from the system. On up to the Arc de Triomphe to watch tourists snap furiously, and meditate upon the fine detail in the Napoleonic tableaus high above the pavement. The view down the Champs Elysées through Tulieres to the Louvre is stunning in its order: from the bush to the greatest architectural city in the world.

The following morning demands a walk through the dew-laden gardens of Tulieres to the New Louvre. Pei's sparkling pyramid of glass connects the Egyptian motif of the Place de la Concorde's Luxor obelisk with the first exhibit of substance within the old Palace walls. The new excavations for the subterranean entrance hall uncovered Philip Augustus' original fortress foundations from the first Louvre in 1200 A.D. The round turret bases are perfectly preserved as are the dungeon rooms. This middle age artifact is part of the hands-on time machine that shoots the visitor back to the beginning, to one of the most impressive exhibits at the Louvre: the Egyptian collection. The new exhibit halls on the north side of the palace, an area that used to be the Finance Ministry, contain two atriums filled with sculpture on multiple levels. The light pouring through the glass ceiling effuses the French sculpture of the Cour Marly with a soft intensity. In contrast, on the second floor is the bright darkness of the Dutch Masters; so with a quick glance down towards the Classical Greek form, one understands the affect geography has on art. Then a retreat to fresh air and a cold beer in a Tulieres cafe filled with tourists from around the world, and the symbolic realization that the phallic Luxor Obelisk, aligned perfectly with the labial Arc de Triomphe, gives birth to this dynamic city: a blending of the world's cultures to create a transcendent metropolis. The sculpture gardens interspersed along the walkway, filled with lithe figures glimpsed through horse chestnut, only serve to reinforce this. Which whets the appetite for further rambles up past the Jeu de Paume to the Grand Palais and finally, the view of a hazy sunset from the top of the Eiffel Tower, over a city caught between its medieval past and the twenty-first century.

The next morning it's off to the Champs Elysées to watch the finish of the month long Tour de France. The Elysées is closed to traffic, lending a festive air to the grand boulevard soon to be packed by hundreds of thousands of Europeans. To see them massed like this, speaking their myriad languages and holding themselves confidently in one of their greatest cities, contrasts starkly with Africa and its seething hordes, and has me secretly referring to them as The Great Northern Tribes. The cyclists are a blur of color as they whir around the makeshift loop between the Arc de Triomphe and the Place de la Concorde. Just before the finish rain makes the track slick and cools off the afternoon. A Frenchman nips an American in the sprint to the finish by the Grand Palais, but the Spaniard Indurain wins the overall title for the fourth year in a row.

A week later it's off to Mexico City. After I take my seat in the business class cabin, a flight attendant stops by and says to the elderly gentleman sitting in the window seat beside me, "Mr. McNamara would you like something to drink before takeoff?" The name doesn't really register until the voice so familiar from all the Vietnam era press conferences while growing up replies, "I think I'll wait 'til after takeoff." What beautiful karma, I thought, for my grandfather in Ann Arbor fell out with this former member of his book club when he moved to Washington to become Secretary of Defense. The club were initially enthused at this choice for Defense, but when he became more rabidly hawkish than most when it came to the war in Vietnam, they were shocked. I knew I had him locked in for a conversation because of the seating arrangements, so when dinner came I began the small talk that usually accompanies the arrival of the food: where are you going, what do you do? etc. He was heading for a conference of business leaders in San Jose, Costa Rica lead by the Nobel Peace Prize winning former president of that country. After warming him up a little I said point blank, "I think you knew my grandfather, Robert C. Angell at the University of Michigan?" He was kind of shocked, but nodded and replied, "a history professor I believe." "Sociology," I said, "you were both in the same book club together, right? At least that is what it said in *The Best and the Brightest*." He nodded affirmatively, yet with a far away look in his eyes, a look that seemed to yearn for the innocence of that time before Washington, before the complexity of one of the darkest wars in the history of the United States. He never spoke to me again on that flight, and I chose not to push it, he being on in years. I returned to my *Harpers* and left him in peace.

The pollution in Mexico City was so thick it seemed like winter had descended on the valley of the Aztecs at the height of summer. The first day is a return visit to the Museo de Anthropologia, surely one of the finest museums in the world. Beginning in reverse, I journey back in time from the relatively recent North American settlements of Hohokam, Snaketown, and Casas Grandes in the S.W., U.S. and New Mexico, to Zapotec, Toltec, Aztec and Maya exhibits, before hitting the Olmec with their huge carved heads, the most ancient of the Mesoamericans. The cascading waterfall in the courtyard splashes incessantly on the flat stones visitors trod, thus connecting all who come with the remnants of a people that didn't even exist as far as the West knew. Tlaloc, the Mayan god of water, reminds us too with his constant patter that the centuries pass with a beat both full and empty of meaning. There is plenty of meaning in the gorgeous artifacts that fill the museum, but they only remind us of the transiency of every life and every civilization: for where are the cultures that created such seemingly eternal cities filled with pyramids, sculpture, ceramic and obsidian wonders? For twentieth-century *Homo sapiens* it is a humbling experience indeed. The remnants of these ancient ones, the colonial architecture of their conquerors and the varied topography of their land, make Mexico one of the most beautiful and intriguing countries in the world.

Through the gardens of Chapultepec, to the Castillo perched on a volcanic peak made famous by its school boy defenders fighting against U.S. Marines scaling the cliffs. Los Ninos fought to the last child, and in so doing inflicted such casualties on the Americans that the red stripe on the dress pants of today's Marines memorializes that bloody siege; as does the lyric "from the halls of Montezuma." The dark mahogany lined salons that housed Maximilian and his entourage, border a balcony with views that, in his dynastic days, would have included the two snow-capped volcanoes that soar close to twenty thousand feet above sea level. Velvet upholstered chairs and divans fill the rooms, but one can't help wondering what was here before the Castillo, when the heights gave a 360 degree view of the once water-covered lake the Aztecs called home, after finding an eagle in a cactus dining on a snake. Atop the second floor of the Castillo, gardens cover an extensive veranda with more elaborate rooms and a circular observatory some two stories higher. The forest surrounding the mount is thick and contrasts markedly with not only the dense humanity of one of the world's largest cities, but also with the stark hills hemming the city in.

The Museo de Bellas Artes, with its Art Nouveau interior and Diego Rivera murals, is a gem. The art nouveau renditions of ancient Aztec motifs, such as eagle heads with snakes in beak topping gold borders six stories high are awesome. Rivera's socialist inspired portraits dotted with Marx and Lenin seem quaintly naive from today's perspective. From Bellas Artes on the edge of the historic city, past Sanborn's Islam-inspired blue and white mosaic edifice, it's into the colonial quarter with mammoth Zocalo and Cathedral built from the stones of the great pyramid at Tenochtitlan. The base of that pyramid, now exposed, lays directly beside the cathedral, and still in view are the coiled carved basalt serpents that lay beside the steps at each level on their way to the now decapitated summit. Just down the side of the Zocalo in this historic meeting of cultures and continents, is the Palacio, its colonial structure undulating from four hundred years of earthquakes and a contracting lake bed. The Rivera murals inside, surrounding a stone grey courtyard and depicting the country's history from indigenous people to revolution, are gorgeous in color and theme.

The valley of Mexico must have been one of the wonders of the world when Cortez's men first laid eyes on it. They say as much in their memoirs, especially Bernal Diaz. The pyramids of Tenochtitlan, set on an island in a large lake under towering volcanoes, must have appeared otherworldly to the Europeans, I marvel, as the 757 pops above the thick smog beside snow-capped Popacapetl, smoking heavily. It is just a matter of time before the peak erases the contemporary experiment in the valley below.

Back in Washington in four hours. The summer that began with the hottest June in recorded history, has cooled to autumnal temperatures and heavy rain from a stationary front stuck along the eastern seaboard. A neighbor's pool that was the lifesaver the two previous months is now too cool.

The counter to such unseasonable weather is the Caribbean basin, my next destination. After a week in D.C., it's off to Nassau and hordes of American tourists even at the height of summer. Amidst the flat sand banks that happen to sprout foliage, tourists search for paradise. But ultimately, these flat islands with their gorgeous beaches become boring. After the sun fries your skin you can gamble or drink or both, that's it. A quick hop back to Miami to catch a flight down to Belize, another English speaking colony along the Spanish Main. Founded by pirates raiding galleons filled with precious metals headed for Spain, this tiny village filled with clapboard houses on the banks of an open sewer, screams authenticity. Tourists are beginning to discover this Caribbean hideaway, and if eco-tourism has a chance to succeed anywhere, it is here. The gorgeous cays off the coast coupled with the Mayan ruins in the north, make a much more interesting destination than the more famous sand banks off the coast of Florida. The pine-covered Mayan Mountains to the southwest add another untouched ecological dimension. This is hardcore Caribbean, unspoiled by tourism.

Then on to Curacao, a dry Dutch outpost in the Antilles. It makes me laugh to see their provocative ads as an island getaway. There are very few beaches on this dessicated island rimmed by a rock shelf. There are some beautiful little coves, but Aruba is probably the place to go for good beach. Downtown Curacao has quaint Dutch architecture, but there is also a huge oil refinery on the edge of the harbor that mars the view and the sky with its belching.

The epitome of what a colonial European outpost was like is found in the capital of Surinam. Paramaribo is filled with classic white clapboard buildings on dirt streets. It differs from Belize City the way Amsterdam differs from London. Neat is probably the word. Set timidly on the banks of a massive, Amazon-like river, it seems on the verge of being swamped. Set in the heart of an impenetrable jungle, Kurtz comes to mind, because who knows what mysteries are up-river toward the Brazilian border. Heart of Darkness explorers might just as well set off from here as from Kinshasa. Surinam might even be a purer experience given a lower population density and far less exploitation of resources. The hour-long ride through the bush to an airport hacked out of the jungle, only adds to the Indy Jones feel of the place.

Continuing on the colonial tour of the Caribbean, the next stop is Port of Spain, Trinidad. From the Dutch to the British empires. Far more developed than either Belize of Surinam, Trinidad's capital has a spectacular setting under lush green hills, the tropical remnants of the mighty Andes turning to the east. The north coast of the island, where geologic erosion creates beautiful white sand bays as cliffs drop precipitously into the sea, is the most scenic part of the island. Classic neighborhoods of brightly colored cottages with rusty tin roofs cover the little city. Their porches are framed in wood lace and occasionally a red tin roof adds color. Five large examples of Victorian extravagance border the savannah that lies at the heart of the city center. These houses, known as the magnificent seven, were built and owned by the exploiters of the island's fecundity, and now represent the glory days of empire amidst the bustling and seriously impoverished contemporary population. The third of the population that is Indian, brought here along with the blacks for servitude, certainly spices up the place with their cuisine. And V.S. Naipul's depictions of the island certainly adds artistic spice.

A day trip down to Georgetown, Guyana is much like a trip back to Paramaribo, except that the architecture and culture isn't as aesthetically appealing. It sits along a big muddy oozing out of thick flat jungle, but has none of the charm of the Dutch colony next door. Of course, the connotations of Jim Jones hang heavily in the thick jungle air. And while as remote geographically as Paramaribo, this place seems at the heart of the heart of darkness, rather than the launching point into it.

Flying back to Trinidad the view is of the muddy waters of the Amazon commingling with all the other large rivers in this northeastern part of South America, as the prevailing current sweeps north-west. This of course makes for a muddy, mangrove lined coast, not a thing of beauty at all, until you get far enough north into the blue water, like Trinidad, or far enough west, like Margarita Island.

Island-hopping up the West Indies through Grenada and Bridgetown gives the amazing perspective of the sweep of those islands strewn between the Andes' end and the isle of Cuba. What conspiracy of tectonics and erosion could create such a delicately beautiful arc of islands? Back to Miami and First World insanity before getting into the heart of it in Washington a few hours later, the true heart of darkness?

Next day it's off on vacation in the land of glacially carved lakes filled to the brim with ice-cold fresh water surrounded by fir and pine right down to the smooth stoned shore. Is this invigorating ecological snap the cause for the differences between cultures and their standards of living? Certainly, there is nothing inspiring about the banks of the big muddy in Guyana or the Central African Republic.

Some of the largest sand dunes in the nation are along the Lake Michigan coast, and under a sky of deep blue it feels like the Caribbean without the intense heat and salt water. The blue skies temporarily give way to thunderstorms coming at high speed across the Great Plains with a gusto that shakes the century old cottage that's been in the family for forty years. I know which topography my genes are more at home in. After a week in this inspiring Midwestern locale, it's off to the northwestern U.S. and another land of enchantment: The Puget Sound.

As the family wings into Seattle: Mt. Ranier covered in glaciers off to the south, Mt. Baker the same to the north and Lake Wenatchee passing below. The ice wrinkled summits of both act as a gateway to a powerful landscape. The drive north out of Seattle is the clearest in history. The view of Ranier to Baker includes the entire Cascade Range. To the west, across a Puget Sound dappled with islands furry with thick Douglas Fir, soar the Olympics. This vibrant body of water crowded with islands is a finger of the open ocean ringed by mountains of fire.

After a bounding ferry ride with a 360 degree crystal clear view, the island with the cabin perched on a hundred foot cliff is reached. The view from the wide porch is south down an arm of the sound, with Ranier catching the dying rays of the sun, its snow and icy immensity countered by the sparkling waters and ferry traffic between islands. Mornings spent swimming in the clear, cold waters, building beach huts out of driftwood and watching sea otters cracking shellfish on their tummies, give way to hot afternoons in the shade of the deck. The hot, cloudless days are unusual for this region, and we feel fortunate to have them. The cool nights demand a roaring fire and occasional trips out to the cliff edge with binoculars to watch pinkish sunsets over the Olympics and keep an eye on bright Venus setting shortly after: she's there with Jupiter, hovering above the diminished snowfields of late summer, before beginning her retrograde to reappear in the east. The summer of '94 and its compacted variety of travel, ends with the ever present lingering orange glow.

October '94: Nature *is* indifference! Winging over the Atlantic on a full moonlit night with a shooting star streaking south: this is the same ocean Pilgrims crossed almost four centuries ago. Later, further expeditions westward and more death and birth and all the while the earth keeps spinning with nary a care for the former or the latter. "Cold hearted orb that rules the night...." But the thought of Paris tomorrow warms the soul: a cafe au lait and a croissant at my favorite place across from the Madeleine will suffice to cure any world weariness (this ironically written aboard TWA 800, which was blown out of the sky off Long Island two years later).

November '94: The trip from Johannesburg down to the Lesotho capital of Maseru is etched in mind as one of the great adventures. Flying in a Fokker prop seating ten, Air Lesotho (yes, one plane) putters down to the capital in an hour and a half of turbulence and puke. I happened to be traveling with several Chinese (they have big sweatshops there) who got so sick they were throwing up all over the cabin. I looked out the window to ignore the vomitorium by gawking at the amazing desert-mountain terrain. The approach into Maseru was enough to make anyone ill, what with plateaus out both windows and the winds tossing us around on our descent with no runway in sight. But it appeared, and my full faith in Lesotho Air prevailed, until the leg back to Jo-burg, that is, when one of the plane's doors blew off, giving us fresh air just when we didn't need it. But Maseru itself, nestled under sharply tiered mesas is reminiscent of Sedona without trees, and timeless in its simplicity. Like Swaziland, an ancient African kingdom left untouched.

I'm in love. Scooting down from dull Pretoria ablaze in purple jacaranda trees (which bloom in anticipation of water, not because of it), over a great desolate desert, the mountains begin to rise in stark grandeur and I know innately that I'm headed for something good. To the south, massive coastal range hugs the southern tip of the continent, while below desert rivers meander through canyons reminiscent of the Green River of Utah and Wyoming. Descending into Cape Town, the dryness of the jagged peaks contrasts markedly with the vineyards filling the fertile valleys. Then, there it is, Table Mountain, and without its famous tablecloth. Directly after getting to my hotel room I head out knowing the weather could change. I'm on the precarious funicular in no time, scooting up the perpendicular sides of the plateau. On top, one of the great views in the world: Robbins Island, where Mandela spent twenty-five plus years is there in the white-capped open ocean; below, the moneyed villas of the rich along Clifton's white sand and crashing surf and sparkling granite boulders, and over to the right a little, nestled in a large bowl created by the mountain, is the small picturesque city itself. Hiking to the eastern side of the plateau without meeting another soul gave the walk an extra special feel, a feel of worship in a sense because the silence atop the massive geologic structure was overwhelming, and the crystal clear views, exceptional. Peter Weir's *Picnic at Hanging Rock* came to mind, and the feel of vanishing from the face of the earth a real possibility.

To think that at the very bottom of a continent filled with such misery and human wretchedness of late, could exist a quiet, meditative place of such grandeur, is almost unacceptable. The following days of wine tasting, hiking, cafe sitting, and roaming around the beautiful waterfront further underlined the juxtaposition. Then driving down the spectacular Cape, past ostriches and roaming baboons, to see the Whitbread around the worlders heading off on colorful spinnaker runs to Perth, made the last evening in that magical place even more special. With scenes of Rwanda carnage lingering in the mind's eye, the only conclusion to be drawn was that tired old cliche of living for the moment. So be it.

January '95: Amazing! The sun is shining in Lima. The bone-dry foothills of the Andes crowd the view to the east, while to the west the sun begins its slow descent over the shanty towns, cathedral spires and the crowded port of Callao, to disappear in pink Pacific brilliance behind a huge desert island just offshore. A ramble through the streets finds poverty and desperation and the smoky smells of barbecued mystery meats grilled by vendors at every miserable corner. The smells make the stomach grumble, but knowing the savory cuts are from monkey, horse, cat or dog stifles the pangs. The Plaza de Las Armas opens up at street's end, relieving the claustrophobia of run-down neighborhoods with brightly lit National Cathedral, first constructed in 1535, and troops of the National Palace marching sharply in dress red in the courtyard of the Governor's House. In the middle of the plaza billows a huge Peruvian flag, and around its mast saunter Peruanos celebrating the twilight glow of a soft summer evening. This is the site of the original city center, built here along the desert coast where two major valleys sweep down from the gold country of the high Andes. From here the gold was shipped to Panama, where it was transferred to galleons on the Caribbean side for the run to Spain. The Rimac river runs just behind the Governor's house, and from the plaza you can hear its chattering rapids as it heads for oblivion in the nearby Pacific. The Qechua name for the river means "talker," due to the gurgling, boulder-filled waters that carved the valley through barren landscape over the millennia. A walk behind the classical architecture of the palace takes one over a decrepit bridge spanning the Rimac. From this vantage point the architecture of old Lima, with its cathedral spires, government buildings and Moorish-style dwellings, contrasts with the dry hills rising nearby, giving the city a transitory, impermanent feel, even after almost five hundred years; as if one mighty torrent could sweep this colonial settlement away in seconds, and restore the dessicated coastal plain to its silent, natural state.

The following morning brings escape to the massive sand dunes along the coast south of town: to fresh air, sea breezes and the massive adobe ruins of an ancient place of worship, Pachacamac. This Qechua word means "earth creator," and the eroded walls and mounds on a promontory of sand rising above the verdant Lurin valley where it meets the sea, have been a place of spiritual significance since before Christ. The Inca built the most impressive structure on the highest point of sand closest to the ocean, and there on the western side of the Temple of the Sun are chairs sculpted in the adobe walls where high priests celebrated the solstice with the sacrifice of sacred Llamas. The priests would smear their faces with the blood of the animals as they observed the sun making its most northerly and southerly points on the unobstructed Pacific horizon. Directly below this temple are numerous complexes, with ruins dating back some two thousand years. What little moisture there is on this dry coast, has made decent progress in that time to erode the massive adobe temples and buildings. There are vast plaza areas for pilgrims between temples, portions of which are still painted with a red and yellow dye obtained from crushing a certain insect. Walls and alleyways and steps still remain in this extensive ruin set above the pounding surf. Like the Rimac, this valley is one of the major routes to the high Andes, and the Incan capital of Cuzco.

Atahualpa, the Incan king captured by Pizarro, offered two rooms of silver and one of gold here at Pachacamac for his release. Francisco sent his brother Fernando to these temples to secure the fortune, but Atahualpa was killed later anyway. In one of the small ruins of the site, Spanish spurs and other metallic artifacts were recently uncovered, thus directly linking the gold hunters to this place of indigenous spirituality. Little good the Llama blood did.

The Asian link to these shores, first noted in visits to the Museo Nacional de Costa Rica, is reinforced by the pottery of the Nazca's. That pre-christian era people crafted ceramics two-thousand years ago with facial features identical to the Asians of today. The pieces are comical because they fit the stereotypical picture of the yellow hordes produced by propagandists during W.W. II: thin mustache, slanted eyes and a generally mean look. Now, what were these craftsmen on the fairly isolated west coast of South America doing creating such images around the time of Christ? From what I've seen there had to be a more recent contact with the Asian mainland than can be accounted for by the Bering land bridge some twenty-thousand years ago.

April '95: Venus this morning high above Rio in pink pre-sunrise cloud, the waves thundering below, favela dogs and roosters stirring, the Corcavado bathed in light, the peaks of Dos Hermaos catching color and Ipanema stretching awake with walkers aplenty; ahh, Rio! Winging south from that primal setting of ancient granite thrusting out of dense foliage (half expecting dinosaurs to be grazing around their smooth bases), the east coast of South America and blue Atlantic fleeced with clouds fills the window; and beyond, the 1,000 mile curve of the planet glimpsed in the direction of Namibia (where I'll be in two weeks), gives one the true feel of the revolving island we cling to. The day does not necessarily blind us with quantities and measures, not when you're at 30,000'. The civility of bordered ranches in the Pampas below brings one back from the edge. Green pasture cut through by darker green forested river courses meandering toward the Rio de la Plata, whose muddy waters meet those of the azure Atlantic just off the silt-brown beaches of Montevideo.

Strolling the cafe-lined streets of B.A. across town to the smelly yet colorful barrio of La Boca, I realize that only two weeks ago the rainy streets of spring Paris and wanderings around the Louvre were my home, and three weeks ago it was desert Dakar. This mingling with the knowledge that in another two weeks the rolling hills of the Transvaal will be my reality.

Sure enough, after the longest commercial non-stop flight in the world, with fantastic morning views of the Skeleton Coast of Namibia, the high veldt is reached. Autumnal light softly reddening Pretoria's historic sandstone buildings highlights a deep blue altitude sky. The blacks dressed in tatters, lounging on grass this Easter Sunday reinforce the contrast of the two previous weeks. And four weeks ago exactly it was the same sunset lighting the snow white domes of Sacre Couer in spring above the city of wandering and musing.

Then Mauritius, volcanic island paradise in the Indian Ocean with green mountains jutting above coral reef lagoons. Similar to Hawaii, with a Diamond Head-like peak named Le Morne Barbant at the abrupt end of a range of forested mountains looming above pounding surf. Port Louis an interesting mix of Indian descendants, French, and South Africans converging. Starkly contrasted with the island paradise is Luanda in its wartorn state. Its shanty town sprawl seemingly quadrupled since last trip a year ago. But there is talk of peace, which is hopeful, but given the recent betrayals of past political agreements, far from certain.

The flight back to Johannesburg over unpopulated green mountains and hills, then shrub and meadow geometric patterning until Kalahari scrub and salt pan desert. There have to be bush people below, watching the centuries pass with only a shrug.

The trip to Windhoek equally desolate, but at least with the occasional dirt road or path cutting a straight swath or meandering across the earthly void. The desert mountains of Namibia randomly thrust above the scrub like the mountains around Gaborone and Las Vegas. The sky filled with fleecy puffs seems to protect this arid land from too much exposure to the deep nothing of the abyss, colored by a deceptive blue.

Then it's by vehicle to Swaziland, across the grassy veldt. The slow climb past fields of corn and massive forestation projects takes us high into the region that historically was too much for the Afrikaaners to get a grip on; thus it survived as a kingdom. The mountainous approach into Mbabane is impressive, following a ridge that drops off spectacularly to the east, down into the lowlands of Kruger National Park, and the flat heat of Mozambique. Rocky hilltops and grassy knolls intersperse as the road drops into a bowl-shaped valley. Africans clothed in multicolored skirts hike the roadsides with kindling on their heads. And then there it is, the capital, in all its five building splendor. It's the King's birthday, so everyone is in his birth village, celebrating.

May '95: Wrapping up business in Washington amidst gorgeous scents of daffodils, tulips, irises, dogwood, ancient flowering cherry trees and the inevitable bittersweet good-byes to family and neighbor-friends newly made. Off again, this time to Thailand, rationalizing the continued mobility by knowing all is transition in the great dream time.

Transiting grey-fog San Francisco served to reinforce that one can never go home. Everyone still doing the same thing or close to it. "There is no present or future, only the past happening over and over again now," I quoted O'Neil to a friend as we sat having coffee two and a half years after leaving. Childhood buddy making big bucks but working hard. Only had time to see me for an hour on a Saturday he was so busy. Mai pen rai. Off across the Pacific for twelve hours to Taipei and then another three to Bangkok. But, at least it's change! The avoidance of the static the main thing.

Hot, humid Bangkok not as polluted as expected, but the traffic lives up to its nefarious reputation. Sidewalks with holes, loose bricks and raised concrete slabs aplenty: all the Third World standards. Noise pollution as well, but take it in stride in zen-like fashion and it's O.K. Of course, in true Asian philosophy everything is in balance, and here in Bangkok the contrasting ingredients include the mind-blowing Grand Palace with its multicolored ceramic-fragment construction techniques, towering Wat Arun rising spectacularly above the murky Chao Praya River, and the appropriately named Golden Mount perched above the merging canals of downtown with views over the entire chaotic metropolis (saffron monks roaming throughout). Not to mention the centrally located position of the city for traveling in south-east Asia; starting tomorrow, with my first trip to Sri Lanka:

Great scenes today here in Colombo: Viharnadevi Park in town very rough, i.e, grass waist high, pooling stagnant water, huge goyan lizards scampering about, trash, then the white city hall looming through the trees, built by the Brits three hundred years ago, and directly across the street from it, gazing at the colonial monstrosity with ultimate patience and indifference: a huge Buddha!

Met an old sage bedecked in traditional sari garb who said he was a gardener in the park! There certainly was no gardening going on. He pointed out large trees filled with huge fruit bats hanging from limbs, sacred Bodhi trees, and a bath for three elephants. Three bronzed mahouts dressed in swami cloth scrubbed and washed the Indian beasts with light faces as they lolled in the cool waters. Then, he insisted on taking me to a Buddhist temple hidden in the back alleys of Colombo. It was a fantastic place, the pure, authentic experience every westerner craves: Buddhas crowding every nook and cranny, big painted gold motifs of the buddha's life, and incense wafting through a courtyard with a tethered elephant with long tusks. This beast, being fed coconut palm leaves, sprayed with water and giving itself a shower of bright green grass which clung aesthetically to its grey hide, had just killed six people in a rampage in the north of the country (where the Tamil Tigers are also on a rampage), and was brought here to save it from being killed by locals. Great juxtaposition under the sacred Bodhi Tree: violence, serenity; tusks, petals. Then retiring to a Buddhist Temple pavilion in the middle of Beira Lake that spills into the Indian Ocean. A Bodhi Tree in planter giving desperate shade coupled with ocean breezes make it the coolest place in mid-day Colombo (with golden Buddhas at all points and a mini-Stupa nearby). Yes! my karma must have been good, because on returning to Bangkok the news reported a truck bomb had been planted by the Tamil rebels beside the tiny Colombo terminal the night I left, yet failed to go off.

Then back to Bangkok for the weekend before a night and day in stinking Manila. But first the flight soars over Angkor Wat, home of the Khmers, and the vastness of the forests of eastern Cambodia and Laos. The Mekong cuts a huge brown swath through an impenetrable landscape, forming the border between those two countries, before spectacularly mountainous Vietnam with its lush green valleys and rice paddied flats appearing long and narrow against the South China Sea. The coastal town of Qui Nhon below, nestled between huge unspoiled sand dunes to the north and south. Wonder how many assault landings there were on those beaches. Fishing village on back side of dunes in a sheltered harbor looks like one out of the thousand newsreel shots being napalmed or blown to shit. Fifty-eight thousand Americans died down there. For nothing. "Our nada who art in nada…" May they rest in peace! As my good friend Henry (Heironymous Bosch) Miller said: "All is chaos and meaninglessness," and that land below with all the blood from both sides spilled on it, is testament to that, as Mr. McNamara has belatedly admitted.

Manila has worse slums than West Africa. But absolutely gorgeous flying in over green mountainous archipelagos dappled across the South

China Sea, Corregidor among them. Swept into the airport over festering tin-roofed shanty towns as far as the eye could see. In the distance, rising mightily to the north of town and still smoking a little, the great bulk of Mt. Pinatubo looms, the very volcano whose ash colored the sunset skies of the Caribbean when I first started this job thirty months ago.

After Manila it was back for one of the great weekends in history, with Friday night spent with a wonderful Thai family at dinner, then a sleep over in their gorgeous traditional Thai style house filled with antiques. Opium beds, Chinese blue and white, and antiques from all dynasties and Thai Kingdoms filled the three intricately carved house structures joined by a porch, all resting on stilts. Then the next night a dinner at a colleague's, followed by a licentious evening on Bangkok's infamous Patpong roads and a delectable dim sum brunch Sunday morning. Then the great, striking contrast came the next day with a departure for Helsinki and its awesome civility.

Simple things so many people in the West take for granted exist here, like cleanliness, greenness, tram cars whose solid sounds on the rails recall everything that a place like Bangkok is not: efficiency, order. Pine tree smells waft through the city streets filled themselves with cafes crowded with unabashed big beer drinkers.

Birch trees swing and their aspen-like leaves shimmer in soft early summer breezes: what a thing to behold. Lilacs and lupines line bike paths cutting through forested terrain around an inlet from the sea that reaches well into the heart of the city. Victorian houses nestled on the shore across from the hotel, and next to one, on a rise above the lake, buried just nicely in birch shade, is a simple cafe with plastic chairs and tables run out of an old shed. To sit there and read, or to just sit and breathe clean air deep into the lungs and watch fleecy Northern Hemisphere clouds sweep in from the Baltic under a midsummer night sun is a miracle. The exquisite cathedral and square just above the busy harbor filled with ferry ships to everywhere is a contrast of Russian architecture bathed in Mediterranean light. Other images that linger are the boat trip past numerous rocky islands with brightly colored cabins perched just feet from the waters' edge, (and other thrumcaps piled high with wood awaiting the torch that signals midsummer night's eve), to the largest fortress in the world on Suomenlinna Island, with its outcrops and tidal pools lined with sun worshiping Finns: quintessentially blond Finnish girls, nicely tanned and perfectly proportioned, wearing peach colored bikinis while sprawled on rocks gazing out to sea.

And now, back in the air after a week and a half in suffocating Bangkok, on the way to Islamabad past intense lightning storms over Calcutta.

July '95: Talk about the anvil of the sun, this place is hotter than Saudi. At nine in the morning it was thirty-five Celsius! Islamabad, the Brasilia of the Punjab, bumps up against the brushy Margalla Hills as they thrust up abruptly from the flat, bleak terrain just north of town. The mountains make for nice sunsets as muezzin wail from a myriad of mosques. The Friday Market is one local event of worth, what with beautiful dark red Afghan carpets intricately patterned clinging to boulders, hanging from tree limbs and covering the ground of each shalwar qamiz (knee length shirt over baggy light trousers) covered trader. Hard to believe that Kashmir and Daal Lake are so close and for now closed to all travelers. Five hikers have just been abducted from Kashmir's Himalayan trails, held by mujahadeen trained Muslim rebels to force the release of their own prisoners from Indian jails.

Burma: delta mouth of the Irrawaddy flooded, rice paddy quilt broken only by green shade trees marking stilt villages fending off the swollen waters. Canals the only roads cutting through alternating paddies of green and brown squares as far as the eye can see. Then the soil rises just outside Rangoon, giving terra firma to trees, dirt roads, crowded thatch villages and stunning gold stupas soaring skyward. Downtown, golden Shwedagon, one of the largest stupas in the world, dominates not only the skyline, but the whole tiny island of soil this capital clings too. Shwedagon glistens huge even way out over the Gulf of Martaban, making this city caught in a time warp seem like some sort of alien settlement.

The flooding in Bangladesh is much different than in Burma, for the villages cling to small islands of soil just feet from being completely inundated. There are no shallow paddy fields to be seen, just deepish water covering everything, then another village isle of shacks with a couple of ancient conical mud and grass huts crowded together some distance away. Outside Dhaka there is no land at this time of year, only a Ganges-Brahmaputra sea filled with a thousand village islands. The huge casualties that regularly occur in this delta, must be from the waters rising just an extra two feet or so.

August '95: Talk about trips down memory lane. Returning to Australia after sixteen years, almost to the week, is a rare thing indeed. Some sort of homecoming, and this time even more impressive because of the great need for fresh air, space and unchaotic civilization. I had to look hard through downtown to find the old decrepit YMCA I stayed in all those years ago as a lad of twenty. Such is the nature of time that everything in the block had been torn down, replaced by shining new buildings thrust up around the lonely boarded up Y. The harbor didn't disappoint, still exactly the same, with rounded sail-like domes of the opera house shimmering in the sun against the clean green-blue of Sydney harbor waters. Then walking through the stunning botanical gardens where I spent so many days reading that wild work: *Storming of the Mind*, by a Robert Hunter, thinking it might possibly be the songwriter for the Dead. Got the old mind reeling in those halcyon days before returning to the west coast and hitching up to Eugene through redwoods towering over roiling cold Pacific waters. God, sixteen years; all that has occurred in that span of time is amazing. Not just in my life but in every life. How time is overwhelming in every second that passes, yet in the end how it amounts to no more than the incessant pounding of waves on a beach, century after century: "Just be the shore and I'll be the wave," as Nils Lofgrin sang.

Then hopping over to Wellington for a day really brought all the rushes back: how I landed there, green, having only traveled in Europe for a couple of months, heading off across the Pacific at a time when no one went to New Zealand or Australia. Remembering how nervous I was after landing even though it was an English speaking country, and how quickly I fell in love with the old Victorian houses clinging to forested hillsides of the university district, the clean streets and the journey by ferry to the northern tip of the South Island in a raging storm across the Cook Straight I now swoop in over; the antipodean winds buffeting the 767 and flattening the whitecaps below are the same ones that froze me to the bone all those years ago out on deck. Towering mountains full of snow across the straights and high above the fjord-like cuts through which the ferry made its way to Picton, create one of the most dynamic approaches to any city in the world. Then the fresh, pine scented air hits the nostrils, and you know you are nowhere near the tropics.

The weekend with cousin in Sydney, eucalyptus green suburbs nicely scented, kookaburas squawking in the treetops, kids scurrying through the brush. The creek just down the hill reminded me of youth in the forests of Maryland, eucalyptus and bottle brush instead of oak and pine. Then the walk out to Cremorne Point from Mosman and the gorgeous houses perched on sandstone cliffs carved by the wind into abstract works of insanely beautiful sculpture; awesome views of the harbor dotted with sail and the Opera House with ferries plying the white-capped waters between Manly and Circular Quay. The mind drifts back to Seattle and the Puget Sound exactly a year ago with its ferries, forested islands, fresh air and craggy Cascades and Olympics. This place is not as spectacular, but the weather is nicer, the water warmer and the neighborhoods hugging the myriad bays with gorgeous views more accessible. The only problem with Oz is its Americanophilia: McDonald's at every corner, and ads on T.V. more plentiful and worse than those found at home. The whole frenetic western death pace lives on here despite the enormous distance from its cultural origins.

But getting back to environs, paradise doesn't get any better than sitting on a Sydney ferry to all points. Riding the foredeck reflecting on cruising down the Chao Praya a week ago, with hyacinths bobbing, houses on stilts and Ayuddiah ruins soaring above the canopy of an island at the heart of the Asian rice basket, is one of the great earth leaps. Sparkling Sydney harbor compared with the silty Chao Praya, hah! Then, in the same thought, realizing I'll have to leave this glorious place in no time and venture back to the heat and humidity and chaotic traffic, is hard to fathom.

Flying out over the Blue Mountains, the great expanse of the continent is revealed. Even in the forested mountains just west of the sprawl of Sydney there are few signs of settlement. When the brightly colored eroded soils of the desert appear further west, the vast, overwhelming expanse of the continent is felt, and the Aboriginal concept of dreamtime understood. The multicolored continent with Ayers Rock as its navel, the myriad islands speckling the Timor Sea, an incredibly brilliant full moon in the east: consciousness in eternity is the dreamtime, but individually we only experience a nano second of the most amazing thing ever.

On takeoff from Kathmandu, the plane has to climb steeply while circling over the primitive city nestled in a green valley surrounded by the enormous foothills of the Himalayas. But soon after, the flight is over the flat, flooded Ganges plain at 30,000'. Looking straight down at sea level, or close to it, from the equivalent height of Everest, gives an accurate feel for the immense tectonic thrust it took to lift such a volume of rock and soil to such lofty heights. Everest level out the window to the north, jet stream winds whipping snow from its rocky summit, reminds one that most jets cruise at this mountain's altitude or below. And to think that a pioneering British women hiked that very peak with no oxygen a couple of months ago, only to die in an avalanche on K-2 in Pakistan last month, is stranger than tragic fiction, but captures the essence of existence.

September '95: Just south of Dhaka, the two swollen monster rivers draining the Himalayas converge with freighters plying their muddy waters, shanty settlements on slivers of sediment anchored by roots of trees: there only by the grace of Buddha. In a glance these villages speak of the ephemeral nature of things, perched as they are on an unstable delta where the so-called soil is really quicksand. I understand now how so many drown here. There is no high ground.

The only difference between California and Bangladesh on the natural disaster scale is that flooding is from the annual snowmelt in the Himalayas, while earthquakes are random. But even predictability cannot be prepared for here. Maybe that's a lesson for those who think predicting earthquakes would change anything.

Phnom Penh is a tiny village compared to Bangkok. Quaintly colonial is probably an apt description, but belies the cruel reality of pervasive banditry and Khmer horrors that still exist in this country cursed by history. The huge Mekong, like every other river in Asia during Monsoon, is flooding the entire region. Like Rangoon and Dhaka, Phnom Penh is where it is because there's a tiny bit of high ground to see it through the annual deluge.

September '95: Hong Kong is not the exotic place I expected it to be, but that's coming from more authentically Asian places to the south. "It's a great place if you like to shop," is the stereotypical comment, but for me the trail system on the mountainous terrain rising dramatically behind the forest of skinny skyscrapers clogging the narrow waterfront, is where it's at. The most dramatic thing about the city is you can escape it so quickly by the Peak Tram. For three dollars round trip you climb steeply up the tropical mountainside to just below Victoria Peak and its 360 degree views of the harbor and Kowloon and the islands scattered across the mouth of the Pearl River. Most importantly, the breezes atop the ridge are cool, the air clean and the quiet on the opposite side of the city, deafening. Hiking over slender skyscrapers and crowded harbor through mountain forest with the hum of the *Homo sapiens* machine below steep cliffs of dark green: sunset over Macau, hazy orange glimmering sea filled with tethered freighters. There's even a creek with chattering waterfall along one walk, all ten minutes from the chaos that is Hong Kong.

Okinawa. Ryukyu Island chain beautiful with its turquoise waters contrasted by dark green foliage; Japan civility refreshing compared with teeming chaos of Thailand. Not a good time to be an American here, though, with demonstrators crowding the streets of Naha, protesting the military presence of our forces and the rape by three of them of a twelve year old girl.

October '95: I hate to keep harping on the stimulative transition between Bangkok and Helsinki, but now that it's autumn an entirely different response is demanded by the simple beauty of changing leaves. That has to be what drives the northern tribes: the stimulation of changing seasons, the reflection change brings, etc., all drives the mind, imagination, intellect. The smells here this morning in the botanical garden, the maples red and orange, fallen color scattered atop dark green grass, took me back to autumnal Oregon during college daze. The point being: around the equator where you don't get big seasonal change, is also where a malaise of sorts sets in, or is it malaria? Compare with Anglo/Chinese dynamic capitalistic fusion of Hong Kong last week.

Herring festival along the waterfront filled with working old wooden sailing ships reminded me that exactly three years earlier I began work with the Nat'l Park Service at the San Francisco Maritime Historical Park on the stunning bay with office in the wheelhouse of an old ferry, and museum piece boats just like these working (the C.A. Thayer an exact duplicate) ones in Helsinki. Finnish fisherman barbecuing fresh salmon next to their boats made it impossible to resist the smells drifting along the cool Baltic seafront: delectable!

A week ago it was strolls atop yellow and rose colored leaves fallen on soft green moss clinging to glacier scratched granite meeting lapping waves framed by the wafting smell of pines; today it was the Mughal brilliance of contrasting red sandstone and white marble at the famous Red

Fort and Jama Masjid Mosque, second largest in the world, set amidst the ancient wonder of Old Delhi. A sage in a small mosque in the corner of the prayer yard presented a small glass tube that had a beard hair of the Prophet in it. He also had a footprint in marble that was reportedly Mohammed's as well. Two weeks ago it was Hong Kong to Okinawa; last week autumnal, Baltic Helsinki: this job is hallucinogenic. Ironic considering it's government employment. In old Delhi there are no automobile jams, but rickshaw, bicycle and wagon cart jams, going nowhere as they disappear down labyrinthian streets filled with seething humanity. The legendary poverty overwhelms as predicted. Outside the gorgeous mosque are rag children holding several month old babies in their own starving-thin arms. Some of the newborns are dead, some drugged; impoverished kids using them to keep from ending up the same.

Over the Red Fort, sun going down in the haze, towering distant thunderheads, silver lined, with circling vultures soaring over the dense, timeless heat and mayhem of this historic city. What is this feel one gets that is India? The weight of history seems to be part of the stifling air.

Taxiing to the National Museum down a three lane boulevard crowded with vehicles, when up ahead a white Brahma bull strolling against the traffic divides the nonplussed autos and buses into further congestion as they obediently avoid the sacred beast.

Harrapan and Mohenjodaro ceramics circa 2500 B.C. are vaguely similar in design again with S.W. Native American. Did the Silk Route stretch all the way from Kabul to Casas Grandes in Northern Mexico? Perhaps the Bering Straights were a northern extension of the trade road before being swallowed by rising ocean waters. But with no remnants of trading villages in Alaska that to this day line the route for thousands of miles across Asia, the traffic had to be maritime in nature.

Mall-like stretch from government house colonially similar to Pretoria, to Arc d'Triomphe-like India Gate monolith; center of political India. Women washing in what are supposed to be reflecting pools, smacking clothes against rocks to dry or clean further, creating background rhythm to vultures spiraling heavenward in spiritual vortex.

From Delhi to Bangkok and then back over the top of that chaotic metropolis (To quote Barry Lopez: "One evening I saw the distinctive glows of Bhiwani, Rohtak, Ghaziabad, and a dozen other cities around Delhi, diffused like spiral galaxies in a continuous deck of stratus clouds far below us") to Islamabad, refreshingly quaint in its modern, contrived way. Pakistan International Airlines is unique in that it offers a recorded prayer from the Prophet Mohammed before all departures: "The Koranic Prayer of our holy Prophet, peace be upon him". Not understanding Arabic or Urdu, it is a nice meditative chant just the same. And before landing the flight attendant always comes on and intones: "Inshallah (God willing), we will be landing soon." Well, if airplane maintenance and a safe landing is up to God, we're all in trouble.

A visit to the ancient, 2500 B.C. cities of Taxila, with mounds dotting the flat valleys recently tilled: on which young boys in flowing shalwar qamiz play cricket with twig wicket and rock balls, their chatter the only sounds breaking the ancient silence. The image that sticks in mind is strolling around the Jaulian Monastery perched atop the craggy hills, the sound of shuffling feet through dust the only sound in this 3rd century B.C. Buddhist site, to climb a crumbling wall for a vista of three boys in a far off, isolated tilled field playing cricket under towering, dry hills. Camels heavily laden with straw roped across their backs slog down dirt tracks too narrow for vehicle and beast in a valley directly below. Poverty adobe everywhere, men relaxing on woven string beds framed with rough-hewn branches just off the road under trees or next to trash piles or in yet another recently tilled field. The random, indifferent nature of everything here is cool. "Whatever, never mind," seems to have been coined centuries before Nirvana made it a mantra. The brilliant multicolored trucks plying the narrow paths that pass as roads are a wonder to behold: pride of ownership reflected in the intricately colorful paint jobs and bangles jingling from bumpers. Walking around the ancient stupas and ruins in the gnarly hills with the wafting wail of muezzin coming from unseen mosques in the surrounding countryside reminds one of the clash of religious beliefs, as Buddhism inspired ruins of ancient age remain in lands long ago conquered by Islam.

Then to pine-covered hills of Muree, an old British hill station settled to beat the heat of the unbearable Punjab in summertime. This autumnal time of year is cool, the fresh sound of wind through tall pines a thing to behold. Old cottages of British heritage dot the piney ridges overlooking the flat, dusty Punjab to the south, with myriad mountains of Kashmir to the east, and lesser Himalayas climbing steadily to the north toward the eighth highest peak in the world talked about earlier, Nanga Parbat. The Muree Bazaar at 7,500 feet is a bustling mix of tribal people and Pakistani middle class come to stay in their vacation retreats before the snow closes the roads through the nearing winter. Bright, red meat hangs in front of dark, dusty butcher shops seemingly built some time in the last 2,000 years. Tribal people in colorful garb are hiking everywhere in this steep terrain with huge loads on their backs. Shepherds lying in grass by the roadside as their flock grazes on steep hillsides scattered with tall pine. Water buffalo rest in the middle of tight roads snaking though a labyrinth of crumbling adobe.

Then returning to Islamabad and hiking in the Margalla hills with the sun setting over gnarly green peaks. On one side the semi-First World with Islamabad diplomatic center, on the other side of high ridge, ancient villages, undisturbed for thousands of years, nestle in the valleys below wind-whipped pine. Then in the waning sunlight, a dark cloud comes overhead and showers the crest bathed in dying light, the fresh breeze carrying the smell of ozone into the nostrils direct to the brain: its response: Yes, yes, and still yes. Joyce's affirmation!

Flying out of Islamabad into Lahore, adobe villages that must look no different from ancient Mohenjodaro cluster in dry countryside between the Jheulem and Chenab rivers. The ancient past is ever present, but in that past is stunning poverty, a poverty Westerners photograph to prove how exotic their trip was.

Waning, burning orange sun reflected in the saturated Everglade-like mouths of the Irrawaddy west of Rangoon, perched itself at the tip of two big muddies; then, moving southeast, the fiery waters align with the ancient city filled with stupas and frame it in shimmering gold.

November '95: Then waking up in blazing mid-day sun over western Australia after leaving Bangkok past midnight. The desert below bright with colors: from reds to orange to salt-pan white, then cliffs and ancient mounds and dry river beds before the slow change to the southeast as the occasional brush turns to trees turns to fields turns to Blue Mountains fully forested and cut through by spectacular rock cliff gorges. Finally, the flat, estuary carved Sydney metro area, European civilization perched on the far southern edge of a massive continent that overwhelms it. Neither the land nor the dreamtime have been tamed. Peter Weir's "The Last Wave" where Aboriginal prophecy speaks of a massive tidal wave wiping out the colonizers along the very coast below, is still pending.

Sitting on a balcony, overlooking the harbor with glistening white sail domes of the Opera House rising out of botanical garden treetops gracing the shoreline, the very acreage where sixteen years ago I roamed, reading voraciously to stem loneliness in a land that was further away from the world then it is now. Thinking of the person I was then, having no idea that I would return to these haunts in a job that paid me to enjoy it, in a luxury I couldn't have imagined in the days of sleeping on roadsides and beaches and staying at the decrepit YMCA. I finally found the old building yesterday when I wasn't looking for it. It was boarded up and abandoned in the heart of a downtown that is being revitalized. But they haven't gotten to the "Y" yet! Thus, for me, a physical link with my youth and a roaming nature that began then and has continued by the grace of god, miraculously survives in the face of progress.

Speaking of which, saw Tom Stoppard's "Arcadia" at the Opera House, and marveled at the scintillating repartee of language and hilarity, mixed with profundity, he's such a master of: "When we have found all the mysteries and lost all the meaning, we will be alone, on an empty shore." The inclusion of the chaos theory connecting two hundred years of advanced civilization with the possible actions of Lord Byron and the wonders of poetry take theater to heights rarely experienced. Which is connected to my dwellings on time, the past and wonder of where I was sixteen years ago from this vantage point. Sydney is a marker of sorts now, for the day I left Australia in 1979 to return to college after dropping out for a year and doing archeology and traveling to Mexico and Central America, was also my birthday: a twenty-first birthday celebrated twice due to the crossing of the international dateline.

Gazing down into the fecund botanical garden with its harbor finger of white-capped water jutting towards King's Cross, thinking about my days wandering and musing amongst its rock outcrops after circumnavigating a continent most Australians have never seen, I agree that chaos is predictable. I think it was Herman Melville who said that the most direct route isn't necessarily the fastest. That statement represents a profound understanding of chaos. Returning to where I was on the edge in a youthful wanderjahre never would have happened if I had taken a more conventional path.

Three days after returning to Bangkok, New Delhi beckons. Actually comfortable in late autumn, though the haze lingers; probably made worse by the cold and need for more dung fires. The image I want to retain forever, and one moment in time in which I regret not having a camera, was upon entering Humayun's Tomb behind a troupe of school girls. There were probably two hundred of them dressed exactly the same in blue skirts with white blouses, each having identical long black pig tails with a red bow on top. As I entered the main gate of red sandstone and headed toward the sandstone and marble turrets of an inner gate of a mausoleum built in 1565 by the Mughal King for his spouse, this sea of girls paraded along the path ahead, with not a single one looking behind. What a picture that would have made! Inside, the tomb itself was almost an exact copy of the Taj, without the minarets and with just a touch of marble, but also built on the banks of the Yamuna, which has now shifted course.

Then on through chaotic Delhi, along the banks of the brown, shallow river to the tower of Qutab Minar, which dates to 1199. It has to be the highest, earliest tower in the world, serving as a superb observation point for spotting advancing armies (the Kalyan minaret in Bukhara was built earlier, in 1127).

Just missed getting blown up at Connaught Circle, the shopping district of old colonial architecture. A huge bomb went off on the very corner I had walked past an hour earlier. The bomb had been placed by a Free Jammu and Kashmir group. Timing is everything.

December '95: The month of the Himalayas! begins with a return to Islamabad, cool under snowcapped lesser Himal. Road trip to Abbotabad, home of the (Piffers) Pakistani military and surrounded by snowy, pine covered mountains. Tribal folk swathed in colorful blankets, wearing Chitral hats, crowd the Bazaar. Low, wooden stalls manned by crouching vendors offer a range of roasted nuts and seeds, while others fry up samoras and chapati. Then the drive up through mountain villages, adobe huts looking cold in the shady side of the valley, while above green pine mixed with deep snow beckons. The snow gets so deep we have to stop or risk sliding over a precipice. Chicken jalfreze, tikka and jinna: savory dishes that fend off the cold and any chance of illness. Exactly a week ago the family was lounging in the shade of a big deciduous tree as the warm tropical waters of the Gulf of Thailand's Ko Samet lapped feet atop clean white sand. Transitions, transitions.

On the flight back an amazing view of the full sweep of the Himalayas, from Nanga Parbat past Nanda Devi and Dhauligiri to Annapurna, then on to Everest and the east where the range actually starts to peter out into sporadic white peaks separated by low, green ridge line after the Bhramaputra makes its turn to the south and its mingling with sacred Ganges' waters.

Hong Kong haze thick, the harbor crowded as usual and the land filling ongoing. Soon there won't be a harbor left. Good to get to Okinawa and its fresh breezes and clean air. The drive up to Kadena is interesting in that the rocky terrain full of caves speaks of the terrible loss of life that occurred here during the bloody summer of 1945. Over two hundred thousand people perished, including fourteen thousand American soldiers. It was the largest land, air and sea battle in history: the carnage made worse by the number of innocent Japanese civilians who took their own lives rather than surrender to the American demon-soldiers, who they thought would rape and torture them first. The caves littering the island were the focus of battle as soldiers and civilians clamored for space inside, with American troops going cave by cave in mopping-up operations.

Then back to pre-Christmas glitz in the incredible shopping extravaganza of Hong Kong. Take the ferry to Macau and Portuguese China. Settled in 1510, this thin strip of land at the end of the Pearl River Gulf was the main European trading point for some two hundred years before the barren island of Hong Kong entered the British Empire. Fortunately I had Murry as my guide, otherwise I would have taken one look at the place from the ferry and returned, it's so ugly. He had just finished a book of paintings capturing the rapidly disappearing authentic old Chinese areas of town, so it was a tour of scenic Macau. The fort high over town, with cannon still seemingly bristling over this settlement of western capitalism, gave one the feel for the romance this place once conjured up. The pastel-Mediterranean colors of the older colonial structures off the coast of China, ready to be handed back in 1999 after five-hundred years, twists ones mind.

Then back to Delhi once more to wander the tree-lined boulevards in a comfortable temperature, shop in Connaught Circle (dodging bombs, another exploded last week!), and wander through the ancient chaos of old

Delhi, before returning to Bangkok and organizing the challenge of a life-time: trekking in Nepal with three young children.

Christmas in Kathmandu! After spectacular views of the Everest region out the right window and a nerve-wracking descent through towering foothills with no airport radar (at least it was clear, Thai crashed our very flight two years earlier in bad weather), the arrival in this ancient valley is shocking in its extreme poverty and filth: compares with the worst in the world. The Chinese inspired temples of Durbar Square coupled with snow-capped Langtang at 7246 meters soaring into the blue heavens over a green valley ridge just north, give this place that should be a hell-hole, the mystique and attractive nature it enjoys.

The first eve wandering through slum streets up to the forested slopes of Swayambhunath Stupa, better known as the Monkey Temple. Getting nailed with red dye on the forehead and flowers in the hair before the difficult climb up steep steps past beggars aplenty and bounding baby monkeys and their moms. Then the view from the top over the valley that used to be filled with lake water until Vishnu slashed the gap we flew in through to drain it. Weathered prayer flags flap while distant mountains clustering around Everest to the east peek in and out of cloud. Gongs boom, bells ring, incense wafts and the buddha eyes atop the stupa gaze.

The next day at huge Tibetan Boudhanath Stupa just north of town with its intelligent eyes and question mark nose and colorful flags and prayer wheels turned by the faithful on a bright, clear morning before heading out to exotic Bhaktapur and its pagoda temples of intricately carved wood and the Benares-like ancient Hindu funeral pyre temples of Pashupatinath awash in smoke. There we stumble upon exotic Sidhus covered in whitewash, playing flutes in various sacred lingam temples clothed only in loin cloth, while along the riverbank the latest crop of dead was stoked heavenward, their ashes kicked into Bagmati river waters that flow toward the sacred Ganges to make way for the next. Some had just been thrown on pyres and their human shapes were unmistakable as the flames licked them black. Living prehistory.

Then a seven hour ride through the heart of Nepal countryside on our way to Pokhara trailhead. The road linking the first and second cities of this impoverished land make the MacArthur aqueduct hiking path look good. Imagine a worse roadbed snaking through huge foothill ranges alongside thundering mountain torrents and you understand why it took so long to go some 110 miles. The Seti River valley where our trail began is impressive in that the river has cut a swath through deep mountain sediments, leaving towering cliffs and its waters white with minerals.

The cloud had been thick all the way from Kathmandu, so we were trying to imagine what the view was, and even pessimistically wondering if we would ever see anything during the month when the total average rainfall is 3 mm, the lowest all year by a long shot. We were rewarded the next morning. The night was crystal clear with a carpet of stars as we watched the sun soar to light the entire Annapurna Massif while sherpas served hot tea at our tent doors. Wow!

After trekking four days through villages linked only by trail, past impoverished children, adobe huts and thatched roofs covering man and beast alike, along snaking ridge lines under towering Annapurna and Machhapucahhare with booming Madi River far below, up stairways of stone made for the gods, past villagers hefting exquisitely bundled sticks, hay or completely covered by harvested foliage so they looked like walking bushes, through thick forest of mist with occasional temples in shafts of light bolting through morning mist, across terraced fields of rice with views south to rolling foothills, it was on to Pokhara and a "civilization" that is filthier than anything found in the mountain villages. But not before meeting a Tibetan lama in a monastery on a peak just behind our last night's camp. He invited us into his spartan chambers, lit candles and incense and blew conch shells and played a human femur he'd plucked from the heat of a cremation pit to prove he had learned his spiritual lessons. Of course his little hilltop redoubt had one of the greatest views in the world.

Then out onto lake Phewa Tal in a canoe under snow-covered, looming Fishtail (Machhapucahhare, never been climbed! sacred now, so it never will be), to an island temple before coffee at a lakeside cafe accessible only by water. Pokhara is only at about one thousand meters, so the lurch of the Massif is awesome considering Machhapucahhare is about 25,000'.

The airport was something out of West Africa! One stinky little terminal in complete confusion. We couldn't sit in the waiting area due to the smell of urine, so we just let ourselves out onto the landing strip and hung around gazing at the huge mountains until a little siren sounded to tell us the plane was landing. It banked in, landed, off loaded, loaded, and we were off in about fifteen minutes. The flight back to Kathmandu had been delayed so we hit the range perfectly at sunset. The view from the cruising altitude of 3,000 m. showed orange-red snow from Dhauligiri past the Annapurna Himal to Manaslu, before the Ganeshas and the triangular tip of neon pink Langtang and the entire range east to Everest blazing in dying rays preceding our descent into the valley of trash and wonder.

I had some gastrointestinal problems, which, given the fact that I'm in India and Pakistan a lot and never have any problems, tells you how nasty it can be. On the last night I was fantasizing about some good, spicy hot Thai soup coursing through my gut: a medicinal cuisine for sure. And just to show how everything is relative, returning to Bangkok was like arriving in Paris. Now I can say I have spent Christmas in Oaxaca, Jerusalem & Kathmandu, three cool spots with mystical overtones spread evenly around the globe. Today is a good day to die!

Jan '96: Hiking the forested mountains behind the chaos of buildings and people that is downtown Hong Kong, eighteen months before the Chinese takeover, I come upon a tiny Buddhist sanctuary buried in green up a dead end path. There is a temple with large, hanging incense coils that must burn for weeks, but not another soul. Through the trees I can see I am as high as most of the skyscrapers: harbor congestion glimpsed between them. Complete serenity in this bustling metropolis of seven million souls. This is the type of experience that hiking rewards you with. I relax and drink in the ambiance of this place perched by a mountain stream in the eye of the capitalistic storm. The changeover will never affect this timeless sanctuary.

Then down to Australia in the height of summer. The Tennis Open is wrapping up in Melbourne, sail covers the blue bay, bodies sprawl on beaches pounded by huge waves, and blue sky devoid of ozone allows the sun to make the skin crawl. Up to Port Moresby, Papua New Guinea, tiny little place that reminded me of West Africa! And not just because of the name. But the foothills of the Owen Stanleys rolling to the north speak of mystery, the untold prehistoric tribes that still live in those hills remind one that very little of the world is known. The world is not getting smaller, its still closer to the world of Joseph Conrad than it is to that of Alfred Toffler. There is the feeling here that one is on the edge of something.

But the return to Sydney brings one back from the edge. First world all the way!

February '96: Journey to Hanoi reinforces the sad reality of the earth's state at the end of the twentieth century. From Hong Kong to Islamabad is a thick layer of smoke. The realization hits me on the flight to Vietnam because it's a perfectly clear day, but the haze below is so great I can barely make out the topography. The beautiful forested mountains of Laos flowing into Vietnam are almost invisible, yet the fires obscuring the scene can be made out seemingly burning out of control in areas that look inaccessible. Maybe it's the time of year for firing fields across Southeast Asia and the Indian subcontinent, but this obscurity has been prevalent for months now, and speaks of the greenhouse effect in a big way; as if this area of the world needs any more heat!

In sharp contrast to this, mid-month it's off to deep winter Helsinki. One of the most sharply defined transitions anywhere. Snow storm while walking across frozen sea inlet that I described earlier at the height of midsummer gorgeousness: flashing back to that mind's eye image while cutting a frigid path across the thick ice to where the cafe perches in summer bliss. The wind numbing my tropical face so I can't see for the tears, and my thoughts become fearfully scrambled and incoherent, but enough mental ability remains to get back across the frozen waste to the hotel's warmth and a sauna overlooking the same body of water. Watching the snow swirl over the rooftops of wonderful little Helsinki already deep in it while sweating in an oven reminiscent of Bangkok. The next morn sitting in The Engel cafe on the main square with snow flurries filling the grey sky framing the majestic cathedral that soars above the small harbor filled with thick ice and ferries. Sipping cafe au lait gazing out on this scene literally freezes one in time and place and the wonder of a job that lets one experience such moments that will be remembered and cherished for a lifetime.

March '96: The day after returning from the frozen lands of northern Europe, we take off for Cambodia and one of the glories of the ancient world: Angkor Wat. With a sitter for the kids the trip to Siem Reap is uneventful, and the accommodations decent. Our guide is the inimitable Mathieu, a Frenchman who's not only married to a Khmer (thereby saving her life because she was educated: the Khmer Rouge considered any educated person an intellectual), but has worked as a photographer for the Ministry of Culture over the years documenting the overwhelming size and variety of architectural and artistic styles of Angkor, most of which still lie buried in the jungle. The immediate impression, and one that is reinforced by Thai newspaper reports, is that the Khmer Rouge are far away, pinned down by a government offensive in the mountains of the southwest. As the sun set the first evening we dashed out to a temple-mountain site that predates Angkor Wat by about three hundred years: Phnom Bakheng, built circa 900 A.D. After a steep climb first up the actual mountain, then up the flanks of the five-step pyramid to the crumbling five-towered sanctuary, with 360 degree views of flat-jungled countryside and moat-encircled-wonder of the similarly five-towered, but far better preserved, Angkor Wat rising from thick forest. A hazy orange, greenhouse effect sun bathes the ruins in an odd light as it sets over the Western Bareay, a perfectly rectangular five-mile by one-mile shallow reservoir, built before Bakheng to regulate water flow through rice paddies to sustain the multitudes that would construct this mountain temple.

The numbers of tourists atop the complex was astonishing, considering the dangerous reputation the area still has. It was almost circus-like, even from the beginning of the hike as two young lads in tatters "escorted" us up the difficult trail, showing us which way was easiest, then at the top pointing out such things as the Thai border and Angkor Wat, before "walking" us back down the mountain. Talk about creating jobs out of thin air; but desperation demands that they do. There are no schools because all the teachers were slaughtered.

The next morning Mathieu, with cigarette dangling classically from lower lip, began the two day whirlwind with a stop at the huge gates of Angkor Thom, topped by large, full-lipped Buddha faces (or the Boddhisatva of compassion, Lokesvara depending on the interpretation), with elephant trunks forming colonnades on either side of the base, and the road into this last Angkor city lined with enormous Naga (cobra) heads with demons riding the long tail of the right hand snake and devas on the left. The huge walls of this ancient city built around 1200 enclose the similarly faced ruins of the Bayon. The mysterious faces peer out into the jungle four to a tower, and there are some 54 towers! Bas reliefs line the outside walls depicting fierce elephant battle scenes against the Khmer's traditional enemies the Chams (Vietnam) and Siamese. The Chams are easy to spot because their helmets are in the shape of inverted lotus flowers. Even war canoe scenes of battles out on the big lake (Tonle Sap) were carved in such detail that while the battle is raging on the surface a multitude of marine life swarms underneath the action. Forest scenes too are amazing, with each leaf and bird in the treetops delicately rendered while just below heads roll. This is all ironic considering this is the last structure built by the great Khmer empire, overrun as they later were when the Thais sacked this city in 1431 and carted all the gold and statuary off to their capital at Ayuddiah, just north of Bangkok, which was in turn sacked by the Burmese in 1765 with all the valuables from the region ending up in Mandalay.

We spent the rest of a long day visiting little seen temples hidden away in the thick forest, many with huge trees and roots growing aesthetically, along and from ancient walls and towers. Many of the sites were mined by the Khmer Rouge when they occupied the area, so we had to stay on defined trail: no running off to pee in the bushes! As if we needed any further warning, most of the poor Cambodians doing ongoing reconstructive work had one or two limbs missing.

Then, a few hours before sunset, when what little coolness there was in the day prevailed, we headed toward Angkor Wat. The problem is, it is so overwhelming in every way that to describe it is futile. My favorite detail were the *apsaras*, erotic dancing devas exquisitely carved in sandstone that cover every panel all over the site (some 17,000!), each one unique. Next favorite were the great Naga heads at every step, with their long bodies forming balustrades of incredible length: the longest of which is at the entrance lining the causeway bridging the moat that encircles the site. The bas-relief panels inside the outside wall are far more refined than the ones at Bayon, and tell the tale of the *Mahabarata* and *Ramayana* in stone....incredible. We gazed at these for hours, with Mathieu interpreting each important scene as the sun's waning orange light bathed the galleries. Then we clambered up precarious steps to the quincunx, or five towered top of the Wat that is supposed to represent the mountains of Nirvana (the Himalayas!), to catch the sunset over the awesome grounds and vast jungle disappearing to the west. Mathieu had photographed every square inch of the place and said we would return the next day for further viewing of Angkor Wat, but only after seeing some of the earliest structures constructed by the Khmer in the surrounding countryside, beginning around 800 A.D.

These structures were far more primitive, most made out of brick, and all consistently Hindu in their allusions to Shiva and Vishnu or Brahma. Bayon is actually the only ruin that is solely Buddhist in its motifs, with even Angkor Wat syncretic in its religious depictions, but still mostly Hindu at base. Buddhism is a usurper here for the most part. Of the temples visited the second day, Preah Khan was my favorite. Labyrinthian ruins lost in a deep forest alive with exotic bird calls of amazing variety: it really symbolized for me the true Angkor experience, because it had only recently been cleaned of jungle and we were the only ones there.

Then later in the day back to Angkor Wat for further looks in nooks and crannies that few rarely see. One of my favorite sights was the incredibly delicate carving in one of the entrance gates originally built for elephant access, marred by Vietnamese tanks just barely scraping through when they occupied the Wat as recently as five years ago.

There are some 200 temples in the area, but we did well to see the fifteen or so main ones in two full days. Some of the more interesting sites are too far into Khmer Rouge controlled areas to be seen safely, but hopefully some time in the future that will all change.

Our adventure didn't really start, however, until the final day of the four day trip. Instead of flying back to Phnom Penh, I was told that taking the boat down the lake was a must, so that's what we did. The early pick-up by taxi took us down along the lake where the "port" was in the dry season. The Tonle Sap is actually filled by the Mekong backing up during monsoon season, but the villages that line what must be the high water mark, are some of the most primitive settlements I've ever seen. In the early morning light you could see whole families circled around fires next to leaf-roofed shacks on stilts. What century is this? Amazing stuff. Then when we got to the port at the end of a terrible dirt road, where the Siem Reap river winds through the normally flooded flatlands, we caught a pirogue filled with locals amongst a thronging floating market crammed with boats selling fish, fruit, vegetables, meats, etc., all in the middle of a shifting nowhere. When the water rises this is obviously all abandoned.

Nothing is permanent. So, we wound our way for some forty-five minutes along this river, with scenes right out of life along the Mekong at every turn, with grass-hatted people casting a variety of nets into the water from slender craft that looked as if they would tip at any second from our wake, but never did. Then, like something out the movie "Apocalypse Now" a long, narrow gunboat came speeding towards us, with massive, manned machine gun on the bow. I have to admit my heart stopped as they slowed to look us over, gun sweeping back and forth along the length of our slender craft. I think there was one other foreigner on board the crowded craft besides the two of us, but even though it looked as if it was the Cambodian Navy, they are apparently just as bad as the Khmers. Anyway, they looked us over pretty thoroughly, before speeding off toward the port. Scary!

Finally we came out of the shrub-covered flood lands into the Tonle Sap. An amazing floating village, this one permanent and cleaner because of the depth of water. There were uniformed kids going to school in boats and even a floating restaurant with pirogues tethered alongside. We dock at the floating boat depot, then climbed aboard a nightmare vessel that was shaped like a tube, with no way to open a window in case it started sinking, not to mention fresh air. We freaked out, and after seeing another boat, fled the death trap. It turned out to be the wrong boat after all, but the one we ended up on wasn't much better. They stuffed everybody they could inside and on the roof: there was no toilet for a five hour trip down the lake, then along the river into Phnom Penh. It was wild! The boat went so fast that every wave sent it flying before landing with a sharp thud. Since the lake is so shallow, it was very wavy. We were both losing it when after two hours of being shaken violently out of our bodies, we reached the river and another three hours of smooth water all the way to the big city. On the lake we passed these long, slender war canoe boats used by the Navy, heavily armed with machine guns, apparently to keep the Khmer Rouge on their side of the lake. Our speed boat was filled with locals, so we weren't much of a target. The cruise down the river was amazing in the sense that it was a cruise back in time: stone-age fishing villages lining the banks, followed by thick forest that went on and on and on. This region certainly qualifies for Heart of Darkness classification, and I was thinking that if the engines cut out, then what? And to think how boring it would have been if we'd taken the thirty-minute hop by air....! When we finally got into Phnom Penh and the boat docked along the decrepit, trash deep, muddy river bank to off-load us, we grabbed our suitcase from the top of the boat, stumbled up into the riverside slums and couldn't find a cab. Only rickshaws! Finally, after roasting in the mid-day sun, we found one, and even though we had six hours until our scheduled flight, we fled to the airport and bailed out of Cambodia on an earlier flight. Enough was enough.

Two days after returning to Bangkok it was off to Islamabad and the wildness of spring in the Margalla hills primitively perched above the contrived capital. Went for a long hike through beautiful spring flowers and cool pine forests to the ridge top for amazing views of the Himalayas of Kashmir thick with snow in the distance. Even snow-capped Nanga Parbat soared through shifting cloud further to the north. The Margalla were full of bird song and rifle-totting shepherds wandering with their flocks. The temperature was as perfect as Pakistan must get. Then off to Peshawar for further adventure: adobe-raw Afghani refugee camps sprawling along the railroad tracks to Rawalpindi, their copper smiths turning out the finest crafts at many a poverty stricken turn. Went to the American Club to catch the World Cup of Cricket and the match of the century with Pakistan playing their arch-enemy India in a one day test in Bangalore. Fazal, my driver, and I watched with intensity while drinking ice-cold ones in the classic colonial club in the heart of the city with sun-setting over the Khyber pass just to the west. On the way back we cruised through the old part of town to take care of some business. The labyrinthian streets of the Khyber Bazaar, full of vendors selling the finest teas I've ever smelled, freshly roasted nuts, and the vibrant reds and oranges of fresh radishes and carrots beautifully arranged, along with the crush of the crowd under the fortress walls of the old Mughal fort built by Babur, Bala Hisar, was something out of the finest, exotic travelogue. Then the run back along the Grand Trunk road (that stretches from Calcutta to Kabul), trying to pass on the decrepit road with vibrant, Peter Max Pakistani trucks with bangles tinkling and shimmering from bumpers, clogging the way. Then over the Indus, ice blue water fresh from the Karakoram flowing alongside the road before cutting through rough, jagged mountain range at Attock, where Alexander crossed on his way to victory along the Jheulem. The Mughal fort built by Akbar in the late 1500's that stands so spectacularly above the steep gorge and churning waters, thick walled and seemingly impregnable, is one of the more memorable sights anywhere. We stopped for tea and a smoke atop a cafe with views of the gorge and Indus: shaddora covered women, multi-colored cloth fluttering in the breeze and jars atop their heads, head for the white water to replenish their village. So much Pakistani military in this part of the country due to the ongoing history just a stone's throw away. If it isn't Kashmir to the northeast, it's the Pathan tribes and continuing wildness of Afghani Civil War just west. Not to mention China to the north and Tajikistan, deep in rebel trouble, to the northwest. Had the most amazing view of Delhi from 35,000' on the return: the Red Fort, Connaught Place, India Gate and the Parliament buildings, all with the added bonus of soaring Himalayas looming above the entire Gangetic Plain. In the span of two weeks, winter Helsinki, wild Angkor Wat, and intense Pakistan were visited. Compact variety of Earth!

The next week it was back to Delhi, seen so clearly just the week before. This time the concentration was on Old Delhi, its narrow, colorful, wildly primitive labyrinth of streets, so tight only a rickshaw can fit through the alleyways. Didn't see another foreigner for hours as I followed my nose trying to escape the minotaur of fear attempting to exit the heart of this slice of the ancient past. Finally solved the puzzle when I spied the towers of the gorgeous sandstone mosque, Jama Masjid, just across from the Red Fort and wild Chandni Chowk. I rested by imbibing an exquisite, fresh pomegranate juice while absorbing the seething humanity: buying, selling, discussing, bicycling, bartering, moving frenetically about like an ant mound. Then a return to the Red Fort for some historic intensity, wandering though the British barracks, and studying the exquisite marble architecture of the royal Mughal court: Rang Mahal, Khas Mahal and the Moti Masjid, where most of the inlaid semi-precious stones of exquisite beauty have unfortunately been removed.

April '96: Oh, Australia! What can be said of one of the last great unspoiled land masses on the face of the planet. Clean, people-free, sophisticated in just the right way, and the most beautiful beaches and water at every turn. Spent the weekend at some friends' cottage up in Pittwater, across from Palm Beach under the towering, pock-marked, Aboriginal relic-filled cliffs of the Kurin-Gai National Park. Peace and Quiet and beautiful swimming in the calm bay waters. Then amazing restaurant hopping back in Sydney: from Indian, to haute cuisine to a wonderful little smoky Spanish dive down in the theater district. All amazing! When one thinks of the over-priced and violent craziness of America, Australia sure seems attractive.

The day after returning from OZ the entire family heads off for Easter break up-country. We pick up a Thai office colleague who has arranged breakfast with a Monk in Lop Buri at his country Wat. The ulterior motive is the prehistoric pottery he has dug up in constructing this relatively new temple. It seems one night while encamped on this spot he had a vision of light beams emanating from the ground. He took this as a sign he should build a Wat on the illuminated locale. But when he began excavating a foundation for the spiritual home, he unearthed a prehistoric burial site. Some of the pottery that came out of the ground along with the bones is over two-thousand years old and predates the famous Ban Chiang ceramics found in the northeastern part of the country. We actually drove to another spectacular Wat near Takhli, under sharply serrated limestone peaks, where the horde was stashed, and bought from the monks about thirty fine pieces of varying age. The karma seems to be good as all the funds we "donated" will go to the further building of the temple grounds. What a blessing!

We left the monks bargaining with my colleague about how much our donation would be, and headed north to Sukhothai, literally translated as "the rising of happiness", Thailand's first capital from the mid 13th century and revered as representing the golden age of Thai Civilization. The contemporary city is small and welcoming, with the beautiful ruins of the capital five kilometers outside town. Great lawns of green grass frame sandstone red pillars and stupas of the lotus bud crown amid moats reflecting all in blissful serenity. Quite a contrast with the next day's arrival full of expectation in the crown jewel of Northern Thailand, Chiang Mai, which turns out to be a mini-Bangkok, with all the traffic and general hecticness.

The drive from the teeming city center up to the 1600 m. mountain temple of Doi Suthep is refreshing due to the trees and views out over the city, but the perpetual smoke from slash and burn agriculture is depressing. A Burmese Wat constructed in 1383 by King Keu Nea atop the peak named after the hermit Sudeva who used to inhabit its slopes, is gorgeous in its gold draped stupas and chanting Monks and shimmering three-hundred stepped Naga staircase. If only it were clearer...

The next day we drive through villages becoming sparse into the wild northwest of the country along the Burmese border, The Golden Triangle, poppy country. Village kids line the tiny road winding toward the first mountain range, throwing water at us as we pass, the first sign of the spring festival of Songkran. Atop the mountain pass, to give the poor old car a rest after all the switchbacks and climbing, we stop to buy crafts from multi-colored Hilltribe folk: Lisu, in fact, at this location. These Hill Tribe folk are so reminiscent of North American Indians it's amazing. The same faces and their cloth designs are all too vaguely familiar. Nice views over the forested hills rolling north and west to Burma. A pickup truck pulls up, and three heavy guys jump out to stretch. One guy starts asking a lot of questions after noticing our diplomatic plates. I'm polite in response, and hey, with kids it's not as if we're out here spying on Khun Sa's drug trade on behalf of the government. They're fairly cordial, but still obviously curious as they head off in the same direction as we do, down a steep, long grade toward the quiet and remote village of Pai. Half-expecting to find them waiting by the roadside, we descend big time for a couple of hours before coming into an extremely quiet little town, with not a whole lot going on. In the evening, after securing a couple of rooms in a guest house, we four-wheel up to a nearby waterfall which the kids enjoy immensely. Water slides, deep, cool pools, all great fun under towering jungle canopy.

The next morn it's off through more intense mountain terrain until we reach the turnoff for the spectacular Than Lod cave, about ten torturous miles to the north in thick jungle, under towering, contorted peaks, some with colorful prayer flags on them, but all looking like something out of the Cretaceous. With a guide hefting a great, bright lantern we enter the dark cavern full of swallows circling en masse at its entrance, where a large, clear river carves the labyrinth. Stalagmites and 'tites looking sparkly in the lantern-light, and incredible climbs up rickety ladders into enormous chambers full of crystal formations and oddities. One curtain-like formation has a faded pictograph of a deer with spear-point headed for its throat. After rafting with the lantern lighting our way into the black heart of the cave, we climb precariously to discover teak-boat coffins in a high chamber. The burials are said to be Piman and are wild the way they are hidden away in the center of the earth. We hiked out the other end of a cave that is said to be the longest in Asia, into the dim light of jungle somewhere just south of the Burma border.

After leaving the ancient lands of the northern Thai border, we had to climb yet another series of high mountain ranges before a descent and drive through further gnarly hills on into the nice little city of Mae Hong Son. A slice of quiet civilization in this mountain valley village. We stay in a one room guest cottage by a lake with a Burmese temple complex, Wat

Jong Klang shimmering in gold and white, and two hundred year old Wat Jong Kham in wood with lace work hanging from the eaves, right next door. We fill our days visiting Elephant camps, seeing a Monk initiation ceremony marching through the streets of an outlying village, riding long-tail boat downriver toward the border to visit Paduang, or Long Neck people in their remote riverside village. The women, like a certain African tribe, begin adding metal rings when they are adolescents, and continue until their necks are so elongated that if they remove the rings their necks would flop over. They believe it is a sign of beauty, and they certainly are elegant as they sit on their bamboo porches weaving gorgeous cloth. They are refugees from the SLORC regime that runs Burma with an iron fist. Apparently they had been forced to Rangoon to perform for tourist groups for no pay. So they escaped here, out in the middle of nowhere, perched above a beautiful set of rapids in extreme northwestern Thailand.

The favorite activity in the region with kids is Pha Sua waterfall, some twenty kilometers northwest of town, very close to the King's summer palace, and one of the last Chinese Kuomintang settlements (talk about living history) along the Burma border. Big, deep pool with nice falls for showering and best of all, no crowds. The amazing thing is just a few miles into the jungle from the falls are Karenni insurgent camps, bases from which these ethnic people continue a fifty-year fight. They began their guerrilla activities by helping the Allied powers against the occupying Japanese, then began their fight for independence against first, The Burmese Government, and now against the current military dictatorship with one of the great satanic names in the world today: The State Law And Order Reconciliation Council, or SLORC for short. Their allies in the fight for ethnic enclaves include the Karen and Kachin peoples along the Thai border further south, whose villages are continually attacked and harassed by the Burmese Army, forcing them to flee into Thailand for safety. All this contemporary history ongoing as we enjoy the luxury of a peaceful waterfall just down the road.

The drive there and back is classic rural Thailand, with rice paddies, water buffalo and chickens just wandering around the wooden villages. After a refreshing swim, driving back in the warm evening air sipping a Singha beer, reminded me of similar eves during high school summers in rural Maryland, returning from the refreshing waters of Dickerson quarry. Half a world, but not so far away.

The long drive completing the circular route back to Chiang Mai began depressingly, with the road under construction and unpaved for at least sixty miles. Good thing we had the Trooper! Beautiful brooding forested mountains with dark valleys to the east, and lighter forest along ridges toward Burma. Valley villages of thatch and bamboo amidst dark green rice paddies whiz by as we climb over seemingly endless mountain ranges on into Mae Sariang and the swing back east toward Chiang Mai. This is a beautiful section of road, with high pine forest dropping into the deep gorge at Ban Ob Luang, the runoff waters from Thailand's highest peak, Doi Inthanon, at 2,600 m. All of Chiang Mai and surrounding towns seems to be out in force along this stretch of river as it widens out, celebrating the first day of Songkran. Driving through the many small towns and villages gets us soaked as the water people are out in force, drowning the roadway and its occupants...pity the poor motorcyclists. In Chiang Mai we stumble onto a nice guest house and head out into the festivities centered around the moat. Everyone and everything is soaked!

The drive back to Bangkok takes nine hours and gives an incredible perspective of this Southeast Asian country. The mountains between Lampang and Phrae are some of the nicest we've seen on this entire trip: lush forest with big old growth trees creating huge canopies. Rivers run clear here even in the dry season and picturesque village after village after village until "rice basket of Asia" country and flat boredom on into Bangkok.

Then finally off to the Philippines for the first time in ten months. With a day off there I desperately want to get out to Corregidor before we return to one short night. The day dawned beautiful and clear with big fleecy clouds hovering over the volcanic peaks that encircle this teeming metropolis: probably as nice as this city gets. Wonderful boat ride out to the island, with the water becoming cleaner and clearer the further out we went. Then forested Corregidor appears, its tadpole-like shape glimpsed from the plane on the way in, the Gibraltar of the Pacific. The Malinta Tunnel that housed MacArthur and the Philippine President, Quezon, during the immense bombardment lasting for months before surrender in May 1942, was fought for with intensity. The Bataan Death March began just across the narrow north channel from the island: thousands perished on it while Japanese soldiers tried to obliterate every living thing on Corregidor. The huge gun emplacements housing 12" monsters were shattered by the pounding they took from artillery raining down from Bataan and Cavite. The behemoths were blown off their bases and still lay in the shrubs like giant's toys. Amazing that anyone survived at all: MacArthur finally heeding Roosevelt's order to leave, spirited away by a PT Boat to Mindanao, then a flight to Darwin, and Quezon being lifted off by submarine and taken to the States. Historians say the only reason the Japanese didn't successfully invade Australia was because of the amount of time it took to take the Philippines, including Corregidor.

May '96: Helsinki cool spring clean, with trees just budding green. Night slowly being erased by a sun that refuses to set. Flying over Russian steppes, villages scattered in the darkness below, their electric glimmer incongruous with the twilit north in pink and lingering blue of the midnight sun.

Back to Fiji almost seventeen years to the day. Gorgeous drenching rain drive from Nandi to Suva past sugar cane plantations, then towering volcanic peaks (some flumes thrusting out of dense jungle), before hitting the coral protected coastline with pounding surf ringing the island. Half the Fijian people are so African, with theories surrounding their origins still open to discussion. Our driver said many of the oral stories passed from generation to generation say they are from Tanzania. If so how did they get close to mid-Pacific? The Polynesians built canoes and sailing craft and traveled through the region, but Tanzanians! Were they enslaved?

Suva a classic colonial harbor, with tired cargo ships and round the world sailors moored under stunning green mountains, with green off-shore islands drifting lazily under huge clouds catching sunlight at their tops while dispensing rain from their bottoms on the southern horizon.

On the return to Sydney it was a deja vu of the flight back to Joburg from Mauritius. Almost an exact parallel of a journey across deep blue water to a far-flung exotic island and back to a sophisticated English speaking city. Just half a world away, that's all. Scalloped cloud pattern all the way to the Antarctic.

June '96: It's hard to believe that one month ago I was in the faintest beginnings of spring in Helsinki, the sun trying vainly to warm the northern climes, and now I'm back in the north of Michigan with trees green but spring not quite over even on the Summer Solstice. Fiji and Sydney recently visited in between add to the extraordinary wildness of traveling almost around the world, and definitely around the Pacific rim with a stop in Tokyo on the way to S.F. Waking to bright sunlight over the calm Pacific then crossing the California Coast directly over little Westport, last town on Highway One before it turns inland over the forested coastal range to avoid the mountains of the lost coast. Then, seconds later, Mendocino appears in its cute quaintness on the headland below and the memories associated with that spot come flooding back like some dream from the troubled sleep you just awoke from. Then Point Reyes as clear as you'll ever see it, white cliffs dropping into sheltered harbor and the estero home of seals and great white sharks and the best oysters in the world at Johnson's Oyster Farm. The Bay Area, home at last.

Stumbling out of the plane after some fifteen hours of flying and being given the keys to a cottage in Carmel. Paradise, and unusually clear of fog for the time of year. Kids playing in the warm waters of the Carmel River lagoon as it pools behind the sand bar keeping the thunderous cold, turquoise surf at bay. The now habitual drive south over and through the Big Sur to Nepenthe for Parisian style lattes the next morning: the fresh air even more stunning and dynamic than Sydney. Meditations during the drive through coast range of golden brown with redwoods nestled in its folds, of Miller and Jeffers and countless journeys down this stretch of road in my own life: family drives after traveling across country, drives from Colorado on spring break, hitchhiking down to Mexico, coming up from L.A. to settle in S.F. for almost ten years and countless trips down from the city. Scenery and smells and memories and strong coffee and chaotic kids set the mind a whirling. The Zen of cleanliness. This place is clean. The white sand speaks volumes with Point Lobos and Sea Otters and surfers and graduating high school kids building huge bonfires on the beach, and rotting kelp and fresh seaweeds of a variety of color adding to the visual and odorous wonder of the place.

The drive up to S.F. and a stop at Ano Nuevo to hike to see the Elephant Seals lying huge and fighting on the farthest beaches. Fog thick all the way up the coast, but then parting miraculously in a triangular shape that mirrors Ano Nuevo making it bearable to walk and enjoy despite the strong onshore breezes. Dead Elephant Seals mummified in the sand drifts are a curious attraction for the kids, as are the surfers heading down to one of the beaches for what looks like a good break.

Back in the city it's trips down memory lane and good coffee and cuisine and beer and vistas of fog coursing through the gate and the wildness of this outpost of America grown large. I was in Sydney just the week before and contrasting these two gorgeous locales so directly brought that very word to mind as a major difference. S.F. is wild. Sydney an English Garden. S.F. has more of a raw edge to it. Sydney is quite sedate.

Over in Marin at a playground under towering redwoods next to a clear running creek at the base of Mt. Tamalpais: As good as life gets anywhere on the globe.

Then the trip to heartland America, with thunderstorms delaying travel at O'Hare. In Charlevoix the rain cascading down and not caring about the weather because the air is fresh and clean, the pace relaxed and the water as cold as newly melted snow. The cottage perched between crystal clear waters amidst pine and birch and maples and latent flowering shrubs is a godsend to the third-world weary. Thinking of where we've come from and what's been seen over the past year is jaw dropping, especially knowing this too will soon be a gorgeous memory that will dissipate like the fog coming off the lake last night at the end of the longest day of the year. It was Carmel on the Great Lakes with cool, light fog wafting through the streets, but with fresh water rather than sea water creating it. Oh, Charlevoix!

Rigging the old sail boat in what has become a ritual. Teaching the girls the stays and lines then hoisting the flapping sails my grandfather's fingers raised and fixed and threaded and raced with. Sailing the boat is connecting with him and this place and the memories associated with it from a very young age: the smells that trigger those memories, and the weather, always the weather.

July '96: A mere two weeks ago we were winging south above the fresh water ocean of Lake Michigan to Chicago then on to D.C. Today I'm winging south again, but this time over the South China Sea with peninsular Macau to the west at the wide mouth of the Pearl River on the way back to Bangkok from Hong Kong. What staggers the mind is the amount of life that can be lived in such a sort span, enough, almost, for a lifetime: Round Lake and Lake Charlevoix to the banks of the muddy Potomac for whirlwind rendezvous with family and friends before refreshing San Francisco Bay and Fourth of July festivities and the launch out over the Pacific to Tokyo before heading south to the rice field green of the Chao Praya floodplain for a few days before the chaotic wonder of Hong Kong Harbor.

Not to mention Jakarta, and the journey into its Dutch past at the ancient harbor of Sunda Kelapa. Red-tiled roofs predominate the small area along the banks of the putrid river that flows into the tropical Java Sea speckled with a thousand islands just offshore. Known historically as Batavia, this area reeks of colonialism, but also an age where the exploiters could afford a high quality of life, which contrasts markedly with the teeming hordes bustling about yet another Asian metropolis trying to scrape a living from nothing. And this is one of the burgeoning economies of the region!

But the almost prehistoric harbor, filled with the distinctive Buginese Macassar schooners that have plied these waters for centuries, carrying wood from Borneo, spices from the Celebes and slaves from and to everywhere. The morning air is thick with humidity as I stroll along the quay bustling with the off loading and loading of these brightly colored craft, wide of beam and tall of sail. Amazingly long, slender pieces of wood obviously hewn from old growth forests in Borneo compose the hulls, while equally long and strong pieces serve as gangplanks for off loading by numerous impoverished folk.

One of my favorite places in the world to wander is found in Jakarta: the National Museum. A small, white colonial building off a major thoroughfare across from the Monas monument, its eclectic collection culled from the vast island network this nation encompasses is extraordinary, but not overwhelming (like most national museums). The courtyard alone with its huge collection of Hindu statuary lining covered walkways or out on the grass is enough for anyone, let alone the great collection of musical instruments, batiks and the different architectural styles of each distinct island. But my favorite section was the Dong Son drum collection. Traded to Java's shores from Vietnam over two thousand years ago, these bronze masterpieces have the most intriguing reliefs cast upon their surfaces I've ever seen: wild bird men in canoes, frogs raised on the typanum, abstract storks flying amidst other fantastic abstract patterns. To think of the age of these instruments and the fine shape many of them are still in, is a miracle. These sit on the floor next to the case exhibiting the skull of the first *Homo erectus* ever found, Java man!

Rising up off the dark green mountainous island of Formosa, with dense Taipei nestled snug in harbor valley, protected from direct Typhoon assault by towering peaks soaring to 4,000 m. along an eastern spine. The northern tip of this tiny nation disappears dramatically into deep blue under a waxing half moon in azure sky. Then a few geologic remnants of the main island form miniature Formosa's of green grass perched atop precipitous cliffs far out to sea. Nature's pounding will obliterate this string of green pearls from the ocean's surface soon enough, for aeons ago they must have been connected with the Ryukyu and Japan proper.

The most impressive first impression of Seoul are the stunning jagged peaks of forest and exposed rock that hem in the northern part of the city sprawl along the mighty Han. Heading south to Osan the first thing that strikes the visitor is every inch of tillable terrain is planted with corn, squash, pumpkin and herbs. It must be a carry-over of the self-sufficiency required to survive the atrocities of brutal war in the not so distant past. The hills in this part of the country are thickly forested with deciduous and pine, while the valleys are dense green with orderly rice paddies cut through with dirt paths. Egrets browse white in the paddies searching for insects and fish.

Osan as American as Lincoln, Nebraska: what with the commissary stocked as well as any Safeway, the base exchange loaded with clothes, kitchen items, pharmacy and electronics, and with Mexican restaurants, Burger King and even Popeye's chicken strewn around base, you wouldn't bat an eyelash if you were transported here blind except for the airmen clothed in camouflage, the Patriot Missiles and the scream of jets above. But that would tell all, wouldn't it?

August '96: Back in Delhi, but this time with a desire to soak in the prehistoric ambiance of decrepit, rickshaw thick and teeming Shahjahanabad, or Old Delhi. After wading through the masses I slip into Digambar Jain Temple, built originally in 1526. The shrines on the second floor terrace are some of the most exquisitely ornate I've ever seen.

The ceiling in every incense thick hall has the intricacy of a Tibetan Thanka. Devotees make offerings to Lord Parasnath (The immediate predecessor of Lord Mahavira, the founder of the religion, who, like Buddha, was a prince who renounced everything to search for the meaning of life in the sixth century) of candles, fruit and rice. Beautiful, wild place. And next door is the stinky Jain Bird Hospital, where mostly pigeons crushed by the hordes on the streets are cared for. The Jains are known for their aversion to killing anything that lives, however humble, and so these lowly, flying rats benefit. Well, kind of, I think I would rather die than be cared for in such a foul(fowl) place.

After leaving the Jain sanctuary it's back out into the overwhelming crush of the Chandni Chowk and a long, slow, dodging stroll through the heart of this ancient capital throbbing with life. Down the length of the Chowk to another respite inside the grounds of Fatehpuri Masjid, another Mughal mosque of sandstone and marble, but smaller and part of, rather than set apart from, the surrounding bustle. I exit through the north entrance of this sacred compound onto Khari Baoli, the scent of nuts and spices by the ton filling the nostrils. I dip into a dark, covered street reminiscent of Jerusalem's underground Arab markets filled with spices, and avoid porters heavily laden with huge packs of spices exiting onto the street. An interior courtyard jammed with spices spilling out of large bags at every turn overwhelms the senses. Ginger, turmeric, coriander and chilies, chilies, chilies are every where, piled up in ground or whole form under grungy slum buildings.

Further walks into the heart of the human maelstrom brings glimpses of horrible poverty, death, and squeezing past cattle as they commandeer the narrow streets. And shops, shops and more shops selling everything imaginable. What a world, what a life, and how ultimately meaningless given the evidence before me of absolute and utter hopelessness amongst the impoverished hordes who continue to breed, breed, breed, thus perpetuating the exponential cycle of absurdity.

September '96: Back to Australia in blustery spring weather, flowers just beginning to peek from the warming soil. On the flight up to Port Moresby the views of the Great Barrier Reef and Whitsunday Islands is stunning. Fraser Island, just north of Brisbane, is the largest sand island in the world. Further north in the protected waters between the reef and mainland, windblown or water washed sand blankets the surface, creating rippling sand patterns stretching between sporadic atolls. These sands, upwelling from somewhere, or being swept off the reef, must be the sands that created Fraser Island over the millennia.

After monsoonal cloud cover obscuring the thickly forested Owen Stanley's of Papua New Guinea, it's back down across the Coral Sea, tracing the beach-lined continent, from Cairns southward. Only to hop a plane a day later halfway across the nation into the Red Center and the Aboriginal dreamtime of Uluru, Ayers Rock.

Shimmering edge between Uluru's blood-red setting sun sandstone and deep, clear blue sky, gives the feeling this monolith is indeed a spiritual entity. Bulbous Olgas in the direction of the waning sun explored the following day. Behind Kata Tjuta, the Aboriginal name for the thirty-six individual sandstone domes clustered west of Uluru, I head off into the Valley of the Wind. The silence of the high, rounded mounds soaring into the clearest sky on the planet, is broken by the piercing call of an unseen bird in the green foliage of gum trees growing in an amphitheater of sandstone walls. In the dark red sandy plains that stretch out 360 degrees around these two geological wonders are spring green forests of stately desert oaks, spinifex grasses that grow in circles, acacias in arroyos and seasonal flowers galore. Tjukurpa, the aboriginal origin myth is centered here, and there is indeed a feeling of serenity in the landscape, of centeredness, of dreamtime understanding as I fix my position on the globe in the mind's eye, and meditate on the noise and chaos that seems to be engulfing the planet: The Last Wave!

Winging again across the infinite sweep of the Aussie interior, chasing the setting sun on the return to Bangkok: red rivulets running north and south, sand waves rippling across a continent, occasionally interrupted by stationary white salt pan lake clouds, scattered across the dreamtime.

October '96: The leaps taken across the planet's surface in this job are poetic. From the center of Australia and its red sand spring amongst sandstone behemoths, to quaint Helsinki tinged with the colors of autumn. We drink champagne and laugh, for tomorrow we die!

On the return from Karachi, that contemporary bastion of chaos and possible model for the planet's future! The Prime Minister's brother assassinated by police in a hail of gunfire just a few days ago, ambushed for no apparent reason. If he's not safe.......

Not to belabor the point, but from the Red Center of Australia to the Thar Desert in exactly one month. The waves of sand below are white with sporadic pockets of trees growing from what looks like the original, grey surface. The sand is on the march.

Once again a beautiful stroll through the Margalla Hills thick with fullbodied pines along the ridges. Views into the historic Taxila valley close as the crow flies. Only a four hour hike! Then halting above a gorgeous valley filled with fields of potato and radish and wheat and corn and the wails of mullah over loudspeakers, each village answering the other in prayer to the prophet. The sound's eerie timeless beauty as the fresh wind rustles the pine needles in the green foothills of the Karakoram.

Ohhh, the planet, the planet, the planet at twilight over ancient adobe villages the shape of neurons whose dendritic dirt roads connect to the next cell of human habitation across the Punjab wrinkled by plate tectonics under towering Himalaya deep in monsoon snow. The Vale of Kashmir hidden in distant dusk valley, full of danger.

The Ganges' massive sand bars are 2/5ths human ash, and 3/5ths Himalayan minerals: the liquid form of God! Big bend of wide, brown sacred river far below, Himalaya white from Dhauligiri to Kachenjunga. Everest and Kachenjunga as clear as clear, with the former's Nepali name,

Sagarmartha, or peak of the world, looming timelessly above the rich history and contemporary squalor of the Ganges Plain.

Then to Krabi for a weekend away. flying in over the jagged limestone peaks of green tufted tops and white sheer rock sides as they peter out spectacularly in the gulf formed by the green, lush island of Phuket. Later driving through these peaks towering above the road and over pristine rice paddies of emerald green with the occasional wet, black water buffalo, wandering through the shallows, evokes the classic south Asian scene depicted in so many watercolors brushed on rice paper. Then catching a rooster tail pirogue out to Prang Na, past brownish white limestone walls rising out of turquoise water, before a squall line of incredible volume obliterates the earth as we wade ashore and take refuge in a beach front cafe. This peninsula of sand and palms pinched between a mesa of limestone at its base and tipped by probably the most spectacular combination of thrusting, Yosemite-like rounded peaks and gorgeous sand in the world, is something to behold. Adding to the spectacle are phallic pinnacles rising just off shore, obviously the inspiration for the large, multicolored carved phallic offerings found at a fertility shrine inside a cave at the base of one of the promontory's huge monoliths at the southern end of the beach. Wow.

The Alps of the south island of New Zealand sweep majestically southwest. Their glaciers crumble into west coast rainforest, Mt Cook soaring clear, last stop before Antarctica. Memories of hitch-hiking and solo-climbing and camping in thick forest next to rushing silt-laden streams under towering peaks. Then, as we approach Cook Straight, Mt. Egmont can be seen in its volcanic cone perfection, a few cumulus hugging its ice cream snow fields, halfway up the west coast of the north island. On the departure the plane wings over the northern part of the south island. Out the window is glimpsed the lake set in mountains I camped beside those many years ago. Remembering reading Henry Miller while strolling through the mossy forest, seeing no one while camped out on the clean lake shore under razor sharp peaks. Then hiking out to the road after a few days to hitch to Greymouth, when after thirty minutes without luck an old man limped out of his little cottage with a hot cup of tea for me. Precious! From the Himalaya to the Southern Alps of New Zealand! What a reach. Tragedy maketh the man. The night before the return to southeast Asia, Betty Carter is singing her classic style of jazz at the Basement in downtown Sydney. I first saw her live in Montreal in 1978 in an intimate club where we sat just feet from her passing joints back and forth. Just short of twenty years later she still blows me away. The actress Judy Davis is there for both sets, showing some taste. Carter's band is continually challenged by her unique improvisations, but pull it off. She's happy, and it's an inspiring night for all.

November '96: Then up to Taiwan and the clearest view ever of that island's forested mountainous backbone, contrasted by the thick air pollution obscuring the thickly populated areas all along the western coastal plain. On to Osan and opting to stay inside to watch the '96 election returns rather than wander the ancient streets of Seoul on a bright, crisp autumn day. Clinton wins handily under the intermittent scream of A-10s and F-18s patrolling the DMZ skies above. The political theater cannot be beat: intense congressional races, and senatorial races down to the wire and too close to call mirrors the competitiveness that drives American society to outposts like Osan.

A race to overnight in Manila before coming back to Bangkok miraculously on time to meet the family in the Hua Lumphun train station just before departure by sleeper train south to Ko Samui and a gorgeous long weekend in paradise. Perfect time of year too as sun's intensity is broken by tremendous tropical downpours. Images of note that stick in mind are swimming in soft surf with a torrential squall pelting the surface with a myriad of drops leaping off the smooth surface: the word sacred wafted into my mind as I listened to the rippling of multitudinous pearls from heaven. Then diving to the white sand bottom and hearing the storm's drumming of the surface while watching multicolored fish dart past only brought home the miracle of this particular planet. Later that night, swimming in pounding surf from a distant disturbance out over the Gulf of Siam, a thin sliver of waxing moon paired with Jupiter appeared in a break in the clouds above. The crystal clarity of the planets and their reflected glow upon thick cloud again brought the word sacred lilting through the brain of one *Homo sapiens* immersed in the churning mother's milk of all living things.

Leaving Samui on the same rockin' and rollin' sea through the gorgeous Ang Thong Islands with one peak that rivals anything on Bora Bora, before boarding the train north to Krung Thep still wobbly from the huge swells. Then into the City of Angels early in the morn. Slums lining the tracks the most interesting with their thick reality of smoky stoves and babies wandering through trash piled high along the banks of black, putrid klongs.......Only to lift off some twelve hours later for Helsinki, that cold-ass city of the far, far north and its autumnal grey sky and pelting rain after the blessedness of planet earth's tropics.

After liftoff from flat, rich, civilized Singapore the Lingga Archipelago just north of the island of Sumatra appear sweeping southeast towards Jakarta, my destination. The islands are pristine green, each framed by a thin turquoise belt and separated by glistening seas. In the distance, along the backbone of volcanic peaks that made this terra firma, a cone peaks high above a thick layer of cloud, a future Krakatoa?

December '96: On a clear winter morning flight to Taipei, just north of the Dongrek Range that separates Thailand from the wilds of Cambodia, the familiar rectangular shape of a Khmer bareay below jars the senses. The brown water of the distinctive reservoir frames a square island at its center, holding a building that can only be an Angkor cousin. Our position is such that Phnom Rung should be directly below, but we're too high to see the historic landmark. Several more bareay come into view, scattered across flat parched land, the green mountains only a minor inconvenience in the push north of Khmer Culture. Further east, Preah Wihaan must be nestled in one of the valleys before the range peters out at the syl-van gash of the Mekong flowing south brown and wide from the Tibetan Plateau. The other side of the river brings Laotian mesa mountains, rising to form pristine, tree clogged bowls, all most likely filled with teeming wildlife, some maybe not even "discovered" yet. Then more typical ser-rated mountains appear toward the Vietnam border, with one fifth of the forest slash and burned by hill tribe folk in one of the most remote places anywhere.

The southeast corner of Chengdu Island due south of the Korean archi-pelago is littered with perfect volcanic cones soaring out of uniform rec-tangular rice paddies framed by raised dikes. Listening to James Taylor's "Sweet Baby James" minutes later soaring over the rugged mainland ter-rain covered in snow: "Those mountains seem dreamlike on account of that frosting." Yeah! Then into dark, bleak Seoul with its Orwellian roof numbered apartment complexes rigidly arranged in microchip fashion in swirling snow among traffic, traffic, traffic on the banks of the mighty Han River.

Each Punjabi village at night on the descent into Lahore is a spiral neb-ulae containing infinite variety and complexity of life within. The next morning it's off in a rented jalopy with Fazal at the wheel on the Trunk road west to Peshawar. Just before reaching that wild west town, we turn north toward the towering Hindu Kush and the isolated small city of Saidu Sharif. The roads of Pakistan have to be some of the most dangerous anywhere in the world. It's not necessarily the traffic, but the deteriorated condition of the roads as they switch back over rugged foothills and high above raging rivers in steep valleys. We take freezing large, spare rooms in the intriguing White Palace Hotel, built of cool marble by the King of Swat as a summer retreat. The marble porches are reminiscent of the Mughal Rang Mahal in Old Delhi's Red Fort, but without the frills. The complex sits beside a raging river under towering rock and snow peaks of pine, with local tribal folk climbing and descending numerous trails that honeycomb the valley: a group hefting huge logs on their backs cross a rickety bridge upstream. The traffic on this main valley trail that meets the end of the paved road next to the hotel is endless. The bustle at the trailhead is ever changing with a variety of goods being brought down from the high mountain valleys and exchanged for supplies dropped by small truck for the long slog up the trails. Smoky adobe homes cling to the steep slopes above the hotel, the chatter of their children echoing across the thin air of the cool valley. The rooms of the hotel actually look like barracks of the British hill station variety, tiered as they are alongside and above the marble palace. Trying to get the history of the place, the accurate history that is, was difficult as the proprietor denied the British had anything to do with this particular retreat. The next frosty morning Fazal and I head off down the thrashed road toward Saidu Sharif and Swat Valley to the north.

We decide to go for a big view due to the clarity of the day and so head up a dusty, twisty, bleak drive up to Malamm Jabaa, a ten thousand foot peak with a deserted ski resort at its base. The only reason this sad excuse for a paved road winds up through desolate villages and barren hills is because of this proposed vacation destination that no one in their right mind would venture to. The entire resort, including small hotel and chairlift is in total disrepair. But it's the highest point one can access by car in Swat, so we climb on and on past tiny mountain villages with dirty famished kids waving and pointing at us. At ten thousand feet the vast vista of high, snow deep Hindu Kush peaks, bleak craggy foothills and wide shallow rivers sweeping in from the Afghani border and Chitral past the shanty towns of Saidu down in the dry valley below, make this view one of the more unusual on the planet's surface: 360 degrees of Central Asia.

And to think Alexander the Great actually fought his way through the Swat valley, at Udegram on his way down from Chitral, and the Dionysian outpost of Nysa. There a few nights before, Alexander's cohort camped in this village formed from the god's name, and found there vines for wine (no other tribes of the region made wine), ivy growing (it was found nowhere else in the Far East), all evidence that their Mediterranean god had indeed touched down in that forested valley some time before. To celebrate, all his troops marched up a mountain, crowned themselves with ivy and went on a Bachic spree to honor Dionysus in this remote place. The Dionysian customs of the people of the valley, the Kalash Kafirs, included sacrificing goats for religious purposes and exposing their dead in wooden coffins hung among the trees. Fascinating! All these thoughts while glancing in the direction of the hazy, dry, Afghan border, across which, the fighting that began with the Russian invasion of 1980, continues with the ultra-Muslim Taleban driving successfully north in their attempt to unite the country for the first time in years.

K-2 is more spectacular than Everest: its triangular, snow and black rock lurch is staggering to the eye. Even Nunkun at 23,000' along the front range seems tiny compared with the monster looming from back along the China border. Back in Bangkok for Christmas, the food eaten in those remote Pakistani valleys comes back to haunt me. A cholera-like vicious diarrhea stays with me for weeks. The black, putrid nature of my shit is a powerful thing to behold. At least it happened at home and not on the road.

January '97: The trip to white sand of Jervis Bay three hours drive south of Sydney through rolling, forested coastal hills: The wave break off Plantation Point the best body surfing I've ever done in my life. The huge waves surging through the narrow opening out to sea way across the bay hit this point perfectly with a nice wide base supporting towering water you can see through. This was a sport trip to Sydney as I caught Australian Open warm-up tennis at the Sydney International in White City, just minutes from the hotel. The blistering sun in a deep blue skin-cancer sky was the quintessential Aussie tennis experience in an intimate venue. A few days later, after a quick, uneventful trip out to Fiji's coral encircled isles, I caught the West Indies playing Pakistan at the Sydney Cricket Ground under an equally classic sky. Drinking beer while watching the colorful uniforms scamper for balls across the deep green grass under fleecy cloud exemplified in a relaxing afternoon the Zen wonder of sport in this sport mad country.

Then the big leap up to Bangkok and the following week to Hong Kong and a day trip through the insanity of mainland China's Guongdong Province: Shenzen, Duonggong, then on into Guongzhou. Whatever aesthetic the Chinese once had is gone. Their cities are booming with glass and steel skyscrapers, modeled after Hong Kong capitalist energy. The architecture is cold and austere, showing little humanity. An attempt to mimic the First World's surface but not its dynamic creative artistic freedoms. Off the recently built freeway, between the major urban centers, is the old China, filled with rice and cabbage farmers, the latter watering pocket size plots of freshly turned soil with the ancient dual-watering-cans-slung-over-the-shoulders-system: the peasants of the ages sloughing off a progress they have neither access to nor interest in. The best part about Guongzhou is the Six Banyan Trees Pagoda. Built around 600 A.D., this sanctuary shielding one's soul from the street chaos of this mega-city, is a spiritual time machine, taking all who enter back to a quieter, more meditative era than the madness that now exists in the contemporary mind of *Homo sapiens.*

Not long now before Hong Kong becomes part of China, and the absence of their traditional cultural aesthetic robs this western outpost of any soul it might have had. The nervousness in the newspapers and on the streets is palpable. China wants to move in troops ahead of the takeover to "smooth the transition!" The people of Hong Kong better be careful! The behemoth is at the door.

Flying back to Bangkok the immense sand dune coast of Vietnam looks appealingly unspoilt. The rugged hills where the narrow country is pinched together surround a pint-sized valley with a tiny airstrip. After reading "GIAP: The Victor in Vietnam," describing the life and military strategies of the North Vietnamese leader in his country's wars against the French and U.S., I recognize this locale as none other than Khe Sanh. The numbered hills surrounding the valley are all in the right place, as is the road slicing through the narrow valley from the east, which a relief column took several weeks to breach. Thinking of the B-52 carnage that was unleashed on these mountainous jungles during the height of the battle, killing North Vietnamese troops by the thousands as they bivouacked, one has to be impressed by nature's quick recovery and burial of humanity's viciousness. Nature *is* forgiving! Or is it just indifference?

February '97: The next week Jakarta and Singapore beckon. This quote read on the way to the latter: "In Chinese history 'the written word possessed the power of ordering the cosmos and of generating reality.' This script conveys meaning beyond language." The word order needs to be studied here, because the Chinese seem to be obsessed with it, both on the mainland and in far-flung Chinese outposts like Singapore. This city-state is amazing in its unparalleled civility, considering the part of the world it's in. Order is bought at a price, however, with a fascistic government. The rest of the capitalist world loves fascism, and the U.S. Seventh Fleet would protect it in a heart beat.

One of the more amazing things about Singapore, besides the cleanliness, is the incredible number of freighters tethered in the straits, awaiting their precious unloading/loading time at the dock before heading off to all corners of the globe. Jakarta, on the other hand, is more the norm for this part of the world: huge, sprawling with shanty towns lining old canals thick and black with contamination. Shacks of tin and cardboard on stilts overhanging fetid waters is an Asian stereotype. The Monas, or victory monument in the center of the city, across from the colonial presidential palace in a huge square of trees and grass, rises in stark contrast to the pervasive poverty, yet affords a fantastic view if the smog isn't too bad. The 360 degrees encompass the hills to the south and volcanoes to the west toward Krakatoa. Also the first of the many islands just offshore north of town can be seen in the turquoise waters still plied by the amazing wooden Macassar schooners sailing the ancient route between Sunda Kelapa and Kalimantan.

Then to Delhi where, because it's going to be the final trip with time off in town, I concentrate on the three temples of Old Delhi's Chandni Chowk, the main road across from the Red Fort's Lahore Gate: Jain, Hindu Lingam, and Sikh. The Digambar Jain temple on the outside doesn't appear to be much: red sandstone interspersed with the proverbial white marble reminiscent of the fort across the way. But on the second floor, and inside the temple rooms, one finds murals of vast intricacy blending with the fragrance of a myriad of spices and smoky incense. The chaos of Chandni Chowk, just meters away over a balcony, isn't even on the same planet. A true refuge!

The original temple was built in 1526, but during the 1800s there was a lot of new building, so most of what you see actually dates from that time. The founder of Jainism is known as Mahivara, a prince who renounced everything to search for the meaning of life in the sixth century B.C. (sound familiar?). This prince also has another name, Jina (the conqueror) and the name of the religion is taken from this. The Jains don't actually think of Mahivira as the founder of the religion, like Christians think of Christ or Buddhists of Buddha, but rather as the last of twenty-four "ford-finders," or Tirthankaras, who help humans bridge the gap between the earthly and the spiritual. It is these Tirthankaras that are worshipped in the temple rooms of spice and incense, with devotees making offerings of rice, fruit and candles.

Jain's believe that all life is sacred, and next to the temple is a tall skinny building that acts as their bird hospital. That's right, they take injured (mostly pigeons) off the crowded streets where they've most likely been clipped or crushed by rickshaws or pedestrians, and attempt to nurse them back to health in scruffy, stinking cages stacked to the ceiling in a long, narrow room. Donations are suggested to view this absurdity, while beggars in the streets go unfed.

Just down Chandni Chowk to the west, the Gauri Shankar Hindu Temple's two steep step entrances are hidden somewhat by the distraction of a garland makers market at street level, even though they act as bookends to it. As one sits to take off shoes to leave with a minder, the smell of flowers mingles with vendor food odors and the hallucinogenic colors of wreaths newly fashioned, preparing the soul for a connection with the sacred up the steps, inside the lingam temple.

Upstairs a broad courtyard opens to the sky, with the main temple bordered by smaller shrines dedicated to the pantheon of Hindu gods: Durga, Hamunum, Yamuna, etc., along one side. Some of these border on the tacky with their bright colors and plastic beads and necklaces, but the 800 year old lingam shrine at the courtyard's center counters this with its awesome authenticity. The brown lingam is a rock penis set in a marble representation of the female genitalia, which itself is in a silver encasement decorated with snakes, Shiva's ornament of choice. It is the most revered symbol of Shiva, and thus represents the cosmic pillar, the center of the universe, life itself. Normally lingams at Angkor and in Thailand are somewhat tall and stylized, but this one has either been worn down by centuries of rubbing and worship, or else is naturally in the shape of just a circumcised penis' tip.

To observe men and women bent over from a kneeling position fervently touching and praying over the phallic symbol: pouring libations of cool water and placing wood apple leaves, marigolds, red powder, henna, rice and sandalwood paste in special arrangements atop it, is a sight to behold. Fellatio is what it comes close to representing: worship of the erotic energy that drives the universe. The water falls into a marble bath in which there are carvings of all the members of Shiva's family: There's Lord Shiva, his bull Nandi, his wife Parvati and his sons Kartik, the god of war, and Ganesh, the elephant god. On the wall behind is a representation in silver of Shiva and Parvati, both wearing gold jewelry. On the side walls niches with single candles light carved stone images of deities. This is a religion that is at least three-thousand years old.

The Sisganj Gurdwara Sikh Temple five minutes walk to the west, and through the heart of human traffic, is recognized by its gold domes glinting under a pollution obscured sun. The Sikh religion originated from the founder of the faith, Guru Nanak, who was born into a Punjabi Hindu family in 1469. Growing up under Hindu and Islamic influences he came to realize that all the suffering caused by wars between the two beliefs was senseless. He strove to end the fighting and bring the two sides together. He preached that there was only one god, that all were children of god and that divisions between Hindus and Muslims was meaningless. Unlike the Hindu Gurus, Guru Nank encouraged people to find god while living normal family lives, without the need to renounce earthly attachments. He based the emphasis of his teachings on moral values and not ceremonies and rituals. His teachings were continued by ten Sikh Gurus. The Mughal Akbar was impressed by their integrity and granted land with a pool that to this day holds the Golden Temple in Amritsar. In 1604 a book by the fifth Guru was compiled and placed in the Golden Temple. The book was a compilation of hymns written by the four earlier Gurus, plus those written by five Muslim and ten Hindu saints. Now known as the Holy Book it contains 5894 hymns and verses.

After checking shoes at the hall around to the right, one passes a Sikh Guard in full turbaned uniform with spear at the entrance just off the tumultuous street who will draw you aside to affix a covering atop your sacrilegious head. Up marble steps with other pilgrims who have just washed their feet and covered their heads, one enters a large hall with live Sikh musicians singing hymns from the Holy Book. Next to them, and the focus of the entire hall, is a marble table with blankets of silk nestling the Sikh Holy Book, the Guru Granth Sahib, which nestles beneath a golden canopy. Underneath this structure, in a marble grotto, is the cage where Sikh Guru Tegh Bahadur was held before being martyred beneath a Banyan tree on this very spot in 1675. He was killed for speaking out against the Mughal Emperor Aurngazeb's use of force to achieve conversions to Islam. A piece of the tree is enshrined in a small room just off the main hall. Pilgrims line up for a peek at the cage, then sit and meditate in this light and spacious hall and dig the wailing tunes.

Right next door, as you exit from the shoe hall, there is the tiniest little mosque overlooking the hustle and bustle with a tiny prayer courtyard and small marble dome. This is the Sunheri Masjid (The Golden Mosque), from whose steps in 1739 the Persian King, Nadir Shah, after defeating the Mughal ruler Mohammed Shah, sat and watched his troops massacre the local citizens, leaving the streets of Old Delhi littered with corpses. Estimates are that the Persian soldiers killed some 30,000, perhaps more, in retaliation for a small uprising that resulted in the deaths of several Persians.

So in a few short blocks heading west along the south side of Chandi Chowk, just across from the Red Fort in Old Delhi, are all the spiritual elements that make up the intricate and profound history of this land.

Transport yourself, if you will, to the next Wednesday, a mere seven days after the intimate exploration of India's teeming old capital along the banks of the Yamuna, to trudging through tall, fragrant pine, encased in snow along the shore of a frozen inlet of the Baltic Sea. On my way to Akseli Gallen-Kallela's studio nestled in the forest bordering this inlet, I decide to take a shortcut across the frozen sea. My first step crunching on the snowy covering makes me nervous, but then, way off in the middle of the frozen waste, in the middle of the inlet, I see an ice fisherman braving the whipping winds, and figure if he's safe out there, I should be O.K. crossing this arm of the sea. Kallela's castle studio is a simple wonder, as it sits nestled in trees overlooking an inlet that in the summer must be magical. It's a wonderland in winter with snow, towering firs and fresh clean air at minus 15 celsius freezing the nostril hairs with each meditative inhalation. The artist is one of my favorites because the landscapes he paints remind me of the birch tree and pine needle-laden forest floors and crystalline lakes of Northern Michigan. One of my favorite paintings of his, called Lynx Den, captures snow corniced boulders amidst the red trunks of pines with a blue Finnish winter sky at the top of the picture: Lynx footprints trudge to an unseen lair. Other pieces capture the intense spirit of this northern tribe as they face the extreme elements of a refreshingly stark land.

Returning across the ice toward the tram stop the other side of the snowy forest, the wind blasts my face. It freezes quickly and the resultant numbness spreads. Turning around and walking backward helps, but not much. In the middle of the ice I panic, and head for the shelter of the trees as fast as I can, hoping no ice holes await: if I were to find water, I'd be dead in minutes. On shore and out of the wind, my torso and face immediately begin to thaw. The thought of the hotel sauna overlooking the inlet that enters Helsinki up to the Opera House, and heating up with drenching sweat inspires me on.

The next week on this whirlwind of weekly travel is a flight to Seoul and Osan. Just off Hong Kong on the way north gorgeous, south Pacific-like Donshuan atoll appears below in the infinite sweep of ocean. Perfection, with white wave break defining the top half, then fading around to the south where a tiny pearl shaped island sits amidst turquoise waters, sliced by a dirt air strip. Then, the high craggy peaks of Taiwan some time later, a few with snow on them, provide a stark, clear contrast to the perpetually thick smog obscuring the island's crowded west coast. It is interesting how *Homo sapiens* sullies the very air and water it needs for survival.

Despite being not nearly as cold as Helsinki, and even sunny for a few hours each day, this country still cannot escape its depressive state. After Thailand, even with its problems, this place is cold and austere, its Confucianism seemingly crushing all aesthetics. The people of Thailand are warm and smile frequently, perhaps superficially, but nevertheless it's enjoyable. Korea isn't friendly; it seems as rigid as the troubled North engulfed by famine. The religion practiced here is the same worship of capitalism found in Japan and, now, China: an all-pervasive conformity in pursuit of material wealth. In the west we seem to combine creativity with the machine, the creative dynamic in fact drives the machine. Here, once the industry has been established, it seems to destroy the unique spirit of these ancient civilizations. The past, represented by the palaces and temples scattered around Seoul, are the wonder of a not so distant past, so quickly forgotten.

March '97: Then to Manila and its crazy American-Philippine mix of congestion. To escape it I take off to Volcanic Taal Lake south of town for some fresh air. Driving through the calles of Las Pinas (to stop at the only bamboo organ in the world in the cathedral there) the whole ambiance reminded me of Mexico and Central America: the reasons being obvious, but still the familiarity was comforting considering it is still Asia.

Then to the largest Jeepny factory in the country, where they literally pound out the shiny metallic bodies by hand, in the dirt. The colorful chrome jeep buses that ply various routes through the city take the place of buses, and certainly are more colorful. Apparently, the drivers compete for business among the young now by installing the highest tech. sound systems in their buses, thus making the noisy streets even noisier with the thump, thump of heavy bass: almost like an endless line of L.A. low-riders. After the subtle climb up to the volcano's rim, the cool breezes swirling around the caldera are miraculous considering it's only 2,000' high. Down inside the ancient crater created by a huge volcanic eruption, taking the top off what must have been close to a ten thousand foot peak, is a fresh water lake with active volcanic cones popping up to form a restless island. Lush coconut plantations litter the crater floor while fish farm nets crowd the waters of the shoreline. Five hundred residents of the caldera died in 1973 when one of the small cones erupted. Life on the edge just a short drive from Manila, its skyscrapers vaguely visible in the smog in the flat lands to the north of Taal Volcano, to say nothing of nearby Pinatubo.

Then, of course, back to Sydney once again, and the fresh air and sunshine and general ambiance of the greatest city in the world drive any depressions far away. Pub life at the end of the summer season is lively and gregarious, the cuisine superb. St. Patrick's day celebrations the greatest ever with The Mercantile Pub in The Rocks closing the street for a day of raucous music and non-stop drinking, the bottles and glasses piled high in the gutters by five o'clock, still with the entire evening to go. And before arriving there sipping Guinness on tap in a tony Surry Hills patio with the advertising community from twelve o'clock on, with a sausage barbecue smoking away so more beer could be quaffed. What a life!

But then, in counter, to pay for the sins of Sydney, it's off to Islamabad over Easter weekend. The eighteen year old Airbus that Pakistan International flies twice a week to Bangkok, is deteriorating rapidly. And to compound my fears we takeoff into the first storm to hit Bangkok for several months. Flying out to the west towards Burma, we hit the worst patch of turbulence ever, with the plane free-falling for what seemed minutes, and people screaming, and a coffee pot that spilled steaming up the cabin with scary hissing so it seems like a fire. I was wondering whether the old plane was structurally up to the incredible punishment. This time it was, but maybe not in the near future. Something in the clouds (ice, hail?) had taken a huge divit out of the plane's nose, because after landing in Rangoon, all the pilots huddled around pointing and examining it for an hour, looking worried. Great! They decided to fly on and we did reach Lahore later that evening with no problems. But leaving Islamabad several days later the wheels locked-up just as the nose began to lift, forcing us to come to a wild, crazy halt after hitting top speed right at the end of the runway. All in a day's work!

April '97: My reward was a quick overnight to Chiang Mai later in the week. After the hour flight I went to the consulate, took care of business, then went to the hotel and headed off to see the historic Lanna Wats inside the ancient city walls framed by a moat that we didn't see on the family trip exactly a year ago. Wat Prah Sing was exquisite in its ornate Lanna style of red with gold flower pattern columns at the entrance to the wat, and on the ceiling inside. Started in 1345 and housing the Prah Singh Buddha from Sri Lanka, the inside of the wihaan is exquisitely decorated with detailed murals of life in the Lanna Kingdom. The old wooden library next to the new main wat, built high up to protect the buddhist texts stored there from paper devouring bugs, is a wonder of simplicity, again with a little gold fringe around the windows but this time painted directly on the brown wood, all to great effect. The chedi at Wat Chedi Luang, built in 1441, is impressive in height and girth, with four Buddha images placed in the four directional niches around its base.

The next morning, before flying back to Bangkok, I whipped off in a tuk tuk to the oldest wat in the city, Wat Chiang Man, founded by King Mengrai in 1296. The main wat has huge columns of teak inside, along with wall murals and the Lanna red base and gold geometric pattern on the ceiling and around the entrance. Next door, in another wihaan are kept two ancient Buddha images, dating from 2500 and 1800 years old respectively. A nice quiet meditative enclosure in what once was a small, quiet town now become like its capital to the south.

Then a few days later we pile the kids in the old Isuzu Trooper and, to counter covering the northern part of the country the previous year, head for a beach and rainforest trip to Southern Thailand. After fleeing Bangkok to the southwest, we soon get sea smells wafting in the windows, then piles of white salt in evaporation ponds amidst windmill sails spinning to pump water. Stalls selling bagged salt and dried fish line the highway, each one exactly like the other in choice of products it's a wonder any one makes baht enough. But, of course, for these folk, it doesn't take much to make a living. Our first stop is Petchburi, and a climb up Khao Wang hill and the intriguing collection of wats and various structures comprising King Mongkut's palace atop Phra Nakhon Khiri (Holy City Hill). This hike was surprising in that unlike the rest of the historic sites in Thailand, this hill was so clean and gorgeous with planted foliage amongst sharp limestone rock and flowering trees covering almost the entire park. Monkeys loll about on the cobblestone paths between the palace, a huge chedi and an unusual architectural collection of temples, with one small prang a bright reddish orange on the furthest point with the best view of the sleepy town. Petchburi, in fact, struck me as one of the more authentically preserved Thai cities of some size anywhere. There are six or seven temples rising from the quaint downtown area, adding to the old Siam flavor of the place.

After the hike we head just five minutes north to Khao Luang Cave sanctuary. Down steep steps into a grotto buried in a low hill, this cave filled with buddha images by King Mongkut is stunning due to the openings in its ceiling, allowing strong shafts of light to stream into the largest cavern and light the various images and stalactites and 'mites. With few people around it is one of the best meditative places anywhere: both finite in its enclosed state, but infinite with the sun streaming in to light a reclining buddha. Not to mention cool in the burgeoning heat of the day.

To pacify the kids it's off to the beach at Hua Hin, and a night in a rough hotel built out over the water in the center of the old town, lined with classic wooden Thai buildings. To sit out on the deck above roiling surf to watch a sunset over Burma and the bobbing fishing fleet just offshore, is one of those fond memories that will never be forgotten. The only problem with the beach was the incredible number of jellyfish in the water. Fortunately, there was a little beach lagoon where the kids could play, and where the stinging nettles feared to tread.

Then the big drive south the next day, down the isthmus where the country narrows to some ten miles wide, and the hills of tragic Burma parallel the road. A wrong turn puts us on the road south to Surat Thani, where we don't want to head, but it becomes fortuitous when a small road we take from Lang Suan to get over to the west coast is one of the loveliest we've ever driven in Thailand. Beautiful meandering river valley descending from west coast rainforest mountains parallels the road before disappearing in the thickening foliage. We hit the pass at the end of the valley and see the forest covered islands of the Andaman Sea spread out to the western horizon. We spend the afternoon shell hunting on a huge low tide beach at Laem Son National Park, named for the huge pine trees that line the cape's shore. This place is way off the beaten track, separated from the mainland by a thick mangrove swamp, its coastline wild with thick rain-forest jungle descending into surf. We discover a bungalow resort with places right on the beach nearby, fresh air from an approaching storm blasting in open windows throughout the night, making the tropical ecosystem refreshing. In the morning the largest complete rainbow I've seen in some time fills the western sky over the green islands. A double one begins to form, but doesn't quite make it when the clouds begin to break and the hot sun soars above the rainforest mountains to the east. Huge white birds of prey glide above the jungle canopy.

Then, in sharp contrast to the unpopulated, untouristy drive down the west coast north of the island of Phuket, our arrival there brings all the worst of this country back to the fore. Urban congestion in the small towns and in its largest city named after the island, almost drive us off. But after arriving at the still too developed Kata beach, having a great lunch and finding a fancy bungalow for the night with a sweeping view over the sandy harbor, we decide to stick it out. The snorkeling was actually some of the best, and seeing a lion fish, its bird-like feather fins startling in their beauty, added to the color wonder of all the other scintillating sights along the reef.

But we had to flee the tourism of it all, and so chose to return to the limestone karst formation of Krabi, and the more rustic and far more spectacular beach at Rai Lei Beach off Ao Nang. Described earlier, the beach at Pra Nang is my favorite, and the hiking and snorkeling and boat-ing the most interesting. We hired a rooster-tail boat to take us out to Chicken Island off the coast. When we got out to the beautiful white sand bar stretched between two thickly forested islands, the tide was quickly going out. We couldn't get to shore because of the reefs, so had to jump out and hike in. Sure enough, the boat got stuck on the coral, and we lolled about for several hours, exploring the reef life (my favorite the black urchins with orange eye-mouths surrounded by five blue lights, like alien craft) and watching one of the most blood-red tropical sunsets ever. Then wading out to the rooster-tail before it got too dark to see our steps, and as the tide slowly rose trying to push it off the coral and into deep water as the sky blackened and the milky way blazed and Hale-Bopp, the comet of the century, left a long tail in the northwest when we got out on the black water toward Rai Leh beach.

After a few days of relaxation, we blasted north taking a short-cut that initially seemed to be a wrong choice because the rough road began switchbacking through thick jungle and around gorgeous karst formations rising white from the jungle green, with absolutely no other traffic to be seen. Kids getting sick, jungle foliage hanging over the road so it actually blocks the view ahead, almost made us turn around, but once over the hills and into a river valley behind, it was a beautiful, bucolic drive north all the way to the Isthmus of Kra, with the occasional elephant sauntering along the road. Running into huge rain north of Chumphon we decide to make it all the way in one day: 550 miles form Krabi to Bangkok, 10 hours.

Up to Hong Kong the next week where history is made the day I arrive: People's Republic of China Troops come across the border into the New Territories. The first step in the slow transition to China's takeover of the British Colony for the first time in one hundred and fifty years. A colony created to addict the Chinese people to opium, so that the British could even out a balance of trade problem. The end is near!

The next week it is Osan and a day off to explore Seoul city on a gorgeous spring day. Took a bus north through the rolling hills and over the mighty Han River to Yongson Army Base in the middle of the city (a sprawling tree covered campus); then by taxi through the relatively compact and orderly city (compared to Bangkok) shielded from the north by the jaggedly impressive Puk'an-sansong mountains. It's hard to imagine that just thirty miles north is North Korea and the current home of one of the worst famines in the world.

First stop is the impressive architecture of Kyongbok-kung Palace at the northern edge of town. Begun in the late 14th century by the progenitor of the Yi or Choson dynasty, this was the royal residence for some two hundred years. In springtime the cherry blossoms accentuate beautifully the grace and zen-like quality of the curved and carved oriental structures. After passing through the Kwanghwa-mun Gate (Gate of Radiant Transformation) guarded today by two massive haet'ae statues, fierce gods found at the entrances to most Asian royal palaces, you walk across a huge courtyard that once held the occupying Japanese government's capitol. The Japanese, invaders many times over the past five hundred years, built this structure in the shape of the Chinese ideograph for Japan, deliberately in the line of power between the interior royal throne and the Kwanghwa-mun Gate, thus symbolically cutting the power of royal Korea. Only recently torn down as a matter of historic realignment, the walk across a cobble yard takes one to the Royal Throne Hall of Kunjong-jon. It is the largest surviving wood structure in the country, with massive pillars of wood holding up a sweeping tile roof with intricate carving under the eaves. The courtyard that surrounds the throne hall is created by a wooden ramada with exquisitely detailed paintings on the high beams. The color combination itself is repeated all through the palace grounds, and consists of a woven rainbow design above what might be a green royal crown pattern.

Behind the throne hall is the Kyonghoe-ru, the largest pavilion in Korea, its massive roof supported by 48 stone pillars. It is wonderfully set in the middle of a lotus pond with little islands planted with long-needled pines. Bordering the pond are flowering blossoms of pink, red and white, framing this marvel under towering peaks in ultimate harmony. The entire palace complex, before the Japanese destroyed most of it in the Hideyoshi invasion of 1592, must have equaled or maybe surpassed the Forbidden City in Beijing. What makes the complex so aesthetically stunning is the mountain rising behind it, hemming in the northern end of the valley Seoul inhabits. The exposed rock intermixed with foliage makes the peak quite intriguing.

More beautiful than this central palace, is Ch'angdok-kung Palace, just up the road. Rebuilt in 1611 after the Japanese invasion of 1592, it served and still serves as one of the residences of the royal family. The carved and colorful Tonwha-mun Gate is entered to access this forest sanctuary in the heart of a metropolis. It survived the Japanese invasion and is Seoul's most ancient gate. Another throne hall sits amidst a collection of more exquisite buildings, surrounded by towering pines and more flowering trees. It is quiet inside the palace walls, and the hike through the Piwon, a 32 acre park that contains the most beautiful ponds and pavilions I have seen in this part of the world, embodies the quintessential Asian aesthetic of architecture blending with natural beauty. One gate, the Pullo-mun, is made out of a solid piece of granite, and walking through it is said to give one endless youth.

On a soft spring day who would ever think Seoul, Korea could be heaven?

May '97: One of the funniest things I've ever seen was glimpsed over successive days in Islamabad. Walking towards the Margalla hills in an incredibly green spring for Pakistan, I began smelling marijuana. Not marijuana being smoked, but fresh, leafy marijuana. As I strolled up a path paralleling the road to the hills, I first saw one small marijuana plant, then another, then a clump, then a forest of plants as high as an elephant's eye. Initially I chuckled and thought this must be the result of one person throwing some seeds out, or perhaps a patch gone to seed and spreading locally. Pinching off some tops and doing nose hits, I couldn't believe how potent the stuff was. I continued on my walk, laughing at this discovery in one of the most drug sensitive capitals of the world, and enjoyed the wild hills above the city and the stunning views of spring snow-heavy Himalayas towering over the Vale of Kashmir to the northeast.

The following day I went for a walk through the posh diplomatic neighborhoods of this contrived town, and much to my surprise found marijuana growing EVERYWHERE. It was growing along the paved side-walks where diplomats and business people jogged and walked their dogs and kids, filled every park I passed, and in one barren lot grew beside spectacular red and yellow poppies. No one batted an eyelash. I couldn't believe some of the forests of fragrant weed growing next to the residences of some very important folks; its sweet smell wafting on a gentle breeze.

On my last evening, as the light waned and ominous black clouds from Afghanistan filled the sky, I caught a scene I will never forget: In a forested stretch of unused land just yards from the Marriott, a group of shawal qamiz dressed youth played cricket in a huge patch of marijuana, the white ball being smacked into thick groves of the plant, with fielders diving into the dope in pursuit. Just off the worn pitch the field was only ankle high in ganja (so they must have played there often), with the shouts and yelps of billowing shawal qamiz blurring after balls.

Then to the First World, Sydney: cuisine, culture and cruising on the harbor. In fact, this was the first harbor of a month of harbors as a measure of travel. The last week of May was Sydney harbor, then on to late-spring-cold Helsinki harbor the first week of June, then to Hong Kong harbor two weeks before the historic changeover (anxiety in the air!), then Monterey and San Francisco Bays for home leave, before settling in on picturesque Round Lake between Lakes Charlevoix and Michigan for two weeks at the Chicago Club, before heading back to San Francisco for a 4th of July on the wind and fogswept Bay under Mt. Tamalpais: fireworks exploding within the fog, lighting it pink, purple and white, with half the pattern shot out underneath the cloud ceiling, making the display one of the eeriest and most interesting anywhere. Kerouac's famous quote, "the only ones for me are the mad ones, the ones who are mad to live, mad to die, mad to be saved, yet burn, burn, burn like fabulous yellow roman candles exploding like spiders across the stars, and in the middle you see the blue center light pop, and everybody goes, Ahhhh!" reverberated through my brain. Here in the home of Further! Amen.

June '97: Ring of Fire Circle Tour! It's one thing to takeoff from Narita with volcanic Mt. Fuji snowcapped in a pink sky, then cross the stunning Northern California coast ten hours later over Redwood National Park, with even more impressive Mt. Shasta deep in snow to welcome you home. But on leaving San Francisco three weeks later, after enjoying the sparkling white granite of Jeffers' Carmel, the Mediterranean feel of Miller's Big Sur, and the exquisite glacier-carved lakes of Hemingway's Michigan, the views on departure are more impressive. The fog was thick on the journey through the City to the airport. But on takeoff the fog had mysteriously lifted, revealing a crystal clear afternoon. We sluggishly rose past San Bruno mountain, crossed churning surf at the base of Daly City's cliffs, then paralleled Ocean Beach until we reached the Golden Gate, where we turned sharply east over the bridge: with views of China and Baker Beach and old neighborhood haunts, not to mention awesome city views, there for the visual feasting. Then the 747 climbed east to Port Costa with Mt. Diablo dominating the south (Why the hell were we heading east? The plane *was* full of Japanese!), then finally turned north over the golden hills interspersed with green of Napa.

We jetted up the Northern San Joaquin, past volcanic Mt. Lassen with a smattering of snow, then awesome Shasta thrusting through fleecy cloud, then crystalline Crater Lake and the various small volcanoes in its vicinity (Mt. Thielson sharp with snow), before the Three Sisters of college daze and that Eugene full of memories where the glacial McKenzie River waters meet the Willamette; which we follow over Salem with Mt. Jefferson and Mt. Hood heavy with snow and glaciers continuing the volcanic line to Mt. Adams and infamous Mt. St. Helens, still desolate except for the waters of Spirit Lake and the mighty Columbia flowing fresh from its namesake gorge, before immense Ranier rising drastically from thick fir scarred by clear cuts as we wing south of the Olympics and their secret valleys of hanging moss and Tolkien trees out over the Pacific. The associated memories of each familiar topographical wrinkle of earth's surface is hallucinatory. The planet which gave us birth triggers memories which give rise to a sentimentality juxtaposed by the savage reality of nature's ephemeral nature.

Then the rugged mountains of Kodiak Island south of Anchorage appear through thick cloud. Later, stretches of desolate tundra as cloud clears while blasting down the Aleutian chain, its equally barren islands scattered across the cold northern Pacific, before more volcanoes at the tip of Russia's Kamchatka peninsula continue the Ring of Fire tour as we speed south alongside the deserted Kuril Island chain and on into Tokyo with good old Mt. Fuji completing the circle.

July '97: Twenty-four hours ago I was downloading Quick Time Video of Pathfinder's rovings on Mars. Now I'm in Phimai, Northeastern Thailand, Third World dirt roads, chickens everywhere, water buffalo furrowing rice paddies in time honored tradition, the pace slow and peaceful: things haven't changed here since they began constructing the exquisite Khmer Prasat of Phimai around 1100 A.D., an absolute gem of white sandstone! One of the vice-regal centers of the Khmer Empire on the Khorat Plateau, Phimai was connected to Angkor by a royal road which still exists. Like a straight Roman road, the ancient route heads southeast from the temple's gate toward the historic capital over the Dongrek Mountains that separate modern day Thailand from Cambodia. Compared with Angkor Wat, which is overwhelming in its magnificence, this smaller version of essentially the same motif, allows one to meditate fully on the artistic excellence of Khmer civilization. One revelation I had staring at the prasat: it's an elaborately decorated lingam, thrusting magically from the earth which gave us birth, toward the heavens. The essence of Shiva! And the foreshadowing of our space program?

But when one considers the price of technology, the dangers of leaving Earth's surface, one realizes the futility of all human pursuits. Take for example my departure from New Delhi one July evening: I knew something was wrong the first time the pilot throttled back after starting our roll, but after two more throttle ups and backs we were getting short of runway! When they finally gave the 747 full throttle the end of the runway crowded with slums came up too fast, and the strain the engines were under became apparent when the inboard engine on the left burst into flames just as we lifted off. It wasn't the fire out the window or the screams of the passengers that was scary as the huge plane sank towards earth and the crowded slums below, but the frantic Thai flight crew unbuckling from their jump seats and running through the aisles in mortal terror. The sinking of the aircraft must have only lasted a few seconds as the extremely competent pilot shut down the flaming engine while gunning the other three to barely lift us over the rooftops. But as we limped to a very low altitude for the swing around to make an emergency landing, there was no nervous relief as the engine out the window remained ablaze. My thoughts were adrenaline lubricated as I awaited the fuel line to blow the wing completely off, sending the huge craft spiraling to earth in a heap to be shown on CNN a few hours later. We made it around O.K. and the emergency landing was nicely organized considering where we were. Fire trucks and a few ambulances were at the ready when we came to a halt at the far end of the dark runway and exited down the chutes. Someone morbidly commented that even if we had miraculously survived the crash we all would have surely died in a Delhi hospital. Then, after being put up in a five star hotel for a night in Delhi (yes, one exists!), we were told by a jet engineer who had been sitting in economy, just behind the engine, that we almost bought the farm!

August '97: Back to old Wellington, home of the first visit to this part of the world eighteen years ago. The weather the same as that '79 arrival and the hotel I collapsed in after twenty-four hours of flying, now a posh office building. A changed city all around with nice cafes and restaurants at every corner. Hiked up to the forested ridge overlooking the entire bay and quaint capital that I climbed as a naive, not well-traveled twenty-year-old. Inhaling the pine scented air and meditating on time's passage between visits to this far-flung land; like Sydney, another geographical time marker. Inhaling and exhaling memories in clean, showery Southern Hemisphere air.

Then it was back to Sydney for a quick night before heading off to Cairns the following morning. Rented a car and immediately blew out of town for the more sedate, funky ville of Port Douglas, but with large resorts lining the famous four-mile beach, even it was too touristy. Continued further north to Mosman Gorge, beautiful clear mountain river flowing deep over boulders much like the Merced in Yosemite Valley. Swimming and playing in the rapids and taking a long hike through gorgeous rainforest reinforced making the effort to visit Queensland, so far to the north.

Then it was back on the road to Daintree National Park at Cape Tribulation. The road soon ran out of pavement after the crossing of the estuarine crocodile infested Daintree River by ferry. Looming Mount Hemmant to the north at 1000m became huge, forcing the road to skirt the pristine beaches to make headway. The rutted, multi holed road was just about to rip the bottom out of the rental when Cape Tribulation and its small village appeared amidst the thick bush. Staying at the backpacking hostel, the clientele were sneering when I parked the car and brought out my suitcase. Perhaps some grudging admiration was felt for a "rich" traveler like myself for staying in such a dump.

But the next morning it was out to the reef on a catamaran. The clear, clean environment of huge, forested mountains dropping into sea fringed with a coral reef collectively called Agincourt, was a powerful sight indeed, justifying its designation as a World Heritage Ecological Site. Between reef and shore the waves were big, the catamaran pitching and yawing violently, and fellow passengers vomited overboard en masse. But once we got behind the protection of the white sliver of sand on the horizon known as Mackey Reef, the waters quickly calmed and we weighed anchor in crystal turquoise waters. The first in off the stern with just mask and fins (others were dressing in wet suits!), I dropped into a world that immediately reminded me of snorkeling the Florida Keys. The clarity of the water, the thick schools of multi-colored, multi-sized fish flocking around behemoth stands of delicate coral blows the mind. At one point, hovering above a school of some fifty grouper swaying lazily, grazing along the sea floor, with a few barracuda lingering near the surface, eying me suspiciously. What a gathering! My favorite sublime scene was a school of tiny blue-green damsel fish clinging close to a delicate coral: they disappear quickly into its skeletal spaces when you come too close. Within the bone-white coral there was a writhing bluish core that also became a vibrant skin. In shallow water on white coral sand, positioning the mask so the glass was half below and half above the water, there was a classic view looking back at the rain forested mountains of Daintree, including the appropriately named Mt. Halcyon, while below the calm waters teemed with tropical fecundity.

September: '97: After the summer civil war in Cambodia it was time to start serving the mission there again on a regular basis. Since Thai no longer flew there, Royal Air Cambodge flew in using a small propeller plane. Gorgeous flying in at low altitude over the thickly forested Kravanh Mountains the Khmer Rouge control, along the southern edge of the Tonle Sap we crazily boated down a year and a half ago, and on into Phnom Penh spread along a huge monsoonal Mekong. The skies were clear on takeoff several hours later, the weather blisteringly hot. About five minutes after lifting off uneventfully I noticed a storm to the southwest of the city, clinging to the flanks of a high peak rising mightily from the dry plains.

The next morning it was all over the news: A Vietnam Airlines Russian built Tupolev had crashed in a lashing storm at Phnom Penh airport less than an hour after we had taken off, killing all aboard except for a small Thai child. It seems that after flying in from Hanoi the plane tried to land but couldn't, then when it circled around to make another approach, wind shear, or plain pilot incompetence, forced it into the ground just short of the runway. The black box taping the last moments of the craft couldn't be found because the local villagers, impoverished after thirty years of war, ransacked the crash site, taking clothes, money and watches from corpses, and any metal that might be sold for scrap. "We might as well be apes, you know," sang Iggy Pop.

The human tragedy continues on a trip to Jakarta and Singapore, where I view firsthand what could be the future ecological debacle that awaits much of the developing world. Usually upon arrival in Singapore there are great views of the city, the incredible numbers of ships at anchor in the straits and the new multi-million dollar airport terminal. This trip the terminal was obscured by a smoky haze covering the region from fires burning out of control on the Indonesian Islands of Sumatra and Kalimantan, the first sign of a terrible tragedy. The monsoonal rains that usually begin this time of year are late due to the burgeoning El Nino in mid-Pacific, thus the fires that are normally extinguished burn on and out of control, making breathing across the entire region a health risk.

Jakarta is just as bad, with commuters donning masks to filter the air. Good luck! This relatively clean city, showing up a place like Bangkok, now has an air quality ten times worse. Only visiting for a few days, I feel lucky to be leaving. The grey skies and haze were so depressing, and the fear of harming my lungs so great, I never left the hotel.

The geographical perspective of Taiwan's close proximity to mainland China is shocking on the flight to Shanghai from Hong Kong. Flying over on previous trips, or even on the many descents into Taipei, it was always too hazy to see the mainland. But this day was crystal clear when we jetted up the coast over Zhangzou, just a stone's throw from Taiwan's major forward island offshore, Quemoy, before the large port city of Fuzou, with another Kuomintang isle nestled right in the harbor mouth. Bizarre! Why haven't the mainlanders just helped themselves to these parcels of land? Surely the defenses cannot be that impenetrable. Across the narrow strait the impressive Niitaka Chain forming the backbone of Fomosa is seen, as on the flight into Taipei, just a little smaller along the horizon.

Thorough hike up Hong Kong's Victoria Peak and environs on the return from flat, overbuilt, congested Shanghai. Waterfalls run full off the ridge top, forest green and pungent after a good rain with fan-tails hopping about, a vibrant green snake slithering off the track into the underbrush, and strange long-tailed sibis birds squawking from low trees; all this natural activity above the packed skyscrapers of a mighty metropolis. Taking the Hong Kong Trail to a steep rise west of Victoria Peak, called Sai Ko Shan at 493m, I absorb one of the great vistas standing completely alone above a megalopolis of seven million, fresh air blustering: freighters plying the narrow channel between Hong Kong and Lamma Island, Lantau peaks soaring further to the west and behind them the peaks above Macau over the Pearl River mouth. Planes descending from the west every five minutes, flying in over Kowloon rooftops and the quick turn and drop onto the tarmac. One of the great landings in the world, soon to be no more with the opening of the new airport. It's very British to preserve such tracks of nature and build the trails necessary to enjoy it. Will the Chinese now begin building on all that glorious natural space atop the ridges? Otherwise, absolutely nothing has changed since the People's Republic took this island built on opium trading back from the British.

Interesting on the return from Hong Kong to Bangkok, the defined contrast between the Thai and Cambodian borders: electricity vs. darkness, calm air vs. violent lightning storm over a troubled, violent land.

October '97: A quick visit to the ancient capital of Laos, Luang Phabang, nestled in green mountains along the banks of a brown, monsoon-wide Mekong. But first it was uninteresting Vientiane, much further downriver and just across from Thailand: a Thai wanna-be. Nong Khai, the noisy Siamese city across the river, is nothing, but it dwarfs this sleepy, post-colonial capital. An Arc de Triomphe copy in the city center is an eyesore, with patterns and designs in bas-relief concrete on the exterior. Inside, in the cavernous car park-like core, all one senses is the smell of urine. The view from the top is extensive, with a fine view of the Mekong winding out of pristine mountains to the west, and the golden Shwedagon-like Stupa of That Luang (built by King Settathirat in 1566) glimmering on a slight rise to the northeast. Closer in it is only rooftops, then rice fields quickly begin and run all the way to the northern hills and the infamous Plain of Jars, site of massive B-52 strikes against the communist Pathet Lao during the Vietnam war.

In town, along the banks of the river, lie two of the more interesting Lao monasteries in the capital. Wat Sisaket is notable for being the oldest in Vientiane, the Thai army choosing not to destroy it in their sacking of 1827, for some mysterious reason. Perhaps it was due to the aesthetic brilliance of courtyard walls covered with tiny niches, 2.052 to be exact, each with a tiny Buddha within! Across the street and closer to the river, is Wat Phra Kaeo, built in 1565 by King Setthathirat to house the Emerald Buddha (which now sits in the Grand Palace in Bangkok after the Thais sacked the city in 1778). He brought the Buddha with him from Chiang Mai where he had been king, and placed it here as a place of royal worship. The temple and its grounds were later destroyed by the Thais during their invasion of 1827, when they left Wat Sisaket untouched. The front and back wooden doors are all that remain of the original, and are both superb examples of Lao woodcarving, with Buddhas and flowers carved in intricate detail in the finest teak. Inside the temple building is a collection of Lao and Khmer Buddhas from around the region, including one of the mystery jars from the Plain of Jars. Were they used to brew alcohol in massive quantities by victorious troops, as legend purports, or are they funeral urns scattered across one slope from 2,000 years ago? Or as my daughter Eliza suggests, maybe they were used to collect rainwater in what is a dry region!

The transport to Luang Phabang is a decrepit thirty-year old Lao Aviation Yak-12 Turbo-prop built by the Chinese. Good enough for the fifty minute flight over rugged terrain, but not much more. Due to the clouds the navigation must have been figured by speed and time, because when we reached a certain altitude after a certain time (just clearing the highest peaks thrusting through a sea of white) the plane nose-dived. In the minutes of whiteout that followed, glimpses of uncomfortably close green ridges whipped past then vanished, leaving all with window seats tightly gripping their arm rests. When we descended through the cloud ceiling we were only a thousand feet above the wide Mekong slicing through a deep green valley. Tiny Luang Phabang and its myriad temples appeared clinging to a sandy promontory, then quickly vanished as we headed for the airport north of town.

Communism has preserved the authenticity of this part of the country. Compared to overly commercial Thailand, upcountry Laos hasn't changed in centuries. It also helps that only some five million people live in a land the size of Great Britain. Founded by Fa Ngoum in 1353, Luang Phabang seems frozen in time. The royal palace, now a museum, houses a fine collection of the ex-royal family's treasures, including a copy of the Phra Bang Buddha statue after which the city is named. Fa Ngoum received it from the Angkor court after he married the daughter of the Khmer King. The original of solid gold is too valuable to be left sitting out and sits in a bank vault somewhere!

An interesting slice of local history with global significance: after the French granted the royalist government of Laos full independence in 1953 (due to the pressures in Vietnam), making it a French protectorate, the communist Pathet Lao and Viet Minh immediately began threatening the royal capital at Luang Phabang. In order to take pressure off the capital, Captain Henry Navarre decided under the terms of the new treaty to confront the Viet Minh at the strategic approach to the city in the valley of Dien Bien Phu. The French defeat there eventually opened up Laos to full communist control some twenty years later, to say nothing of Vietnam.

After the communist revolution of 1975 the 600 year old Lao Monarchy begun by Fa Ngoum was abolished, and the royals, including King Savang Vatthana and Crown Prince Vongsavang were eventually packed off to reeducation camps in the north east where they died of mysterious "natural deaths".

But the real attraction of this tiny little town hidden in the forested mountains are the various wats of exquisite design. On the first evening a walk along the main avenue that parallels the river was in order. In the quiet darkness of this primitive town, we stopped outside Wat Sene and observed a scene most Westerners would die for. Inside the wat, lit by flickering candlelight, were rows of monks in saffron being lectured to by what must have been the Abbott. The red color of the interior walls highlighted by gold stencil bathed in warm candlelight, with the monks periodically breaking into chants, all viewed from the anonymous blackness of a quiet main street, was one of those moments you want to freeze frame.

The following day we saw too many gorgeous wats, with the most memorable being the royal Wat Xieng Thong, built in 1559 by, you guessed it, King Settathirat, at the tip of the sandy promontory. At the top of a wide staircase ascending from the swift brown waters, this wat of classic Luang Phabang style, with its sweeping, overlapping roofs also mirrors many Lanna Thai characteristics: red with stenciled gold coloring on interior and exterior pillars and ceilings, with the interior walls filled with paintings and mosaics of the Buddhas life. This influence is a natural one as Setthathirat's father King Phothisareth (1520-1548) married a Lanna Thai princess. Their son claimed the throne at Lanna (Chiang Mai, Thailand) until his father died. When the Burmese invaded Lanna he renounced that throne, claimed the Lao Kingdom and brought the Emerald Buddha with him to be housed in Wat Phra Kaeo in Vientiane.

Another of the many wats that particularly stands out is Wat Visoun, reconstructed in 1898 from a wooden temple built in 1513 but destroyed by marauding Chinese. The doors on each side of the building are decorated in exquisite gold leaf characters from the Ramayana, framed by a blood-red background and contrasted by the dull whitewash of the building's exterior. Inside, behind the largest Buddha in town, is the greatest collection of ancient Pali stelae mixed with Buddhas in a variety of poses, flecked with gold leaf, some rotting, that I've seen anywhere in southeast Asia. Most of the artifacts are at least four hundred years old, and are unguarded except for a sleepy guard at the front door.

Hopped aboard a slender pirogue for a two hour cruise up river to Pak Ou caves, named for the confluence of that river winding down from near Dien Bien Phu, with the Mekong. Talk about a journey through the heart of a bucolic, primitive nation. Twenty-five kilometers from Luang Phabang, cruising past isolated villages, sampan fisher folk and net tossers from shore, the most spectacular cave, Tham Ting, is found in a vertical limestone cliff rising from the swirling rain swollen water. One jumps off the boat to get into it, and once inside it is burning candles and thousands of three hundred year old small and large Buddhas amidst the stalactites and stalagmites. Royalty used to boat upriver for new year ceremonies in this and another cave above it, Tham Phum. That cavern actually has a small stupa inside and again, hundreds of candles lighting a multitude of Buddhas.

The cleanliness, fresh air, churning behemoth of water and thick forests of Northern Laos are all inspiring after the deforestation and exploitation of Siam.

Crossing the Mekong at 30,000' and 400 km. downriver, 24 hours after leaving Vientiane. Is that the same water flowing past we were alongside yesterday? Crystal clear Annamite mountains of Vietnam, stunning river valley winding through steep hills thickly forested to headwaters with views of sand dune coast a mere stone's throw across the narrow waist of the country.

In autumnal Korea something I've never seen before: the inside lane or shoulder of every road is covered in freshly harvested rice, spread out to dry!

Autumnal Helsinki, cathedral of color: squirrels, woodpeckers, pheasants.

Om mani padme hum!:
"o lotus seated god of the celestial jewel." chiseled mani stone prayer.

What's interesting about trekking in the Everest region is that from the moment you lift off from Kathmandu by either helicopter or small plane, land at the 9,000' trailhead village of Lukla for the hike into the highest mountains on earth, you enter an extreme world you can't be confident in leaving until touching back down again in Nepal's capital. Jon Krakauer speaks of the "Death Zone" above 25,000' in his book on the '96 Everest tragedy, but in reality the entire area is one. The margin for error is minuscule, even for the amateur alpinist.

When you think of the number of trekkers that fly to Lukla every day during the peak season of October/November, crowding into Soviet era Mi-17 helicopters with Russian pilots, or into sixteen seat Twin Otters suited perfectly for the precarious landing on the thirty-five degree dirt runway perched atop a cliff-face, it's a wonder more aren't killed merely arriving and departing. The airport is closed when the cloud ceiling drops, the decrepit control tower apparently radioing Kathmandu. But when our helicopter choppered in under descending thick cloud that hid what a quick glance at a topographical map showed were 19,000' peaks towering over either side of the glacial blue waters of the mighty Dudh Kosi valley, I wondered if the control tower had bothered. It's a fifty minute flight skimming over 11,000' ridges, so the weather might have quickly changed. Ours *was* the last flight of the day. If you're fortunate enough to land at the trailhead, all you have ahead is the altitude and cold that claims many lives in the next 9,000'!

What *is* fun about helicoptering are the views of beautifully terraced mountain flanks, picturesque villages connected by trail amidst the most massive foothills on the planet and glimpsing views of the mighty peaks and glaciers as you transverse the range east to the Solu Khumbu itself. But one has to wonder about the Russian pilots. Who in their right mind would come to one of the poorest nations on earth to fly? They must be incredibly desperate for work. I joked that they had a sign in the cockpit window saying: "Will fly for food!" But they got us to Lukla and back safely, praise Buddha for that!

Considering I'd come from two and a half years living in the swamps of Asia, it wasn't surprising when lightheadedness hit as we began our trek alongside the roiling Dudh Kosi. Sea-level to 9,000' with two nights in Kathmandu obviously wasn't a slow enough ascent! Psychologically the peculiar feeling puts you immediately on the defensive, making the climbing and altitude gains to come even more daunting. Fortunately, our sirdar, Chumbe Sherpa, well-trained with years of experience leading climbs on some 8000m peaks, slowed us down considerably once we climbed to the 12,000' altitude of the Solu-Khumbu's largest village, Namche Bazaar, so that we might acclimatize properly.

The trek from Lukla is memorable for the many river crossings over slender bridges. Competing with yaks for room on decrepit bridges that might collapse into a raging glacial torrent at any moment, is an experience not to be missed! The last bridge on this section, spanning a deep gorge over the Dudh Kosi at its confluence with the Bhote Kosi, is at least 200' above the river! The locals have placed huge stones in the middle of the precarious span to keep swaying to a minimum. From the vertiginous height of mid-span you can glimpse a few snowy peaks soaring over the thick, pungent stands of blue pine upriver, while far below turquoise waters churn. But move on before the next yak train arrives!

After an exhilarating crossing of this last bridge, the real work begins. A two thousand foot climb to Namche through chir pine and the occasional oak, reddish orange in autumnal fire, is the brutal initiation to the high country. What is surprising about this part of the Himalayas is the thickness of the forests. The propaganda had pretty much described this entire region as deforested by the locals in their service of trekkers, but in this busy hiking corridor, that just wasn't the case. Of course, much of the forest glimpsed is completely inaccessible, such as the slope below Nupla (19420') . The waterfalls spilling from its thick ice fields drop thousands of feet through dark green dabbed with oak fire, so its steepness protects the resource.

For a "big city" Namche is nice: tea houses and a market to purchase the clothing you forgot: wool pants, beanies, snow pants, etc. But the most important thing about this village are the acclimatization days. The more the better. But they're not boring days. The Nepali Army has this amazing piece of land with a commanding view. It thrusts out over the Dudh Kosi valley, with the high skinny bridge visible way down below as it spans the deep gorge to the south, while to the north is a fine view of Everest peaking over Lhotse. This was my favorite view of the entire trek because of the unparalleled expanse: starting at pluming Everest (Sagarmartha: "mother of the universe" at 29,028'), then swinging past spectacular Ama Dablam ("mother star shaped pendant," actually more stunning than Everest at 22479') and razor sharp Thamserku (21800') south to the Middle Hills and huge cumulus building from the heat of the flat Terai, you feel the tectonic lift of an awesome range that truly begins where others end. This 180 degree sweep, from the highest point on earth whipped clean of snow by jet stream winds, out past myriad peaks and forested hills to the flatness of the Ganges plain, is something I'll never forget. In fact, the last peaks towering over the green foothills, the two sentries above Lukla we flew in between, rise to 19,250' and 22,000' respectively: five and eight thousand feet higher than the highest peak in the continental U.S, Mt. Whitney, with the latter 2,000' higher than the highest peak in North America, Mt. McKinley! And these were the lowest peaks.

After two days acclimatizing it was goodbye to "civilization". Our next camp was set in the small village of Phortse Tenga (three rock houses with thatched roofs at 14,000'). This camp along the rocky banks of the Dudh Kosi thick with stands of silver pine (with blue pine cones), was memorable for two reasons: our first brush with the dangers of altitude sickness, and the reality of swimming rats!

Apparently a European gentleman had been up Gokyo Ri (17,700'), but had ascended without the necessary acclimatization days. He started feeling poorly on his return to the summer grazing settlement of Gokyo (now overrun by trekkers), so poorly that he was placed in a Gamow Bag. The bag is large enough to cover the entire body, and is pumped manually to increase atmospheric pressure; the idea being this alleviates the symptoms by mimicking a lower altitude. He was stabilized in Gokyo that night, then set off by himself to a lower altitude the next morning, claiming he was okay. Several sherpas found him spitting up blood trail side, so one of them decided (nicely enough) to escort him lower. Even so, he began deteriorating rapidly and was brought into Phortse Tenga on the sherpa's back. The evening we arrived a helicopter had been summoned by runner, and as we set camp a chopper buzzed the treetops, maneuvering carefully in the tight valley as it looked for a place to land. After finding a rock fenced field upriver, it settled down, keeping the blades rotating until the man was hefted out and dumped inside. Then off they went, whizzing back to Kathmandu, leaving us nervously contemplating the hike ahead.

Swimming rats are real! After the helicopter evacuation I went for a stroll along the creek. Finding a large granite boulder to sit and meditate on, I began staring at the swirling rapids. After a few minutes I glimpsed something below the surface. Thinking it was a fish, then a diving bird, then a river insect, I finally realized it was a rat! It had a long naked tail, and swam with such alacrity that I wondered if I was hallucinating. I blinked a few times but there it was, diving into rapids, disappearing for awhile, then bobbing to the surface downstream! I watched it surface one time, then turn downstream like a kayaker, casually floating through churning white water before eddying out at the bottom of the rapid! I was concerned about my mental state for a few days until one of my trekking companions discovered a reference to these creatures in a Lonely Planet guide to the Himalayas. Lucky for me.

Later that night I fell asleep quickly, only to awake an hour or so later. I felt terrible! Hard to put a finger on what it was exactly, just a pervasive negative feeling. That, of course, got the old mind reeling while camp slept and the river roared. I began anxiously monitoring my body to see what the diagnosis might become, while a snippet from Matthiessen's

Snow Leopard reverberated through my skull: "The deep muttering of boulders in Black River—why am I so uneasy? To swallow the torrent, sun, and wind, to fill one's breath with the plenitude of being...and yet...I draw back from that sound, which seems to echo the dread rumble of the universe."

After endless tossing and turning I eventually fell back asleep only to awake the next morning feeling absolutely terrible. My head felt like someone had hit it with a baseball bat, strangely numb! Rather than complain about it I had some breakfast and several strong cups of coffee and began feeling better. I'd convinced myself that I would see how the morning hike went, then make a decision about my personal status whether to ascend or not. As we hiked through gorgeous autumnal forest interspersed with hemlock and cut by numerous cascades (with the occasional reddish barking deer and iridescent impeyan pheasant—the national bird—making an appearance), I began feeling better as we gained 2,000' at a cautious pace. The mysterious symptom of that night psyched me out for the rest of the trip, making me overly concerned with altitude sickness, but not unjustifiably. A healthy paranoia.

When we eventually arrived at Gokyo Lakes (16,000') to camp (passing the tea house in Panga crushed by an avalanche two years earlier killing all 35 Japanese sheltering inside), I was gaining some confidence. But that was blown the next day when we hiked up Gokyo Ri for the great expansive view of the entire Everest region. At 18,000' it is *up* there, and despite how well I previously felt, half way up the peak my body couldn't deal with it. I honestly thought I wouldn't make it up, but persisted with the slowest hiking I've ever done in my life: I would take five steps and stop, sometimes spending five minutes just getting my breath back. Then, just below the top, as our sherpa came down from the top to take my pack and assist me, after each five-step segment I would become dizzy. Scary when you've never experienced it before! I didn't know whether to proceed or turn back. I plodded on, taking in the awesome views of Everest and Nuptse in mixed cloud, the gnarly Ngozumba

Glacier below, and the pristine moraine lakes of Gokyo, to aid my ascent. Once on top I didn't have the confidence to hang out and enjoy the view. The new realization of the body's extreme edge freaked me out, so after ten minutes I headed back down. The psychological relief was enough to make me feel somewhat normal. I even did a Kerouacian Japhy Ryder (the poet Gary Snyder in *Dharma Bums*) gallop down the mountain at top speed with the sherpa, both of us cracking up at the absurdity of it (racing past hikers slogging in ascent): laughter as communication, for he spoke no English.

The weather deteriorated for several days after reaching Gokyo Ri: snow squalls, below zero temperatures, with all views obscured by cloud. In order to avoid depression the sirdar moved us to a sheltered tea house across the glacier, so even though our tents were up, we could huddle around a yak dung fire, and at least read and talk to pass the time. It was really the first time we had spent in a tea house, and although the warmth of company and fire were nice, for the most part they are dirty places, with food preparation suspect. Most of the sickness that occurs on treks is due to the unsanitary nature of these establishments. Although tents are colder, they are also cleaner (no head lice), and our cook was meticulously clean. The hot iodine wash-water that was placed in the meal tent for us at each sitting was one of the great preventative medical measures I've experienced. On an eighteen day trek in a region as unsanitary as this, with fecal matter everywhere due to the lack of rudimentary outhouses, and toilet tents for trekkers the norm, such a simple thing saved our party from serious gastrointestinal problems. On my family's previous trek two years ago in the Annapurna's, the trekking company had wash water, but with no iodine. I got sick.

Many tea house trekkers complained of there being no water to even wash with, let alone iodine water. A classic example of this dearth of water is watching a trekker coming out of the rare tea house outhouse and grabbing some snow with which to wash the hands. So it becomes only a question of time before you get sick, not if you will or not. And that's only one of the problems for the tea house trekker. Jon Krakauer in "Into Thin Air" mentions a tea house in Lobuche (which was our next stop) where he caught a bronchial cold and head lice, neither of which left him 'til getting back to Kathmandu. After acquiring these two problems he wisely moved into a tent.

The same would've happened to us if we hadn't been in tents in the disgusting tea house village of Lobuche, because we were tent bound for two days due to a blizzard! If we had been forced to stay in a crowded tea house bunk room for that time, I'm sure someone would have become ill. The poorly ventilated dung stoves are a real problem, and after breaking the boredom of tent life by visiting the very tea house where Krakauer and his ill-fated party stayed, I began feeling light headed and nauseous myself. Now, was it the altitude (16,269'), something I ate, the smoky tea house, or the gnawing stress of the cold and depressing weather? The problem is, you never know. Should you start back down to lower altitude immediately, knowing that a German died in his sleep the previous night in a village back down the trail, or stay because it might just be the hot lemon tea you had from the unsanitary tea house kitchen.

I continued feeling strange through the late afternoon and evening as the snow piled up, with no appetite whatsoever for dinner (which was never a previous problem). One of the early warning signs of altitude sickness is nausea and lack of appetite, but we had been at or above 16,000' for five nights at the time, so why the delay? The mind starts reeling, of course. Just when you thought you were over the acclimatization hump, there it is again. (But after reading Krakauer's book, with even sherpas getting sick from altitude sickness, I realize that it can strike at any time and at the highest levels of physical and professional competence). I recalled waking up that morning to the hiss of snowfall and the soothing jangle of yak bells, feeling great except for a small headache. After taking Tylenol I felt okay in the sleeping bag, but then the nausea began developing. At dinner I told the sirdar my symptoms and he looked at me with concern. Not encouraging.

Then burrowing in the warm bags for what I knew was going to be a nightmare night, both awake and in dream, with two feet of snow outside and more still falling. If my symptoms worsened a quick evacuation would be impossible. I remember falling asleep quite quickly, then waking an hour and a half later after the weirdest dream. All I can say is it was comparable to dreams you have with a very high fever: insane, absurd, with no comfort to be found. All this compounded by the thunder of avalanches in the distance. Instead of sleep being a sanctuary, it becomes, at least for me anyway, and others seemed to admit to "troubled nights," a nightmare you have no desire to enter. So you toss and turn in the pitch black of the tent, obsessing on the extreme location, the recent death, the weather keeping helicopters at bay, the snow so deep a hike to lower altitude is an impossibility, etc. Then you think of the four Croatian climbers with badly frostbitten feet stuck in their tents just up the trail at base camp, in order to make your own situation seem less extreme. Edgy stuff. A trek to Everest base camp isn't just about the physical challenge, for me it was three quarters mental, and boy, it was brutal.

It was the darkest night of my life, without question, staring at the tent ceiling, listening to my heart pounding in my chest, fading in and out of strange, dark dreamland. Even though we had planned to begin a hike to base camp the next morning at four a.m. (fortunately shortening the night), I was already planning my retreat to lower altitude from the perspective of midnight. The relief of being awakened by sherpas with tea inspired me to at least give the base camp expedition a try. If I didn't feel well I could always turn around and head down with a sherpa.

On the trail, when the light broke in the east, the psychological relief was like making it through a night fighting off vampires. And in old Yin/Yang tradition, the crack of dawn hike up alongside the Khumbu Glacier, with the 8000m peaks catching the very first light, was so inspiring on the clearest morning of the century, that my health worries evaporated. Amazing considering that as we hiked toward base camp a helicopter was flying up and down the glacier, retrieving the frost-bitten

Croations from their high altitude camp, one by one. The day turned warm due to the reflection off the deep snow. The hike up Kala Pattar (18,300'), terribly difficult with no snow, was unbelievably tough because we had to cut trail. But the views of Pumori, the Khumbu Ice Fall, Everest pluming perfectly and mighty Nuptse, were so awesome in the deepest blue/black Tibetan sky, that I barely noticed anything earthly, such as my poor heart beating like its never beaten before.

So our karma was good for the most important part of the trip, spectacular in fact. Chumbe said it was the clearest, warmest day he had ever experienced up there: the deep snow serving to paint the stunning scenery even more so. Again, a Matthiessen quote wafted into the mind while taking in a pluming Everest: "Rock, and snow peaks all around, the sky, the great birds and black rivers—what words are there to seize such ringing splendor? But again something arises in this ringing that is not quite bearable, a poised terror, as in the diamond ice that cracks the stone."

And it wasn't to last, but I didn't realize until later, when the story was finally written, what it was that changed it. Atop Kala Pattar, on that most exceptional of days, with views to last a lifetime, one of my partners trudged off to take a dump directly underneath a promontory of rock graced by prayer flag and chorten (small stupa). I didn't see him until he was well into his business, half hidden by a boulder. It took me several seconds of disbelief to comprehend what was going on under the fluttering, tattered white flags. I pointed out to him that he was shitting in a spot sacred to Tibetan Buddhists, folks who believe the spirit of a place should be honored (and especially this one, with its unparalleled view of Sagarmartha). Hillary's words to Rob Hall, the leader of Krakauer's ill-fated expedition (criticizing him for starting commercial treks to Everest) rang loud and clear: "Engendering disrespect for the mountain"! Bad karma caught up with Mr. Hall in a big way, and in retrospect it was to catch up with my fellow trekker too.

I didn't think anything more about it until two days later, when the left side of the disrespectful one's face began swelling due to a tooth abscess.

He had penicillin and even ran into a doctor who said it was the right kind for the infection he had, but to no avail. It got so bad and so painful that he eventually had to make an emergency hike to Namche and catch an expensive helicopter ride to Kathmandu, aborting the last third of the trek. I had also noticed when hiking behind him that he rarely rounded *mani* stones (*om mani padme hum*! carved into them) or prayer flags (*cho tar*: block-printed with sutra) set in the middle of a trail in a clockwise direction. The sherpas always did, even going out of their way to round them in the proper manner, keeping karma and thoughtfulness right. This guy would always take shortcuts, totally oblivious to what the *menden* (long narrow walls containing stones inscribed with Buddhist scripture) signified (to say nothing of spinning a *mani* wheel). According to Krakauer's book, the Fischer and Hall climbing parties seemed to have a similar problem in the spring of '96.

The porters that were contracted by the sirdar to carry our tents and sleeping bags (our duffel bags of clothes were transported by yaks) were probably the most amazing folks we encountered. First off, they were free-lancers, and therefore more representative of the average impoverishment of the Nepali people. Unlike the sherpas, sirdar and cook, they were given nothing by the trekking company. They hiked in flip flops while carrying huge loads in deep straw baskets strapped by rope around their shoulders and foreheads. When we hiked over the Chola Pass at 18,500', with its expansive snowfield and glaciers, they would tie string around their rubber thongs for traction! And that wasn't all they had to endure. In the many snowstorms we experienced, not to mention the clear cold nights of sub-zero weather, when we trekkers were inside two down bags snug and warm, these three guys were living in caves. When we arrived at camp they would dump what they were carrying and head off to the nearest cave, most manmade by previous porters walling off the underside of a massive boulder. After lining it with fresh picked shrubbery for insulation (sparse at high elevation), they would forage for a certain shrub growing along hillsides whose root burned well enough to give off a modicum of heat.

Talk about tough. These guys must have antifreeze for blood. Bare feet on snow for hour after hour! Boots are so far out of their economic reach that purchasing a pair would be tantamount to buying a Mercedes.

The trekking company gave us a suggested tipping guideline sheet for the end of the trek, because most have no idea what to give the various hierarchical figures. We deduced that our tips were ten percent of what these guys were paid for the eighteen day trek, so we figured what each was making. And remember the trekking season in the Solu Khumbu is only October/November, for the most part, so if they're very lucky they might work three treks of this magnitude for the season and the year. We gave the porters nine dollars each, the cook's helper the same, the sherpas fifteen, and the cook (because his food was so good and no one got too ill) and sirdar thirty. With Americans and Brits and a South African in our party we tipped nicely. Most Europeans of course do not, and they are the ones who make up the bulk of the trekkers in this area, by far. That's the income for these folks for the year, and then it's back to growing potatoes, spinach and cauliflower. It must be their only income, because their existence is one of subsistence.

Despite the crowds in the peak season on the lower trails, the fecal contamination problem and the supposed deforestation, hiking in the Solu Khumbu and elsewhere in the Nepal Himalaya is an economic windfall for the people. Ironically, the smug self-sufficient backpackers, of which there are many, aren't supporting one of the poorest economies on the planet.

It's a spiritual journey too, even if you didn't plan on one, like my trekking partner. The extreme nature of the terrain forces itself on your mind and body, and much like Native Americans who went into the woods on vision quests, there is not much you can do to avoid its affect. After my dark night of the soul, where I could taste death in the icy cold, followed by the subsequent elation of a stunning day amidst the world's highest peaks, I began having intense *deja vus*. It was as if the anxiety, altitude, cold and other physical challenges punctured some cerebral membrane, revealing the future in the present at almost every turn. Every campsite, view and monastery on the retreat was as if I had seen it in some dream or previous life. Spooky! So even though I just went up there to hike the high mountains, the nature of the place showed me something else. Then again, it might've just been the delusional effects of too many days over 16,000'!

On departure from Kathmandu, it was only natural I had a window seat on the left side of the plane. We took off, circled over Kathmandu as usual to gain altitude, then headed southeast, with the entire Everest region out the window, the dry Tibetan Plateau stretching northward. I could trace the entire eighteen day trip in a glance, from Lukla to Gokyo, over to Khumbu and the glacier trudging down from the ice fall underneath that pluming peak scoured by jet stream winds.

November '97: On the way to Pakistan, time and again we fly over the vast green maze of the Ganges delta, just 80 km. downriver from infamous Calcutta. Bengal tigers make their home in these mangrove swamps, but it makes sense because throughout this 18,000 sq. mi. drainage of the sub-continent there isn't a trace of *Homo sapiens.* Conservationists say 520 Bengal tigers are concealed here, the largest concentration left. Apparently the impoverished villagers that do inhabit this swampy terrain are regularly attacked and eaten by the tigers. One of the tigers' favorite methods of attack is swimming out to fishing boats, where the crews are fast asleep on deck. And if it isn't the tigers eating the locals, it is the sharks and salt-water crocodiles prowling the myriad winding waterways. If you had a choice between scrounging a living in the slums of Calcutta or living in the Sunderbans swamps close to nature, which would you chose? Remember the more subtle killers that also exist where the Ganges and Bhramaputra rivers meet the Bay of Bengal: cholera and malaria! "Nature red in tooth and claw," as Mr. Tennyson once wrote!

Some of the most interesting land/sea formations are along the Burma coastal border just south of Sittwe. Mountain ranges spear into

Combermere Bay in a north south direction, eroded so that some are no longer connected to the mainland. Further south sharp semi-cirular mountains form cones and sickle islands. Inland, mountains in similar curved arcs, their green forests combine with shadows of the dying sun to define them sharply against snaking estuaries. The Chin Hills and Akhan Yoma Mountains that follow the Burma coast are savagely slash and burned. Huge white scars mark the mountainsides while fires burn every couple of kilometers. However, looking north towards Bangladesh, then south towards Rangoon, reinforces the fact that there are still huge regions in this world untouched by civilization. As in Laos, capitalistic exploitation on a grand scale has not made it here. Even though indigenous slash and burn is intense in these hills, it's an irony that the free market capitalism of democratic countries destroys nature at a far greater rate than communism, excluding China of course, where the constant haze covering that state hides the ongoing destruction of the land.

December '97: Flying into Seoul recently crippled by economic catastrophe: the cities of Korea look like computer chips due to the uniformity of their apartment blocks. A stifling regimentation that discounts any individuality.

The Earth is immense! Flying into Vladivostok in a round about way to avoid the dangers of North Korean airspace, we head east from Seoul and fly up the west coast of snowy Japan: Fuji soaring above everything at 12,500' with that elegant and distinctive shape.

The snowy, fir-thick Sikhote-Alin Mountain lands of Russia's Far East, north of Vladivostok are an example of the vast untouched tracts of Earth that still exist. Lake Khanka, frozen white off to the northeast, marks the border with Manchuria. In Vladivostok the word is the man-eating Siberian Tiger on the edge of town has just taken another victim. Russia so Fourth World it makes one wonder what all those Cold War trillions in defense dollars were spent on.

"I stopped at Vladivostok. About our Primoriye Region and our [Russian] east coast, with its fleet, its problems and its dreams of the Pacific I shall say but one thing: it's all appalling poverty! Poverty, ignorance and paltriness, such as can drive one to despair. One honest man to 99 thieves who desecrate the name of Russia."—Anton Chekhov, letter to a friend, 1890.

Nothing has changed since the great playwright wrote those words over a century ago. Glancing back on this isolated outpost after takeoff to the north, the low sun shimmers gold off the water and ice surface of Peter The Great Bay and the Sea of Japan.

For the holidays it's off to volcanic Bali, with its black sand beaches, exquisite temples, and tourist infrastructure, but not many tourists. It seems the ecological smoke disaster beginning last summer turned off so many tourists that this renowned tropical island is fairly quiet. Rather than confront the touristy and crowded area of the island's capital, Denpasar, we catch a van ride after landing to the artsy village of Ubud, on the terraced rice-paddy flanks of what was volcanic Mt. Batur. The first thing one notices cruising through small villages and along the tiny roads is the overwhelming number of temples. Every village has several and every family compound has at least a small one. The thatched pagoda-like towers are called merus, after Mt. Meru of Hindu nirvana fame, which Angkor Wat itself is modeled after. In Ubud there are shops aplenty along the quiet high street that must usually throng with visitors buying the masks, paintings, wood carvings and batik this island is famous for. Every night there are Balinese dance performances of the Ramayana with full gamelan bands setting the tone.

Just out of town is the intriguing Hindu site of Goa Gajah, or elephant cave from the 11th century. A carved rock face of a demon with its mouth agape leads to a shrine for Ganesh (therein the cave's name), with linga and yoni also found within the candlelit confines. Just in front of the cave is a huge bathing pool with water gushing from carved female spouts, reminiscent of those all over Kathmandu and Patan. Further down the forested slope past the pool are Buddhist relics of carved rock and more meditation pools. We hiked even deeper into the forest down a well marked path and came upon a gurgling river sweeping through the jungle. Problem was, we couldn't stay and enjoy the scene due to a local bathing naked in the torrent.

Just east of this temple is one of the oldest rock carvings on the island. Called Yeh Pelu and only excavated in 1925, this carved cliff face is full of scenes of everyday life (the only religious figure being Ganesh), a journal of 14th century Bali: folks hunting and cooking and even some humor. One scene depicts a man killing a beast with a knife, while next to this a frog imitatively disposes of a snake in the same way. The walk down through exquisite terraced rice paddies alone is worth the visit. A little rickety thatched house for the caretaker of the paddies rises on a dirt hill, while below various crops in different stages of growth color the rich dark earth light green amidst soaring palms.

North of this region of Hindu prehistory on the island is the small town of Tampaksiring, the locale of the most impressive ancient monument of Bali, Gunung Kawi. In the bottom of a gorgeous valley one comes across relief carvings of ten temples cut into the lava walls on either side of a rushing river. Modeled after the Ajanta and Ellora caves of India, these stunning reliefs surrounded by a valley of paradisal quality were apparently carved in seven meter high niches for 11th century Balinese royalty. Around the base of each set on either side of the boulder littered river are monk cells of labyrinthian complexity, again carved out of lava. We went for a walk up the valley along a narrow trail edging a rice paddy terrace. Waterfalls spilled out of verdant growth topping the lava wall on the opposite side of the river, while palm trees crowded the sky and red flowers of an unknown variety added a dash of color to the verdant scene. We ended up at a gushing water fall that had cut a hole through the lava and fell into a deep pool, misted ferns and flowers clinging to the basalt. Paradise!

Then up to the source of the Pakerisan River at the temple of Tirta Empul. Founded in 962 AD, this temple with its spring bubbling up within the grounds was built to honor the god Indra, who legend has it tapped the spring to release the elixir of immortality, *amerta*. The strange thing about this temple is that the previous President of Indonesia, Sukarno, built his vacation Palace on two rounded hills directly above it, with a high skinny bridge connecting each residence. Strong vibes indeed, for he was Balinese.

The next day it was back in the van for the drive up lava swept flanks to the rim of Guning Batur. Batur is actually the present day name of a smoking volcano rising within the larger rim of an older caldera that must have grown a mountain the size of nearby Gunung Agung (3142m), the highest on the island. The massive explosion was obviously prehistoric, but looking at the size of the crater it left, approximately six miles across, it must have been one of the largest in the history of the planet. Immense! Must have been even larger than Krakatoa in the Sunda Straight far to the west.

That afternoon we chose to hike the active Gunung Batur (1717m) within the large caldera, setting off from the ugly village of Toya Bungkah along the black sand shores of Lake Batur (filling a third of the caldera with fresh water). The hike up through barking dogs and poverty stricken shacks of the outskirts of the village and into tall fragrant pine trees along the volcanoes base, was invigorating. After a near vertical scramble up the tricky, slippery slope of crumbling lava and a red sheet of more recent ash, we all got near the top. Smoke and high heat gushed out of vents all around the rim of this recent geological event, its last eruptions in 1971 an '74. The largest eruption from this particular peak was in 1917, when it wiped out the village of Batur (now underneath the frozen lava river the road crosses on its way to Toya), killing thousands and destroying some sixty-thousand homes. The views to the east of the two other volcanoes of the region, 2152m Gunung Abang, right next door, and the massive Gunung Agung further down range, along with the large lake below and the broad rim, gives an amazing perspective of volcanic activity past, present and future in one glance!

After the long slog back into town we put swimming suits on and try to find the communal hot springs somewhere along the lake shore in the heart of the village. After a bit of a wander we did find it, crowded with villagers in various states of undress, soaping themselves and lounging in the bubbling hot waters escaping from a volcanic vent along the shoreline. The hot spring emptied into the cold waters of the lake through a small canal, so you could swim in deep water to cool off before entering the springs to sooth aching muscles.

The following morning brought the bumpy ride back across the lava fields and up the switchbacks to the rim and its million dollar views. We decided to head to the black sand volcanic beaches of the north coast and head west along the caldera. A classic Balinese Temple by the name of Pura Ulan Danu, perched precipitously on the rim's edge with meru pagoda towers enhancing the views back east in the direction of the three gnarly volcanoes is picture perfect. Rebuilt in 1927 due to the destruction of the former temple, Ulan Danu is considered the female temple to the island in contrast to Besakih at the base of Gunung Agung. Temples are not oriented north south, but mountain-sea. Further along the rim, precisely where the road begins its long wind down to the north shore, is another temple called Pura Tegah Koripan, perched atop at least three hundred steps at a high point on the caldera. There was no view for us, but a mist filtered through pines, lingams and statuary in the temple enclosure felt like San Francisco's Legion of Honor on a foggy day.

Then dropping down to the north coast through forest and village, with intermittent thick cloud and views all the way into Singaraja (lion king), the old Dutch Port that used to be the main access point by ship to the island in the old days. A few red tile roofed Dutch buildings are found in this sleepy little place on the Bali Sea. We end up on an uninteresting black sand beach with murky water for the night, not exactly the paradise Bali is supposed to be, before bailing and returning to the cool mountains and temple of Pura Ulu Danu under the volcanic peak of Gunung Catur (2096m) on the shores of lake Bratan. A spectacular site, the thatched-roofed meru temple was founded in the 17th century and dedicated to Dewi Danau the goddess of the waters. Pilgrimages are made here to ensure the continual flow of fresh water to the villages below. There is also a Buddhist stupa off to one side to keep all the gods in this part of the world happy. Not seeing much to get excited about in the way of a place to stay, and somewhat revolted by the numbers of tourists, we decide to continue on to Sanur, a place of abundant tourists, but with a beach and snorkeling for the kids.

From there we head out on a day trip to the famous temple of Tanah Lot, the most photographed temple on Bali. Perched exquisitely on a little island just offshore, this site is a sea temple, built in the 16th century. The commercial traffic around the area is enough to make anyone sick, so there's a price to pay for a visit to this sublime sanctuary backed by steam rolling surf. South of the airport and Denpasar, the major tourist gateway, at the extreme southwest tip of the Bukit peninsula, is the inspiring cliff top temple of Ulu Watu. Perched atop a sheer face one hundred meters above some of the best surfing on the island, it's a sight to behold.

January '98: Taxiing into Dhaka, turbaned "security" man on ancient bicycle armed with what looked like an Enfield rifle slung over his shoulder. Burma, Bangladesh; eighteenth, nineteenth century, what's the difference?

With a day off in economically depressed Jakarta, I blast down the volcanic spine of Java to the Indonesian cultural capital of Yogyakarta, with giant Mt. Merbabu and smoking Mt. Merapi (2911m) thrusting out of cloud to the north. Not necessarily to visit the arts and crafts or the sultan's palace, all of which I halfheartedly take in, but to make the pilgrimage to the eighth century Buddhist stupa of Borobudur, some forty kilometers northwest of town at the foot of active Mt. Merapi.

One of the three great Buddhist temples of southeast Asia, the other two being Pagan and Angkor, this huge walk-through mandala was built by the Saliendra dynasty somewhere between 750 and 850 AD, almost three hundred years before Angkor. The entire site was abandoned soon after its completion, its burial in deep volcanic ash possibly the reason for the hasty departure. In 1815, when Raffles ruled the island during the English interegnum, the site was cleared, revealing the awesome stupa for all to see.

On the drive up to the Menorah hills that form the verdant backdrop to the site, it's all serene rice fields filled with straw hatted villagers and white brahma bulls plowing black volcanic mud. The first hint that you're headed for something good is the temple of Mendut just off the road under an immense and ancient Bodhi tree. The rather blocky structure has carved relief panels of superb Hindu-Javanese style on the exterior walls together with a subtle foreshadowing of the mini-stupa motif found up the road lining its multi-terraced roof. Inside is a very unusual Sakhyamuni Buddha, for it is seated Western style, in a chair with feet on the floor instead of crossed in the typical lotus position! It is the largest statue to be found in its original place in all Java, and its intricate carved fingers in the *Vitarka* or *Dhammachakka* mudra, express the first public discourse on Buddhist doctrine: "turning of the wheel of Dharma". Three meters in height and flanked by Boddhisatva Lokesvara on the left and Vairapana on the right, with incense wafting through the semi-darkness, it is a powerful impression indeed and prepares one mentally for the large mandala to come. This and another temple called Candi Pawon, two river crossings closer to Borobudur, formed an east-west purification process before entering the main temple. More typical of Central Javanese Temples with its pyramidal roof, it has pot-bellied dwarves pouring riches over the entrance, signifying it was most likely dedicated to the Buddhist god of fortune, Kuvera. Even though folks want to reach nirvana, there's nothing like praying to the material needs of this world why you're here!

The approach to Borobudur is spectacular, rising as it does from serrated palm leaves and light green rice fields under jagged Menorah Hills behind. Built as a broad symmetrical stupa, this monument was built as a Buddhist vision of the cosmos in stone, beginning in the day to day world of passion and desire, then circling higher and higher past motifs of the Buddha's life to eternal nothingness, or nirvana, represented by the 72 Buddhas encased in latticed stone stupas around the pinnacle. Above the 1500 highly decorated relief panels depicting an outdoor textbook of Buddhist doctrine, some 400 Buddhas stare serenely out from open galleries at the cyclical bucolic scene of life on plains continually fertilized by volcanic eruptions.

The synchronicity found here between Hinduism and Buddhism is glimpsed atop the final gate into the highest level of latticed Buddha Nirvana with a Cheshire cat-like Kala, representative of an entropic universe, swallowing the visitor as time swallows all. The balustrades sweeping down alongside steps at the monument's base are strangely reminiscent in style to those of Tenochtitlan in ancient Mexico City. The Makara waterspouts at various midpoints on the terraces are also similar to Mesoamerican motifs in their swirling monster heads of teeth and snarling lips, as are the corner waterspouts chiseled into the head of Jaladwara.

Leaving Borobudur is difficult due to the pull of its magnificence, but there is an equally strong pull coming from 40 km. to the east, the other side of the airport: the ninth-century Hindu temple group known as Prambanan. Constructed some fifty years later than Borobudur, Prambanan might have been built by the Hindu power of Java of the time, the Sanjayas of Old Mataram in the north, as a religious counterpoint to Borobudur, or the closer Buddhist temple of Candi Sewu, just three kilometers in a direct line north toward Mount Merapi. As with Bali, these temples are built in a mountain-sea line, which also happens to correspond nicely with a north-south direction. There is a blending of Shivaite and Buddhist motifs here as with Borobudur, suggesting to historians that there was a marriage between the two dynasties of differing beliefs of the time: Saliendra and Sanjaya. But, given the fact that Buddhism arose out of Hinduism, and similar motifs are found in India and Nepal, the blending is a natural one.

What is left of the Prambanan complex after one thousand years is the eight minor and eight main temples of the central courtyard. Around this courtyard were some 244 temples, all of which lay in ruins. But the courtyard, with its stunning central Shiva Mahadeva tower as the focal point, is more delicately wrought than the tower portion representing Mt. Meru at Angkor. The main spire soars some 47m, its 34m wide base carved with small niches framing lions flanked by heavenly trees and stylistic bird men. Over the gateway into the central chamber is wonderful Kala again, the grim reaper of Hinduism, time eating up everything in its path!

Encircling this tower and its two flanking temples dedicated to Brahma and Vishnu, equally delicate in architectural style, are scenes from the *Ramayana* and *Mahabarata* carved into an inner wall, relating how Lord Rama's wife Sita was abducted then rescued by the monkey god Hanuman and his monkey army in the former, and the heroism of Lord Krishna in the latter. The *Ramayana* ends with the monkeys building a bridge to Sri Lanka, then continues on the inner wall of Brahma's temple next door.

Atop steep steps in the central tower's main chamber is the four armed statue to the Hindu creator/destroyer, Lord Shiva, ironically perched on a Buddhist lotus leaf in syncretic fashion. There is a cell with statuary on each directional side of this temple. In the southern cell is a statue of Agastaya, an incarnation of Shiva as divine teacher; to the west is Shiva's son Ganesh with his elephant head beautifully wrought; followed appropriately on the north, or destructive Mt. Merapi side, by Shiva's consort Durga.

At Candi Sewu, a Buddhist Temple due north of Prambanan in a direct line to Merapi, a muezzin from an unseen mosque broadcasts his calls to prayers across ruins dedicated to a blending of religious beliefs. The mini stupas with erect pinnacles that thrust skyward at Buddhist Candi Sewu, and the inverted Hindu lotus flowered domes with erect linga carved from one piece of stone at Prambanan (another blending of and direct linkage of form), mimic the rounded volcanic shoulders of Mt. Merapi. Further east a few kilometers is another complex of temples built around the same time as Prambanan, Buddhist Candi Plaosan. Again, Kala of Hindu mythology is found over windows here while inside are fantastic carved Boddhisatvas in seated positions looking out windows to the west, toward Borobudur?

On takeoff from Jakarta we fly out over the Sunda straight, the historic, strategic volcano guarded passage between Java and Sumatra. There, clustered clearly in mid-straight with other remnants of famous Krakatoa, and forming the only above water fragments of a submerged rim, is beautifully formed Anak Krakatoa (son of Krakatoa) at 150 m. Its cone is shaped like a volcano ready to erupt rather than a spent one. It still rumbles and spits fire, but on this day looks quiet. Fleecy white cloud rather than smoke ices its summit above vibrant tropical waters. Then it's over Palemban, Sumatra, buried in swampy coastal plain, and sight of last month's tragic Silk Air crash, killing all aboard. The brand new 737 fell out of the sky from thirty-thousand feet and disintegrated when it slammed into the Musi River just north of town. Thinking of such a death spiral is a humbling thought as we jet on to Singapore at thirty-three thousand feet.

Further north, in vast tracks of mangrove swamp cut by huge rivers winding their way through to the sea from Sumatra's volcanic spine, occasional whisps of smoke rise through the canopy. There is no trace of humanity as far as one can see, so who are these *Homo sapiens* isolated here in an untouched land impossible to penetrate? What are they hunting? Who says the world is a known quantity?

Amazing flying up the Gulf of Thailand past gorgeous Ko Samui, Ko Pha-Ngan and Ko Tao, then the thin waist of the Isthmus of Kra, across which you can see the glimmering, island dappled Mergui Archipelago of the Burmese Andaman Sea. Due west of Bangkok, over the Burmese border, there is quite a spectacular peak called Myinmoletkat Taung (2072m), dominating the region. If only the air was clear enough to see it from the city!

Flying up to Yangon the following morning, the mountains on the Thai/Burma border south of Mae Sot are exceptionally beautiful, and seemingly untouched by human hands. No wonder the warring tribes of Burma: the Karenni, Kachin and Karens find it easy to hide from the military dictatorship along this wild border. There is clear cutting and slash and burn in the coastal plain but it mostly stops at the base of the mountains.

February '98: Australia fair! Sydney becomes smaller with each trip, not quite enough now to occupy ten days, after experiencing everything there is to see and do over two and a half years: great people, restaurants, cafes, beaches, scenery and ferries for sure. Ultimately, though, when all is said and done, not a whole lot going on. Like leaving the paradise of San Francisco to take this job, it's time to move on, even from one of the most beautiful cities on the planet.

In Islamabad, but not for long as the Khyber Pass beckons. After the drive from the capital, spent the afternoon exploring the labyrinthian markets of Peshawar's ancient crossroads. Followed the ancient fortress walls that still somewhat enclose the city: built first by the Mughals, then Sikhs, then finished off by the British, who actually tore down some of the congested interior of the old city to give it some breathing space by creating a few wide boulevards. Bala Hisar fort still looms majestically over the frontier town teeming with humanity, guns bristling in the direction of the Khyber.

In the Tribal Lands west of Peshawar are fortress-like adobe walls of various family compounds scattered across the terrain. Watch towers at each corner with sniper holes speak of the Hatfield and McCoy mentality that exists here. Built with money made from smuggling heroin, weapons and liquor from Afghanistan, these tribal folk live outside Pakistani law and answer only to themselves. Then inside the actual pass, proper forts built by the British atop high peaks keep a menacing eye on all that passes below. At one point we take a look at the creek bed squeezing between two granite outcrops, where in the past camels had to be unloaded to fit through. Imagining Alexander's main contingent marching through here 2300 years ago before fighting up in Chitral almost makes me faint from the wildness of ongoing history. The steam railway built by the British to keep the Russians in Afghanistan at bay (The Great Game) is an amazing achievement running up to the border from Peshawar through twenty tunnels and switchback sidings. But, as with most human endeavor, the money and effort were ultimately for naught.

Up on top of the pass under stunning snowy mountains, it is bleak dry hills and more and larger adobe compounds: compounds that drugs have built. At the Michni post I'm invited up to the fort overlooking the entire border region and the many Pakistani fire stations on border peaks around the Afghani town of Torkham. Afghani refugees roar past in crowded buses for the escape to Pakistan as the Taleban gear up for their annual spring offensive.

March '98: Helsinki sea inlets a frozen wonderland of thick ice under blue sunny sky. Mothers walk babies bundled in their strollers out where ice fisherman sit patiently by their holes. A polar bear club granny comes out of a sauna and heads down to a dock kept clear of ice by a whirling water machine, then plunges in. Unfazed by the icy cold, she floats for five minutes amidst ice bergs before returning to the primitive heat. An ice-cutter ferry ride out to Suomenlinna Island through thick slabs is a treat of creaking, cracking and rumbling as the weight of the ship breaks up the thick flow. As the wind stings my face I once again ponder the weirdness of being in sweaty Bangkok twenty-four hours later.

Soaring under black northern hemisphere night heading east over the Kazakhstan border lit by a full moon: a sea of bitter white interspersed with village lights clustered for warmth and oil field gas aflame sprinkled north where they blend with a sparkling universe. Otherwise, a vast bleak snowy expanse under the vault of heaven.

In the morning, S.E. Asia covered in the tiresome seasonal, slash and burn haze. Burma's Akhan hills going up in flames. No more views in this part of the world until the monsoon arrives in three to four more months.

Flying over an atoll of turquoise brilliance just south of Hainan, I wonder what I'm doing in this part of the world at this moment suspended by technology under a clear blue South China Sea sky. A voice responds: "Imagine the depressing alternatives." Amen.

"What is the color, when black is burned" Neil Young appropriately sings through my headphones while winging over Da Nang on the thirtieth anniversary of My Lai. Evil is evil! The soldiers of the time listened to such songs on Radio Saigon hours before death. Anvil shaped and colored thunderheads rise along the Vietnam coast, while inland Laos is in haze from ubiquitous slash and burn, a vague Mekong far below.

Upon arrival in Bangkok, it's off to Myanmar for a long weekend. The quick flight into Yangon is depressing due to the low visibility. Still, the huge white stupas this land is known for litter mountain peaks and rice paddies as we come in low on our approach. The infamous State Law and Order Reconstruction Council (SLORC) has recently changed its stripes. After cleaning corrupt military officials from its ruling junta, they have been replaced by equally corrupt generalissimos under the banner SPDC, State Peace and Democracy Council! The winds of change are a blowin'! One thing about Yangon that immediately strikes the traveler from Bangkok is its cleanliness. Like Singapore, dictatorships certainly are fastidious in this respect, not a soi dog in sight! Our guide tells us they are taken to the edge of town and shot and buried in mass graves. The sidewalks are spotless, though, a nice improvement from the trash of Thailand.

The city itself is quaint, locked as it is in a post-war time warp. Military trucks rumble through the streets, a huge walled fort with gun holes taking up a huge portion of the leafy downtown area. That's another thing that is nice after Bangkok, trees! Lots of trees line the streets and several lakes that picturesquely situate themselves amongst the low buildings of this Irrawaddy Delta town. The most spectacular structure in town is the Shwedagon Temple, noted on previous visits, and soaring in gold leaf to the lofty height of 98m from a small hill in the city center. The myth is that it is 2500 years old, and it could be given the number of earthquakes that have rocked this region. Archaeologists seem to agree that the Mon actually begun this very stupa in the tenth century, with the latest version being rebuilt in 1769. A casual evening stroll around the stupa in a clockwise manner, watching the locals burn incense and the sun set against the gold spire is as magical as this planet gets.

Arriving in Pagan by propeller aircraft we see the one thousand year old forest of stupas on a plateau stretching along the banks of the wide Irrawaddy some 800 km. north of Yangon before landing. Upcountry Burma, even amidst the semi-tourist area of Pagan, is quiet, clean and peaceful: all the better to meditate on the exquisite stupas intermixed with palm trees and farms. We are the only ones staying in our hotel, and the view from the porch is of three huge, fairly ornate stupas lining a ridge top just a stone's throw away. We spend the day clambering in and out of a multitude of stupas of various ages. The first visited is one of the oldest, Shwezigon, its chedi design copied again and again throughout the plateau. Built between 1084 and 1113 it was originally constructed to enshrine one of the Buddha's teeth as well as mark the northern boundary of the city of Pagan. Several beautiful carved standing Buddha's surround the chedi perched as it is above the huge Irrawaddy. A little village stands between the structure and the river, their stick homes and pens full of pigs a reminder of how quickly the great civilizations revert to the basics. Driving back toward the old city we stop at one of the hundreds of nondescript temples and chedis lining the road and climb atop it for one of the great views of this plain of stupas. We're just far enough outside the main cluster to get a feel for the colossal nature of a religious building spree which took place over 250 years. The most photographed and one of the finest temples crafted on the plateau, Ananda Pahto, built in 1105, was our next stop. Its gilded spire and whitewashed hulk dominate the skyline of this ancient ground, while inside massive teak doors, four 9m Buddhas stand at the cardinal points in a state of nirvana. Not far away is probably the most massive structure in Old Pagan, Thatbyinnyu Pahto, or omniscient temple, was built in the mid-12th century and stands at 61m! Views from other temples of these two structures surrounded by a forest of spires with a hazy sun setting over the mountains across a huge swath of the Irrawaddy, is a memory to stash forever in the mind's eye.

Then to romantic Mandalay? Not any more I'm afraid! The old palace and forbidden city are interesting, as is the view from the top of Mandalay Hill north of town where we catch another hazy sunset. Ultimately, though, it's just another noisy, unattractive Asian city. Even the trash we were used to returned, making the place seem more like Thailand!

The most interesting thing besides the huge gates leading to the forbidden city which the British bombed during the war to oust the Japanese, was the Mahamuni Paya. Purported to be two thousand years old, and brought from the coastal Rakhine/Akhan kingdom in 1784 to legitimize the new capital just down the river from Mandalay, at Amarapura, the cast bronze image of the Buddha is so intense in its 15cm. of encrusted gold leaf, that one feels the true devotion of the multitudes who throng the temple. The next day we actually headed downriver to the old city of Amarapura, although there is not much left of it. We continued on for a walk across the longest teak bridge in the world that connects an incredible monastery full of maroon clad monk novitiates with a quiet island with Kyauktawgyi Paya chedi rising above its forested interior. A hired boat poled us back along the teak bridge crowded with folks making their way to the village, while fishermen cast wide nets in shallow waters. A quick drive to the shores of the Irrawaddy brought one of the great views of classic Burma: the city of Sagaing and its hills above the wide, brown river absolutely covered with white stupas and various monasteries.

Gazing down at the mouth of Joseph Conrad's "Meinam" or Chao Praya River described at the beginning of his "Secret Sharer," I see no Paknam Pagoda: "corresponding to their insignificance to the islets of the sea, two small clumps of trees, one on each side of the only fault in the impeccable joint, marked the mouth of the Meinam we had just left on the first preparatory stage of our homeward journey; and, far back on the inland level, a larger and loftier mass, the grove surrounding the great Paknam pagoda, was the only thing on which the eye could rest from the vain task of exploring the monotonous sweep of the horizon."

Jakarta deep in economic turmoil, so I go on a tour of the huge Mosque the day after twenty thousand filled its floors to celebrate the end of Ramadan. But that doesn't keep them from slaughtering brahma bulls and goats to a blood thirsty god. The smell of fresh blood from the slaughter pens next door filter through the sacred light. In the afternoon I go for a pirogue ride around the great Macassar/Buginese Schooners at Sunda Kelapa. My paddler actually takes me out the mouth of the harbor into the choppy sea, which we ride back into the port with a setting sun adding to the exotic feel of this ancient harbor.

Then back to Yangon again through slash and burn haze thicker than ever. A photo from space must capture this annual disaster. Smoke billowing off the sharp edge of a ridge line some ten miles long, filling two leeward valleys with smoke so thick you can't see a thing. Is this natural? After all, these Hilltribe people who Tourists drool over with their brightly colored clothing and back to nature lifestyle have been burning these forests for millennia! Out over the coastal plain toward Moulmein is some clearing, revealing the serrated dragon teeth mountains which thrust from rice paddies to spectacular heights. Gorgeous!

April '98: Flying to Ho Chi Ming city over Cambodia, I trace that crazy ass boat trip from Siem Reap down the Tonle Sap Lake to Phnom Penh from 25,000'. Huge Mekong sweeping down from the north to join Tonle Sap River at that ever-troubled capital.

Off to Vietnam to finally pay homage to the place. On approach to the airport, winding Saigon River full of sampans and net tossing fisher folk brings on savage flashbacks of news stories filed from those very banks during the late sixties and early seventies. I might not have fought here, but I was weaned on this war! Snippets of *Apocalypse Now* dialogue and Heart of Darkness allusions flit through the mind's eye: "Mistah Kurtz— he dead!" Dusty roads of the *Quiet American* stretch toward the Cambodian border past concrete hulks that must be the remnants of French watch towers Pyle and Thomas took shelter in way back when. Oh, Pyle, look what your naivete wrought! Craters the size of Volkswagen bugs litter the rice fields, still too deep to plant in but useful as duck ponds! Near to the craters are family cemetery mounds. The recent burials are whitewashed, but the older ones seem to be slowly returning to earth as fertilizer.

Tree lined boulevards of Ho Chi Minh City gorgeous after Bangkok! And the streets filled not with automobiles but with bicycles and motorcycles. Cars are in fact quite rare in the downtown area, and coupled with the breeze blowing in from the Saigon River and the sea, makes for an airy and pleasant environment. The Vietnamese women on motorbikes dressed in Ao Dang, the classic slender dress in white or light blue they wear, is a stunning sight indeed with long, jet-black hair flowing down their backs in contrast. The French colonial architecture is also exquisite, bathed by a setting sun its Mediterranean yellow takes on a transcendent beauty. Visits to the Jade Emperor Chinese Pagoda awash in incense and gorgeous gilded wood carvings inside, with caged birds and Bodhi trees creating a sanctuary amidst the congestion of Saigon's streets outside. Phuoc An Hoi Quan Pagoda in Cholon with its myriad conical incense sticks that burn for a month hanging from the ceiling exudes a strong Chinese influence, which has a more Buddhist/Taoist flavor than the Buddhist/Hindu feel of Thai wats.

The peace and serenity of the pagodas was contrasted starkly the following day by a trip to Cu Chee and the infamous Viet Cong tunnel complex the Yanks tried to bomb, napalm and tunnel-rat to extinction, all for naught. The V.C. would just build around collapsed tunnels destroyed by B-52 craters the size of small houses! There were three levels of tunnels as well, but the B-52 bombs couldn't wipe out the third layer! The tunnel rats, American troops that went into the tunnels to root out the V.C. with knives, pistols and grenades, had to confront trap doors opening onto sharpened bamboo stakes, heavy swinging balls covered in nails etc; a regular tunnel of doom. And when they successfully navigated into the heart of the tunnel complex, they would inevitably find everyone gone, as the tunnels opened up under the Saigon river, where the VC could swim away to safety. Amazing stuff! And so close to Saigon city it must have frustrated the hell out of the American command. Of course, the construction began during the French war, so they had some twenty-years of preparing the tunnels before the Americans even arrived!

The War Museum in Ho Chi Minh is full of anti-American propaganda, but it is justified! After all, it was a fight for nationalism, not necessarily communism. Ho Chi Minh and the Viet Minh were trained by the OSS (the predecessor of the CIA) in southern China to overthrow the Japanese occupiers during W.W. II. Ho thought Truman would agree to a unified, independent Vietnam after the war because of this. But Truman gave the French back their colony, thus inflaming the Vietnamese, which lead to the two subsequent wars that claimed some three million civilian lives, not to mention huge numbers of French and Americans. Ohhh, the mistakes of history, and the meaninglessness after all is said and done.

On takeoff from Saigon, flashback to C-141s rolling down this same runway past the same concrete bunkers that used to house Phantom jets, heavy with body bags. "Be the first one on your block to have your boy come home in a box!" as Country Joe and The Fish sang.

Then Da Nang and Red Beach, the sight of the first American landing in this gorgeous country, in March '65. First stop, however, is a trip to the ancient Cham relics housed in a French designed Museum built at the turn of the century. It is filled with a plethora of fantastic sandstone carvings of lingas, altars, Garudas, Ganeshas, Shivas, Brahmas, Vishnus and an image know as Uroja, "the mother of the country," who gave birth to the kingdoms which ruled Champa, represented by breasts with hardened nipples. All these artifacts ranging form the 7th to the 15th century were discovered in the many Cham ruins found in central Vietnam, the most famous of which, My Son, Tra Kieu (Simhapura) and Dong Duong (Indrapura) are just a half day south of Da Nang. The early pieces in the Cham canon are playful and must have been highly influenced by seafarers from the Indonesian archipelago, for they are very similar in style to Balinese sculpture. But after the 10th century, the influence of the Khmers seems to take over, and the carvings become a little more conventional, and very similar in theme and style to sculpture at Angkor. The northern Vietnamese eventually wore the Cham down and occupied the length of the country by the 15th century, in the same way they wore others down in the 20th century!

Then to historic Hoi An, an old trading port untouched by time 30 km. south of Danang. During the 17th, 18th, and 19th centuries it was one of S.E. Asia's premier trading ports, a port of call for traders from Portugal, Holland China and Japan in the early days, and America and Great Britain later on. The two and three hundred year old Chinese homes which still stand give the feel of centuries past: their ying /yang convex tiles, and ying/yang "eyes" on doors guarding houses from harm mix with village folk walking the narrow streets devoid of automobiles with rice hats and baskets slung over a shoulder, take you back to another age for sure. The covered "Japanese Bridge," so called because the Japanese traders living in one part of town built it over a stream to connect their neighborhood with the more mainstream Chinese section, was erected in 1593, and still stands sturdily, guarded by a pair of monkeys at one end and a pair of dogs at another. Perhaps the builders were born in those two Asian animal years!

A climb into the fresh air of the stunning Marble Mountains in the afternoon, with intriguing hikes into Buddhist sanctuary caves that in the Vietnam war were used by the V.C. as hospitals. A plaque in one of the caves describes the heroics of an all female platoon that got on top of one of the peaks and mortared the U.S. Marine airfield north of China Beach, destroying 19 aircraft in one night. Beautiful temples grace the flat bits of land at the top of the main peak, and the views out over the Vinh Diem River and south to Hoi An are blissful, not to mention the views out to Cham island off the coast, and up China Beach toward Hai Van pass etc. But contemporary views are deceiving, there was a lot of V.C. activity in this area due to the large American bases and the fact it was the first place the second imperialist invasion took place. A lot of Americans died patrolling this gorgeous countryside, not to mention the native folk.

The drive up the coast from Danang to Hue is one of the prettiest drives in Asia. The first portion of the trip up over Hai Van pass gives sweeping views of the beaches both north and south of this historic natural divide. There was endless V.C. activity on this road during the early part of the war before the Tet offensive. Many an ambush on trucks resupplying troops took place here, and many an American was killed. Langco bridge, one of the few bridges to survive the Tet offensive's preliminary bombings still straddles a pretty inlet of the sea meeting rolling hills and cute fishing villages nestled in sand dunes. The drive on to Hue through rice paddies along the decrepit railroad that runs the length of the country, is full of colorful roadside activity and more inlets stuffed with birds: green, green, green!

Construction of the citadel in Hue was begun in 1804 by the first Nguyen emperor on a site chosen by *fengshui* along the banks of the Perfume River. His official duties were carried out in a Forbidden City-like citadel within a citadel called the Royal Enclosure. The Thai Hoa Palace within this enclosure is like one of the palaces inside Beijing's Forbidden City, outrageously beautiful. And it is well named as well, for the 80 carved and lacquered pillars holding up an ornate roof echo the northern Thai style of wat decoration. But the real attraction for me was the Tet offensive and its most memorable event, the taking of Hue by the V.C. Their raising of the communist flag from the tower built of brick in 1809 for 25 days, is forever etched in my mind along with the ferocious street fighting between Marines and the communist invaders. 150 Marines were killed in two days fighting block by block against a foe that had ten days to dig in. The slaughter of Americans finally stopped when the O.K. from on high was finally given to destroy the historic city to save it. That and the simple use of tear gas drove the V.C. out, but left some 10,000 civilians dead in its wake. The terrible destruction is still there to see within the ramparts of the old city. Those areas that were completely wiped out are now used as fields for the growing of vegetables. Time goes on......with the sea gypsies who live aboard sampans off the islands of the Perfume River giving the entire scene an exotic quality.

Then out to the serenity of Nam Giao (Temple of Heaven, just like in Beijing), once the most important religious site in Vietnam. Nestled in pine and frangipani, this is where the Emperor offered sacrifices to the Emperor of the August Heaven every three years. And on to the Royal Tombs of the Nguyen Dynasty (1802-1945), especially the elaborate grounds and graves of Tu Duc, the longest serving from 1848-1883. The detail in the very Chinese influenced architecture is exquisite—which is unusual for me to say because normally I find it too gaudy. And speaking of gaudy, the French influenced architecture of the tomb of Khai Dinh (1916-1925) shouts to all who visit that he was a great and powerful puppet of the French! But speaking of *fengshui*, my guide, Cong and I had the most magical conversation as we both straddled the very center line of the top step beginning the descent down the hill from this tomb. The view is actually quite sublime with high green hills topped with old American and South Vietnamese fire stations surrounding a quiet valley. He is very well read but has never been allowed to leave the country. I spoke of my Grandfather's falling out with his old Ann Arbor friend Robert McNamara, a fact which quite impressed Cong (the fact that people once friends could so openly disagree). This lead to my purchasing the anti-McNamara book, *Dereliction of Duty*, for Cong back in Bangkok and having it surreptitiously brought to him by a another traveler to Danang. We couldn't stop talking at this magical juncture, going on and on about his experiences in the war in Danang, the current deleterious situation and even the lay of the land and how it affected the war's outcome. Wild! Only darkness and the closure of the puppet's tomb stopped us.

On into Hanoi whose old quarter impressed me the most with its motion, capitalism, narrow streets and bars with tiny chairs out front where one sits like a child with a cold one while bikes and scooters throng past. The Temple of Literature a big favorite too, with its delicately wrought gates. Khue Van Pavilion at the far end of the temple is an exquisite example of Vietnamese architecture. Eighty-two stelae perched on the backs of fortuitous turtles line one courtyard and list the names of all exam passers at the national level from 1442 to 1778: a sanctuary from the bustle of the capital's bike and scooter crowded streets. But not many cars! A visit to Uncle Ho in his Mausoleum had the stern guards smacking my disrespectful hands out of my pant pockets. Ho looked great! His white hair nicely trimmed and his skin in pretty darn good shape. You have to be impressed by the guy who defeated both the French and the Americans. He was total Zen too, as a visit to his simple stilt house where he spent most of the last twenty years of his life shows. He was a monk with no children, but the father of a country!

Hanoi on takeoff: using shallow bomb craters for a different crop from rice, thereby highlighting the numerous hits this particular region sustained. Writing, traveling, teaching........the best of all lifestyles!

To Hong Kong and Shanghai for the last time and happy for it. Enough is enough. A week ago I was in Hue, two weeks ago, Jakarta. In one week I'll be in Sydney and in exactly one month, San Francisco......

Crystal clear afternoon cruising down the South China Sea past a bone-white atoll rising from deep blue water. Clear that is until approaching the Vietnam coast and all the slash and burn haze from two months of firing

S.E. Asian forests spills out over the sea. But still clear enough to see forested and white beached Cham Island, Hoi An historic port and fishing village of last week, Marble mountain and China Beach wide and clean stretching north and south below. The bridge leading to Hai Van pass just north of Da Nang where I photographed three young boys by the old railroad trestle a week ago is directly below as we cruise past at 35,000' Amazing to reflect on memories generated by planet earth from on high. Racing to the other side of the plane I see Langco bridge, protected by Lt. Warr and company during the Tet offensive before they were rushed north to take back the city of Hue in his book *Phase Line Green*. Hue is obscured by haze to the north, but the Perfume River is seen winding out to sea.

Therapy complete? It's just a beautiful country now, with none of the angst I used to feel when flying over it. The Annamite mountains bordering Laos and hiding the Ho Chi Ming trail are stunning in their lack of deforestation.

May '98: Leaving Bangkok at o'dark hundred, a farewell waning moon with Saturn perched on its sickle hangs low in the eastern sky as I stroll down the dark lane leading to Soi 31 in search of a taxi to the airport. Another chapter closes only to followed by more!

The morning I arrive stateside from steamy, polluted Bangkok, my hands touch metamorphic-smooth red Franciscan chert on a hike under a cobalt sky along cliffs plunging into the always stunning Golden Gate: reminding me that only two weeks before I took a farewell walk along Manly Beach up past Shelly Cove to the dreamtime sandstone cliffs carved by wind into webbed patterns perched above thundering turquoise surf after ferrying over from Sydney.

Then the week following Sydney I was on the granite-smooth mountains encircling Seoul. One exposed ridge of solid granite on Inwangson had the occasional gnarled, stunted pine growing aesthetically from the odd crack, as if it were a bonsai pruned by an unseen ascetic hiding atop Snyder's *Cold Mountain*. But up there the spiritual was the last thing on the Korean military's mind. The peaks around Seoul form a natural defensive barrier against the marauding commies to the north. So, even that far south of the DMZ, the ridges of those mountains are patrolled constantly to guard against any type of attack, be it mortar or frontal assault! The sublime side by side with earthly conflict, none of which is new in this world: century-old walls line the ridges where today's troops stand guard.

Then coming off the mountain trail into a typical Korean neighborhood of cinder block houses crammed next to and on top of each other. The local folks stare at the white boy fresh from the trail stroll through their narrow streets lined with tiny shops selling every imaginable item: fruit and vegetables spill onto the street and the occasional truck sells huge fresh fish direct from its bed.

Then on the flight back to Bangkok on my very last trip out of Thailand the troubled history of the entire region is cemented into my brain once and for all: B-52 craters scattered across a forest clearing in Laos, as if it was only yesterday…flashbacks from Franciscan chert! Then I clamber around the rocks from China Beach to Baker Beach, stopping to skinny dip in the clear cold surf as it washes into long slender caves burrowing under the multi-million dollar homes of Sea Cliff: heaven is the Golden Gate on a clear spring day, the Marin Headlands as green as they get.

August '98: Strolling along the C&O canal on a wet, humid summer night after driving all day from fresh, clear-cold waters of northern Michigan, I realize that exactly twenty years ago, on the verge of turning twenty, I took a similar drive to the refreshing north. Then, as now, I stopped in Ann Arbor the way we stopped this time and visited graves and Angell Hall etc. Touching base with the ancestors before moving on…Yet, this time, to show how quickly the mighty have fallen one hundred years later, we stay in a dump of a hotel across from the railroad station where my namesake great-great-grandfather made his triumphant round the world return from serving as Minister to China on February 24, 1882:

"We arrived at Ann Arbor......and received a most hearty welcome from Faculties and students." How quickly the families of the revered become non-entities.

Jungfrau to Mt. Blanc, from Lake Charlevoix to Lac Leman! Sweeping, clear views of the Swiss Alps flying into Geneva on my first trip out of Frankfurt. Mt. Blanc glistening white in what I later find out is a rare coating of thick ice that has killed eight climbers over the weekend. Chateaus line both shores of the huge lake carved by glaciers as we near the city of perfection. Memories of being in Sion just up the U-shaped valley exactly twenty-one years ago, getting drunk and breaking into the castle that rises spectacularly above the small town there, surge through the mind. Take a nice drive up to the mission in Bern along the lakeshore and through beautiful farms of apples and pears and vineyards: all the while Mt. Blanc soars across the glacial waters, playing peak-a-boo with the foothills. Up on the road to Bern, the countryside is as picturesque as the drive through Pennsylvania farm country taken just a few weeks ago, just the mountains are a little higher! Bern stunning in its locale on the bluff above the swift turquoise waters flowing fast down from Interlachen, making an S turn around its base. Civilization!!

Two weeks before, truck bombs killed hundreds at the missions in Kenya and Tanzania, and it was tragicomic when we pulled up in a truck with no diplomatic plates outside the mission in Bern. Since neither of us had any idea where we were going, I had a big map unfolded in the window as we slowly headed toward the chancery with surrounding streets cleared of cars and armed Polizei at every corner. They almost opened up on us with Uzis while private guards frantically waved for our truck to keep moving. We pulled over just past the perimeter, but they were still understandably agitated. One of the guards finally said it was O.K. when he got word from the Marines that they were expecting us. When we opened the back of this large truck, with the armed Polizei huddled around watching, there were two small diplomatic bags inside.

After the dark humor of the potential truck bomb it was off to lunch in Gruyeres, home of the famous cheese and fortress town encircling a strategic hilltop under towering peaks that is as spectacular as Switzerland gets.

Flying into Athens a few days later, the pollution was appalling. Homer's sea is still wine dark, but the dirty air obscures all. It was ten years ago to the week we were in exquisite Lindos, Rhodes with baby Emily. Now she's eleven and living in Germany! What a crazy, wild existence.

Flying into Rome a caldera filled with gorgeously tilled fields: fertile soils indeed! Then crystal clear caldera Lago di Bracciano north of the eternal city set amidst late summer brown farms of the coast. On landing St. Peters rises majestically above the Vatican City as if we were landing back in time. Later, absorbing the massive wealth of St. Peter's and the Vatican museum over several days served to reinforce the folk singer Phil Ochs' great spin on Nietzsche's famous quote two thousand years after Christ: "God isn't dead, he's missing in action."

On the way back north, Elba, home of banished Napoleon, floats in a late afternoon sea of silver. The encircling rim of the Alps glimpsed from the rugged Ligurian Coast are a barrier to not only weather (keeping the northern clouds at bay) but also the culture of the stern northern tribes. Lake Como snakes spectacularly into the mountains with many a village scattered along its shores. Mt. Blanc from the week before looms downrange to the west, while the slender Matterhorn pokes distinctly above a myriad of snowy Massifs.

September '98: Tblisi, Georgia: bleak, post-Soviet Third World. The airport is something out of 1935, a Casablanca set, but all too real. Soviet era planes with multi-paned noses are parked neatly around the tarmac, as if awaiting imminent departure. My colleague tells me none of them have flown for years. He said they don't even bother parting them out because there is nothing to put the parts in. I pointed out a few recently painted planes with Air Georgia in modern script gracing their sides. He said they're trying with Airbuses, but the old Soviet fleet is not safe.

Crimean Peninsula comes into view with Yalta spewing brown grunge over the Black Sea. Churchill, Roosevelt, Stalin! Fifty plus years ago! That famous meeting seems like another century, right up there with the Austro-Hungarian Empire! Time is a strange thing indeed. Geography is a little more grounded, and the stunning Table Mountain-like cliffs plunging from the Peninsula's flat top into the city and pounding surf around to the west toward Sebastopol makes up for the pollution.

Flying up the Sea of Marmara, hundreds if not thousands of white birds in huge V-formations set against a dark blue sea backdrop are heading across toward Turkey at half our 10,000' altitude on the descent into the mosque-spire-forest of Istanbul.

Getting into Wien as a late summer sun goes down lighting the grand old pastel colored buildings lining the quick running Donau canal. Then after tossing the suitcase in the hotel it's off for a twilight walk around Schwarzenburg Palace and a long meditation at the impressive fountain built by the Soviet occupiers in honor of themselves as it's bathed in a variety of colors. The Karlsplatz is cause for another contemplative moment, its majestic columns and baroque carvings enough for an eternity of study. The Art Nouveau style of Otto Wagner's Stadt Pavilions close by are cause for further architectural inspiration before heading up the ring road past the Hofburg illuminated in immensely exquisite gravitas. The Ratshaus too is gorgeously lit as I wander through the gardens toward the famous Bergtheater, delicately lit statues and memorials revealed sporadically amidst leafy darkness. A sublime eve if ever there was one. Then a return to the hotel room where CNN froths over Ken Starr's salacious impeachment report to congress.

Next morn, spectacular Ljubljana, Slovenia nestled at the foot of huge Austrian Alps with thick, pine-forested foothills.

The following day Skopje, Macedonia. When I rode the train down through Yugoslavia fifteen years ago on the way to Athens, this place was a dusty, forgotten town. Now troops from all over NATO serve as trip wires in case the Bosnian and Kosovo slaughter heads south. Alexander's birthplace.

The next week again soaring in over the Hellespont glistening in late afternoon sun. Troy is just down along the coast across from the Hellespont, while Gallipoli is almost directly below, along the historic Dardenelles finger of the wine dark sea. Off to the west, a solitary giant rising from the dark waters, the historically Hellenistic island of Samothrace looms large, while beyond the mountainous fingers of Thessaloniki peninsulas are glimpsed through the haze, Mt Athos rising highest and clearest. Then Istanbul spires fill the window along with Golden Gate like bridges spanning the Bosporus, making this a spectacularly situated city.

Back in Wien it's off to Schönbrunn Palace and its Versailles-like gardens and dancing halls and gaudy bedrooms. The contrived nature of this wealth of Austro-Hungarian Kings rings false somehow. The architecture and art is impressive and the gardens grand, but is all too contrived set amidst the green Vienna woods. The gaudy art style of the baroque reaches its pinnacle in the outrageous National Library set inside the grandeur of the Hofburg. The highly acclaimed cafes of Vienna are again, grandly conceived and gorgeous, but the quality of the coffee is sorely lacking.

Scruffy-brown Caucuses bump up against Black Sea dwarfing a lone freighter plowing east toward the Georgian coast. Then glacial white behemoth of Mt. Elbrus, the highest peak in Europe at 18,500', pokes above fleecy cloud. Mottled white of late summer snowfields hug the western slopes of surrounding ragged peaks soaring above the flat Georgian Plain; while huge, dark valleys slice deep into its side.

October: '98: Hopping on the Metro in Springfield, Virginia, after taking care of business following an eight-hour flight from Germany, we cut through the heart of my birthplace. The faintly familiar begins with thick forest and shallow creeks meandering underneath the tracks. Then hazy memories of the large apartment buildings lining the ridge to the north, followed by clearer memories of the distinctive brick warehouses crowding the rail line. Faint turns to concrete with the Masonic Temple looming ahead above late summer trees untouched by autumn. The conductor's voice chants, "Next stop King Street," as if replaying my delivery to Earth forty years ago by a god bellowing in the same manner. I was born on King Street in Alexandria!

The rail station is as familiar as when I was four years old, scrambling with my English Grand Pop on the W.W. I tank once parked on the grass out front. That's the only thing missing from a scene that hasn't changed in all those years (along with my late Grandfather). In elementary school at nearby Charles Barrett we took a field trip on a train that left this station. I remember posters of Ella Fitzgerald in Porgy and Bess crowding the walls on the trip to Union Station and back. The trestle Amtrak and freight trains still use is now rusted, but it's the same one my family drove under again and again on jaunts from Old Dominion Boulevard to Old Town. And the little playground, now all fixed up with new play structures and wood chips, is still there on the right between the trestle and the base of the temple. I remember that playground being incredibly bleak when I was young, full of mud puddles and destitute kids.

The Masonic Temple and its hidden legions of toy soldiers reenacting some of the world's great military campaigns inside, still rises to give what I remember as one of the great views of the Washington area. All these memories coursing through the mind's eye during a short stop at a Metro station.

Exactly a week later, cruising down the Turkish coast above the narrow Dardenelles glimpsed from above the Sea of Marmara a few weeks ago. Geographically the strait is amazingly slim, just wide enough for a couple of freighters to pass each other. Then Gallipoli again at the elbow of the Hellespont's thin arm. Images from Peter Weir's movie of the bloody Aussie debacle, the British using them as pawns in a diversionary move, crowd the mind. And the haunting soundtrack of Albinoni's Adagio in G

Major even in 1998 recalls the sorrow of all military campaigns, let alone every life lived, as we wing over the brown plains where Troy flourished from 5,000 to 3,000 years ago. The wine dark sea offshore is littered with bleak, late summer isles, whatever forests there once were harvested long ago to build the fleets of empire. Lesbos below with a turquoise uterine harbor filling its midsection, a tight vaginal passage opening toward the Temple of Delos in the Cycladic heart of the Aegean, birthplace of western civilization.

Rugged ridge jutting toward the isle of Samos halted abruptly by a deep channel separating it from mainland Turkey. Samos greener and more mountainous than other islands to the north. Then stunning deserted tentacles protruding from the southwestern coast, the few tiny villages spotted more Greek looking in their white-washed simplicity nestled in protected harbors.

Then Greece itself and the Island of Rhodes appearing below. Its deep harbor once spanned by the colossus busy with huge cruise ships moored en masse within. The crusader castle immense even from cruising altitude, the now green moat silhouetting it beautifully. The memories of exactly ten years ago come flooding back. Flying in from London on a cheap charter flight with baby Emily, one and a half years old. Strolling amidst the huge walls and fortifications and narrow lanes of the city within before heading down to the pleasant village of Lindos and its dramatic Temple of Athena perched on cliff edge high above dark blue.

To have the luxury of crisscrossing the planet while tracing past journeys is a state I never could have imagined: reminiscences from on high. Began government employment exactly six years ago with the Nat'l Park Service on San Francisco Bay, with an office in the pilot house of the historic ferry boat Eureka and one of the greatest 360 degree views in the world. Now, a whole world later...time passing in sweet sorrow.

Further along the Southern Turkish coast there is no sign of *Homo sapiens* among the bleak, huge mountains. Could very well be 6000 B.P. from this altitude. And whose to say if things will be any different on eternal

Earth 6,000 years from now. And speaking of eternal, Mt. Hermon pokes above the desert haze of the Lebanon-Syrian border as we begin the descent into Tel Aviv, home of eternal strife.

Back in Israel after almost fourteen years. Tel Aviv almost exactly the same in its borderline Third-Worldness. After the grey of northern Europe the beach and warm waters of the Mediterranean feel good as I float on my back wearing shades, watching the sun go down. Later, trying to find the hostel where we stayed those many years ago after N. was given the choice of leaving the States voluntarily or being deported after being busted for illegally working on a tourist visa. I found the area along Ben Yehudin now filled with upscale hostels for the backpacking crowd, but not the exact place where we set off for Moshav duty in the far-off settlement of Tsofar in the Negev desert along the Jordanian border.

Remembering returning to that Tel Aviv hostel three months later and half-dead after venturing down the Nile to Aswan and back overland. Made the mistake of eating a sandwich bought from a train-side vendor on the return to Cairo. The following day on the bus across the sand-bleak Sinai I seriously thought I was going to die, my gut was in so much pain. Sand drifts across the road and the resultant delays making it all the worse as I focused on the Israeli border as my salvation. The relief felt on crossing it later and catching another bus up to Tel Aviv allowed me to psychologically turn the corner and beat whatever it was that was trying to savage my body. Convalescing in the Tel Aviv hostel for several days got me on my feet again before we departed back to depressing London weather.

I journeyed up to Jerusalem to further track the past, passing the hulks of troop transports where the road begins to climb and the trees thicken that have been there since the '67 war. Guess leaving the shattered vehicles there reminds Israelis of how close Jordanian troops got to Tel Aviv. Jerusalem has changed dramatically over fourteen years, the Israeli construction of settlements on every hilltop as part of their campaign to produce "facts on the ground" before any final peace deal mar the once beautiful rock-forested hills encircling the old city. Inside the city walls the same Palestinian vendors crowding the narrow pathways, the same tourists crowding the same historic, spiritual spots. The Wailing Wall filled with black suited bobbing fur hats and Hasidic curls of Orthodox Jews praying en masse during the holy week of Succot. And likewise the Temple Mount closed so Palestinians could not hurl stones down on those at the base of David's 3,000 year old wall, as they have in the past. After a meditative walk through the turmoil of the holy city, rediscovering the grubby hostel where we spent Christmas eve fourteen years before and recalling the wail of Muezzin on Christmas morning 1984 as we awoke on a hard, mildewy mattress with a pillowcase flecked with paint peeling from an ancient ceiling. Ahh, travel!

Just outside the new Jerusalem choking on facts on the ground, I spot from the bus the resultant tragedy such a policy has meant for the Palestinians who have lived there for hundreds of years: in a valley below a newly constructed highway sliced into bedrock was a deserted village of some twenty dwellings. From the architecture I could tell it was Palestinian, for their abodes really haven't changed since the land was called Palestine: adobe dwellings with a flat roof circled by a low wall, normally used for sleeping under the stars during summer heat. They had obviously been thrown out some time ago, as scrub and a few trees were growing in the streets. Where are they now? Why were they moved to begin with? Why have the Israelis left these buildings standing, when given the slightest excuse elsewhere they blow-up occupied dwellings? Seeing that lonely village set on a terraced hillside under a brand new highway topped by new suburban sprawl, I thought of North American Indians crushed by the advance of manifest destiny.

Back to Tel Aviv in the afternoon for another sunset swim to wash off bitter Middle East realities, personal memories and the dust of ages. Then realizing the similarities between Miami Beach and Tel Aviv, two Jewish beach towns with very similar climates facing each other across two large bodies of water. Is it a genetic predisposition that lures them to sand dunes and warm waters? If it is, who can blame them.

Soaring in above the Vistula river as it flows into Warsaw, it strikes me that many European cities are similarly set in flat terrain, making repeated military invasions inevitable due to the ease of movement possible: no natural barriers, no place to hide and begin a guerrilla insurgency.

Out the port window the Nile Valley is a glowing snake slithering through ink-black desert on the way to Addis Ababa. Orange crack of dawn pierces the starry night over this ancient land as it's done since the beginning of time. Over the Ethiopian Plateau we drop through a grey ceiling above a bright green quilt of farms and huge, extinct volcanoes rising from the Rift Valley; grass hut villages make it feel like a different planet after the staid landscape of northern Europe. After having been shown the world, I arrive at the very spot where our *Australiopithicene* forbearers sprang from mother earth.

The National Museum is always a good place to begin a visit to a new country, and the one in Addis, despite its stereotypically shoddy appearance, is a good bet due its "Lucy" display. The famous 3.5 to 4.0 million year old bipedal *Australiopithicene afarensis*, discovered in the northern exposure of the Rift Valley at Hadar before it hits the Red Sea, is unceremoniously displayed, laid out in a dreary glass case. For one of the most important finds in human history, the indifference of the Ethiopians is refreshing. There is so much that is ancient in this land that the bones of a bipedal-humanoid-monkey just don't seem to excite. What with its Kings purportedly descended from Solomon (the Queen of Sheba having been impregnated by him on her visit to Jerusalem, then giving birth to King Menelik back in the Ethiopian kingdom of Axum, who later returned to meet his father in Jerusalem before absconding with the Ark of the Covenant back to Abyssinia!), and the Ark of the Covenant hidden in one of the churches in the gnarly northern mountains, what is of interest in a collection of ancient bones?

Some of the other intriguing items in the decrepit museum were a plump Venus of Lilliendorf-like clay figurine (also reminiscent of the one found at the 8000 B.P. adobe village of Catal Hayak in central Turkey) and tribal garb reminiscent of North American Indians. Maybe the Lost Tribes of Israel did fan out over the globe, given the Semitic ties this part of Africa has to Judah and Samaria!

Another interesting anecdote from the museum's tawdry display cases was the discovery of where the Dreadlocked Rastefarian Christian sects of Jamaica got their name: from the original title of the last Emperor of Ethiopia, Haile Selassie, descended from Solomon: Ras Tefari, Prince Tefari! I got a chance to see Selassie's throne and, after discreetly asking around, found he was still buried in the latrine he was unceremoniously dumped into after being killed in the coup d'etat of 1974.

I was awakened the following morning by strange chanting over loudspeakers at 5:00 AM. At first I thought it was a Muslim muezzin, for there is a substantial Muslim population in Ethiopia, but this call to prayers was slightly different, perhaps more primitive in its guttural intonations. I later discovered the Christian Orthodox Church of Ethiopia does have a muezzin calling the faithful to prayer, but in the ancient Geez language, which is faintly connected to the Coptic Church of Egypt, and therefore Greek. It certainly had a haunting feel about it, especially when bellowed over the quiet predawn city at 8,000'. Then, some three hours later I was awakened by the tremendous roar of lions! Talk about strange! I knew I was in Africa! I later visited the seedy city lion house full of the Ethiopian variety. They are a little different from the normal African lion in that they're smaller, scrawnier and darker, but with a mighty roar, especially when big hunks of bloody meat are about to be tossed into their cages.

The contemporary travel writer and social critic Robert Kaplan has recently coined the "stretch-limo" analogy when discussing the state of the world. It alludes to the wealthy minority populations of the First World going about their business in a Third and Fourth World sea of poverty. Ironically, I caught a lecture of Mr. Kaplan's on C-Span while in Addis, and coupled with my stay at the new five-star Sheraton built by a Saudi-Ethiopian billionaire, I immediately understood it. If you are like me, one who enjoys leaving the confines of a hotel to explore whatever city you might be in, hotels like this new Sheraton actively discourage such activity: they think they're keeping you safe from the rowdy streets. This particular hotel discouraged the wanderer by not allowing local cabs to even wait outside a secure gate it takes some five minutes to walk to (they would rather you pay exorbitant sums to contract out a new sedan by the hour from their motor pool). When you finally pass the perimeter, finding a taxi is next to impossible because they're not allowed to loiter and no one in the sprawling slum across the street could afford one anyway.

Out on the street, either looking for a taxi or just wandering, the multitudes of impoverished descend in full upon me from this shanty town, begging, cajoling, whatever, because I'd just waltzed out of the most stunning structure within a thousand square miles...I hate being pegged so easily! The unadventurous quickly retreat back inside the limo world of the Sheraton, but most don't even attempt a walk.

Jumping off the runway into the clear, blue, dry air of the Rift Valley with vultures circling, circling (turning and turning in the widening gyre....things fall apart: the center cannot hold) through the indifference of eternal nature: from the evolution of bipedal Lucy to John Glenn's return to space aboard the Space Shuttle. Rift Valley lakes colored by flocks of pink flamingos wading in the shallows. Terrain drys drastically on the way to Lake Turkana (Rudolph), home of two million year old *Homo habilis* who lived side by side with the ancestral *Australopithicines* for one million years or so, where the desert begins big time. A volcanic isle mid-lake has three different water colors in its three distinct craters. *This* is ancient land.

The terrain rises sharply at the edge of the Rift, onto a green forested plateau that extends all the way to the shores of the White Nile's headwaters, Lake Victoria. Deserted forested islands fleck the great lake on the descent along its northern shore into Kampala, Uganda. Like much of central Africa, the green of the region is offset by bright, red dirt roads leading down to the shore. Not a boat in sight on the watery canvas, and no waves pound the mostly marshy shore. Great swaths of papyrus clog narrow harbors as we come in low to land at infamous Entebbe, where the Israelis duped the Ugandans into believing the C-130 filled with Israeli troops belonged to Idi Amin. They rescued hijacked Israelis right there at the terminal with the loss of only one, current Prime Minister Benjamin Netanyahu's older brother. Stranger than fiction.

Then beautiful finger lakes and scattered villages and green rolling hills of Rwandan slaughter. One hundred thousand Hutu tribesmen accused of genocide are crammed in jails awaiting trial for butchering 800,000 of their Tutsi countrymen. I catch sight of a few of these miserable facilities, their courtyards crammed with humanity, as we come in low over the city. I always heard Rwanda was the Switzerland of Africa, but in reality it is deforested rolling hills full of farms. One would never think such carnage occurred here, given the surface serenity of the verdant countryside or the sleepy, red-dirt street capital stretched village like along a low ridge. From Lucy origins to a century full of genocide! Evolution?

Southeast of Lake Victoria the Serengeti is shockingly bleak. Memories of the Kalahari come to mind, but that famous desert was flat, whereas this "plain" is anything but. Huge escarpments plunging into lakes beside volcanoes, make the Serengeti a touch more spectacular. Olduvai Gorge of Leakey fame is just a little to the north, and if this is the birthplace of modern *Homo sapiens*, maybe we do come from hell; or perhaps hell is merely the nature of nature.

Then, thankfully, a few forested mountains rise from the parched ground of dry season, green isles amidst a brown sea, followed by more severe escarpments highlighted by lengthy shadows cast by a setting sun. Cute little volcanic nubs that never blew interspersed by crater lakes that did. One huge crater with crystalline water has a 360 degree ring of pink flamingos just off its shoreline—not bad from 35,000': a pink reef.

What a vast, empty landscape! Hundreds upon hundreds of forested Tanzanian miles pass by without a sign of humanity in this supposedly overcrowded continent. Unlike the Serengeti to the northwest, this land looks habitable. A few villages marked by smoke are spotted, but this land is mostly human free after the congested fertile soil of Rwanda. Glancing north, the snows of squat, volcanic Kilimanjaro catch some color as East Africa goes dark before landing in swampy Dar es Salam, perched on the muggy Indian Ocean.

Just three months earlier the mission in Dar was attacked by a truck bomb. Its facade was obliterated and ten nationals killed, mostly guards on the perimeter. My escort was checking into the mission that fateful day after arriving from Washington. She was buried up to her neck in rubble and had the tip of her nose sliced off by a projectile. Fortunately, there was a water truck in front of the truck bomb when it exploded. If that vehicle full of water hadn't absorbed some of the explosion many more would have died, including my escort. Her husband worked in the Nairobi mission which was bombed the same day, killing twelve Americans. If he had been at his desk instead of in Washington with their son, he would have died along with everyone in his office. As Eric Clapton sang with Cream: "If it wasn't for bad luck, I'd have no luck at all."

Heading back into Addis a few days later, a shimmering Turquoise crater lake glistens like a jewel in the parched landscape. Up ahead, Mt. Megezez and Mt. Gugl are gargantuan volcanic guardians of the Rift Valley as it opens towards the Red Sea. Pulling up to the terminal in Addis, anti-aircraft guns bristle in the tall grass, a reminder of the renewed conflict with Eritrea. When I visited Asmara four years ago, the peace treaty was still freshly signed. Now, the Eritrians have taken by force a northern slice of land they claim is theirs, so the Ethiopians have responded by bombing the already shattered Asmara airport again. "Things fall apart......"

Then a quick hop upcountry to further explore this magical land. Eighty-five percent of the Nile River flow comes from the Blue Nile thundering over Tis Abay Falls after it spills from Lake Tana, home of island monasteries of ancient Judaic-Christianity. The "smoke of the Nile" spray of the falls soothes the skin in the hot, dry high altitude air as it wafts through lush stands of trees. Birds of various colors flit through the spray to the edge of the pounding water, and calmly perch there as millions of gallons surge past. The mesa-mountains bordering this famous river valley are reminiscent of the American west as they soar up over ten thousand feet. A variety of tribes in colorful garb lined the dirt road on the drive down from Bahir Dar, with all males carry one long stick to swat their cattle. One sight had me yearning for a camera: the eternal female from the time of Christ in white robe and red sash around the waist with pitcher balanced atop her head walking through a field of wheat.

Very early the following morning I hired a boat to Kebran Gebriel monastery perched on a thickly forested island far offshore. When we beached it was like taking a step back in time as the soothing sound of cooing doves filled the air, huge spiders clung to tremendous webs in the treetops and a multitude of eagles bobbed on branches hunting for fish. Except for the doves it was totally silent. A twelfth-century circular church with dark eight-hundred year old paintings of St. George inside was set atop a hill with a view of the sun rising over calm lake waters. A gnarled monk in white robe chanting in ancient Geez enhanced the scene as I strolled around the central block holding the holy of holies in the church's interior: a copy of the Ark of the Covenant. Papyrus boats unchanged since the stone age swept past on the lake below, sharing the expanse with huge white pelicans and Nile Perch flopping noisily on the radiant surface.

The Lake Tana region is the locale of most of the Falasha peoples descended from Jews from before 650 B.C. Jewish historians know this due to the style of worship and sacrifice they practiced in this region for thousands of years before being airlifted to Israel as part of an *aliya* program to reunite all Jewish people in their homeland.

Back ashore I go direct to the airport for the short flight to Lalibela, home of the churches carved in basalt. On the Fokker 50 flight there is nothing but beautiful green mountains strewn with conical grass-roofed huts with stick walls. Occasionally, clusters of these classic African styled huts form villages with cattle and crops surrounding them. Nearby to these settlements is always a grove of trees encircling a round Christian church.

The Lalibela airport is a dirt strip and a two room shack terminal! Terrible cratered road from the airport through beautiful dry terrain. Halfway to the village, in the middle of nowhere, the decrepit land cruiser begins to smoke and dies. After several failed attempts at restarting it, my driver and I humbly prepare to hike the final five kilometers uphill through the parched, basalt pillared countryside. Just as we're about to head off he decides to give it one more try. It miraculously fires up despite fried wiring! A day begun with a water journey to an ancient monastery, to be followed by further visits to underground churches carved from rock, called for a miracle! Vibrant poinsettia bushes scattered throughout the poor village of Lalibela offset the dark, grass roofed, two-story-high-conical-huts made of rounded boulders found only here.

Lalibela (2630m) mesas and dryness like the southwestern U.S. except for eight-hundred-year-old subterranean churches carved from stone. King Lalibela ruled in the 12th century, and according to the Ethiopian Royal Chronicles a dense cloud of bees surrounded him at his birth. His mother claimed these bees represented the soldiers who would one day serve her son, and chose for him a name which means, "the bees recognize his sovereignty." A mellifluous name indeed! It was his ambition to build a new Jerusalem that gave rise to the rock-hewn church project, and the Chronicles say they are modeled on churches God showed to Lalibela when he transported him "to the first, second and third heavens." The first European to ever see the unusual places of worship was a Portuguese priest, Alvarez, who visited the site in 1521. He described the Lalibela churches as marvels, but lamented that no one in Portugal would believe they actually existed.

There are twelve rock churches in two major groups, one for each of the Apostles(?) and each with its own emphasis. They are separated by the so called River Jordan, a dry streambed running between the seven churches of the eastern cluster and the five found in the western cluster. Different cross motifs: Maltese, Greek and even the Hindu swastika grace many of the walls inside the sanctuaries. The fact that these churches were each carved from the basalt ground by first trenching around and down to form a block, then cutting doors in the base and hollowing it out from the inside, is one of the engineering marvels of the world. In fact, Bet Medhane Alem, the largest church hewn from rock in the eastern cluster, is the largest monolithic church in the world, supported as it is by thirty-six pillars inside. Situated defensively on a hilltop as they are, these churches under a high, serrated Drakensberg-like escarpment with a view out over a Canyonlands-like depression, are one of the most stunningly situated historical sights on the planet. If they were in a more accessible country they would be one of the most visited monuments as well, so perhaps it's better they're so difficult to reach. Each church has its own unique, delicately wrought Ethiopian Orthodox cross associated with it kept inside since the time of Lalibela! The monks within each church bring each individual cross out for viewing atop a staff when you enter!

St. Giorgis, the thirteenth church and most majestic is separated from the two major groups by the Jordan. What makes it so stunning is its cruciform shape rising 15m out of a deep square of removed rock. Atop the roof across the deep "moat" it was carved from, is a cross in bas relief, thus giving the structure a double-cross effect. You descend into the depths by a rough hewn cut in the rock, eventually arriving at a gate far below the surface. A tunnel lined with small caves filled with the bones of monks is passed through before entering the light and wonder of the courtyard and the smoothly chiseled structure itself carved out of the earth. An ancient female monk with a blue nurse-like cap with a cross on it sat on the ground in one corner of the courtyard picking stones and grit out of what must have been donated grain, while just behind her toe bones protruded from a hole in the wall.

The fact that these churches were carved down into the rock and hollowed out from within by the skilled hands of *Homo sapiens*, makes this style of Christianity different. It is rooted in the Earth in an almost pagan way. There is no aloof, abstract striving toward heaven with soaring cathedrals here, more an ascetic meditation in a darkened cave. The skeletons of mummified monks, skins stretched taught over ancient bones, fill cavities in the rock walls around many of the churches. The monks lived, meditated and died in these carved homes beside the churches: carrying the meditative nature of the cell into eternity.

From the Tonle Sap in Cambodia to Lake Tana; Everest adventure exactly one year ago, and now the Ethiopian Highlands; this planet is beginning to feel tangible. I have been given one of the great gifts of all time.

I love countries where every clock you see has the wrong time, even when it's working! My favorite restaurant name in Addis: The Hard Luck Cafe, fitting for a city whose sidewalks are filled with the severely wounded from the war with Eritrea, begging for anything they can get.

Flying back from Djibouti, looking out over the vast, empty Danakil depression at the northern end of the Rift Valley (the lowest point on Earth at -116m), I continue to have my doubts about global warming from manmade sources. Natural cycles, yes, but flying over the endless terrain not far from where Lucy perished 3.5 million years ago, reminds one that such a high percentage of Earth is unpopulated, especially when the massive oceans are included. Just as the Serengeti and Kalahari and Sahara and all of Saudi and Russian Siberia and Canadian wilderness and immense steppes of central Asia and Amazonia are mostly devoid of humans, so the places of greatest human concentration spewing out poisons into the atmosphere are, in comparison, quite small. Because most of us inhabit cities, we are also blinded by them, thinking all the earth is congested; it isn't!

December '98: After driving from Helsinki to Moscow over two days of endless forests of birch and pine and village after village of cute wooden houses graced with delicately carved lace window frames gently askew on crumbling foundations, I am blown away by the stunning sight of the capital and its brilliantly lit monuments from the heights of the university. Talk about coming out of the hinterlands and into what on the surface looks like civilization! The low expectations I had of the Russian capital were pummeled upon seeing the mighty bridges, glowing hallucinogenic domes of St. Basils, the fortified monastery and the grand architecture of Stalin's seven sisters.

In order to pay homage to Lenin, I awoke early the next morning and took the labyrinthian underground to Red Square. It was the classic Russian scene with snow flurries enhancing the mighty red walls of the Kremlin, while grey coated soldiers goose stepped at an eternal flame at the fortress's base. When I walked up past high stepping soldiers toward the vastness of Red Square itself, I encountered a blockade of more soldiers sealing off the Square. Instead of turning around like a few other visitors, I went up to them and said "Lenin?" One of the dour looking lads who probably hadn't been paid in months due to the dire economic situation said, "Identification?" When I presented my diplomatic passport someone had told me to carry at all times in this dangerous city, he waved me inside. Passing through the guards and strolling up the small incline into the square itself, I saw the onion domes of St. Basils through flurries soaring above a deserted expanse. I had all of Red Square to myself! Spotting what looked like a brown marble mausoleum just before the red fortress walls of the Kremlin, midway across the square toward St. Basils, I made my way toward the object of pilgrimage. Two soldiers were standing rigidly beside the door leading into the structure, and still not sure whether it was open, I approached them hesitatingly. As I got closer I saw the door was indeed open, so I boldly walked past them into the darkness of the mausoleum. Turning left upon entering I saw another soldier, so turned toward him, then took a right down some stairs toward two soldiers standing guard at what turned out to be the actual opening of the resting place of "the man." It was scary being in his crypt completely alone, with only stiff, suspicious soldiers as company. Upon seeing the glass coffin and the fairly well preserved Lenin I immediately thought back to Uncle Ho in Hanoi and how much better he looked. Of course, Lenin died in 1924 to Ho Chi Ming's 1969, so time had definitely taken its toll despite the best efforts of the preservers. When I climbed up several flights of stairs to gaze at the old geezer who changed history in such a dramatic way, I was soon kept moving by a bark from the guard beside me. Guess they don't want folks seeing how badly he is deteriorating, or they want the line to keep moving, even though it was just little old me. After my private meeting I exited into the garden of fallen patriots lining the red walls and made my way back into the square now filling with a number of grey coated Russians, readying to march through the swirling snow in the still empty square. Classic!

One of the images that will stick with me always is the view from the bridge down the hill from St. Basils, back toward the Kremlin and its three domed churches lining the ridge above the frozen river. The fortress walls and their impressive guard towers coupled with the power projected by the Kremlin itself, contrasted by the sublime domed churches within is without doubt one of the wonders of the world.

Soaring north over snow-deep German villages nestled between frosted forested mountains after a Siberian express has roared through, then over Hamburg and Lubeck I trace the train/ferry route I took from Copenhagen 15 years ago to Munchen and on to Athens.

As I write I spot Aland Isle out the window and reminisce more about that time in my life and the fabulous booze cruise to the Finnish island through the stunning granite and fir tree passage from Stockholm. The southwest Finnish Archipelago: thousands of islets framed by white tinged with orange from a sun already setting just after noon. Over "land" nothing but frozen lakes interspersed with trees frozen white. Turku marks the tiny influence of *Homo sapiens* in this northern tundra.

The next day, shuttling over to good old Stockholm and back, I see the waterway I reminisced about yesterday, winding through myriad grey granite isles aesthetically capped with pine. Even though it has been a decade and a half since I sailed those waters, in reality it's a wink of an eye:

"Time is a jet plane, it moves too fast, oh and what a shame that all we've shared can't last...." as Dylan would say.

How often do you look *down* on a half moon rising over the curve of the earth while straddling the Kazakh/Russian border? The curve to the north is highlighted by an ever-so-faint hint of light. Stars glimmer just over the top of the earth, seemingly at the same altitude we're cruising, as if they could well be our destination rather than Beijing. Riding the same Finnair MD-11 we used to take to Bangkok, but this time: China!

Before the sun peeks over the horizon, it is light enough to see a vast sea of white that might as well be the Arctic, but it is Mongolia. Ulan Bator brings with it forested mountains to break the monotony of undulating white, but the tiny city itself is just a smudge of black with twinkling lights against the pristine snow. Then the Gobi desert and its dryness devoid of snow furthers the monotonous landscape before huge serrated peaks jump off the desert floor north of Beijing. As we begin our descent, a hundred mile line of the Great Wall clambering precariously along a mountain range brings a smile to a jet-lagged face.

To think that one hundred and nineteen years ago, my great, great grandfather was in Beijing acting as Minister to China! What the city must have been like then! Magical indeed. He and his family left San Francisco on the *Oceanic*, a steamer with sails, and arrived in Yokohama nineteen days later. The navy gunboats *Ashuelot* and *Richmond* then escorted them to Tientsin, where they boarded houseboats for the trip by canal to Peking! Ahh, those were the days. Now, at the close of this century, his namesake is back in Peking! But what an ugly metropolis.

Beijing is just like all cities in Asia now, bustling modernity with polluted air. It used to have two fortress walls just inside the two remaining moats protecting it. The good wisdom of the communists tore the walls down, but fortunately left much of the moat system. What a place it would be with those walls still up! Especially with the wonders of the Forbidden City, Temple of Heaven and Summer Palace adding to the mix. It could have been one of the remaining great ancient cities of the world with the walls and more of the old dwellings still standing, but no. Towering high rises just for the sake of it blot the major thoroughfares, just as in Shanghai and Guongzhou and Shenzen, making China's rush to join the modern world a crying shame, aesthetically that is.

Behind the Forbidden City, atop Coal Hill topped by five temples and once apart of the royal enclosure, I was struck by the similarities with Mandalay. The royal enclosure in Mandalay is about the same size as the Forbidden City, but, of course, not nearly as stunning or intricately wrought, fire or no fire. And Coal Hill itself is similar to Mandalay Hill, with its view over the city from a fine Buddhist temple. Both enclosures are also surrounded by mammoth moats. But the bat motif in the Forbidden City, like the bat motif in Vietnam, is a sign of good fortune, unlike the fear of bats in Burma!

In Hue the royal enclosure of that forbidden city is called the Purple Forbidden City, as it is here in Beijing. The color purple is associated with the north star, the cosmic center of the world.

And continuing to compare the great historic capitals of Asia, I think Seoul is a prettier and better situated home for the royals. The temples and palaces of Seoul are on a more human scale, are thickly forested, and are set at the base of those stunning mountains (when you can see them). The architectural parallels in the temples with multi-colored coffered ceilings and gilded pillars, however, reveal the direct link between these two civilizations.

Blasting out of Beijing the long line of the Great Wall scaling severe terrain is viewed clearly below: guard towers every quarter mile or so clearly glimpsed as the wall perseveres across deserted countryside for mile after mile; no wonder it can be viewed from space! To the northwest snow-capped peaks soar impressively over the battlements which still guard the northern approaches to the valley of Beijing. Dessicated, serrated terrain north of the wall looks difficult for marauding armies to get through, period! Which brings you to the question, why build the wall along those sections already guarded by nature? The very steepness of the wall in so many places proves the natural impassibility to all but a sizable army. At Badaling, the portion of the wall I clambered a thousand feet to the top of, at least the structure was built to guard the Juyong Pass, a major thoroughfare bordered on each side by high peaks; not just across bleak, steep terrain already impassable. Northwest of the wall begins the arctic-like snowy steppes which lead into icy Mongolia. Chinese/Mongolian countryside comparable to the American heartland: just dotted with villages of uniform housing for surrounding fields rather than one farm house and barn for 500 acres.

Getting back to the global warming issue, cruising across this immense landscape that is empty of humans for thousands of windswept miles from the Himalayas to the North Pole, how can the tiny percentage of congested human habitation affect this huge orb? Then the empty Gobi stretches on and on, reinforcing the point. From the perspective of the snow-white immensity of Mongolia, that Genghis Khan and his riders fought as far south as Saigon (Champa) and as far east as Europe just 800 years ago, is unfathomable.

And then the mighty forest of Siberia: endless, untouched! You cannot tell me there isn't a wealth of wildlife down there: Siberian tiger included. Derzu Ursala lives!

Flying over depressingly dark, frozen Russian country between Novogorod and St. Pete I was driving across just ten days ago, I recall a conversation with one of the Russian linguists accompanying the convoy concerning the mentality of the nation. He pointed out that despite the wealth of natural resources the country enjoys, the Russians would rather have total control over it all and make maybe ten percent profit, than share profits with a western country more efficient at extracting the resource in a sixty-forty profit agreement (Russia getting the sixty!). Of course, the ten percent profit they are making now on either timber or oil is being siphoned off by corruption of some kind. It's an admirable nationalism that actually impoverishes the country, much the same as Cuba.

January '99: Geneva in winter devoid of tourists! What a delight wandering the narrow cobblestone streets of the old walled city up to St. Stephens Calvinist cathedral. Antique shops and cafes bursting in summer are absolutely deserted, and the simple joy of taking a cafe au lait while contemplating the magical setting of this place set on the outflow of the Rhone from Lac Leman in a snowstorm is magic.

Exactly six years after joining this crazy outfit, the anniversary view out the window is of the snowy Apennines and Mt. Corno and Mt. Amaro soaring mightily up over the hazy dome of St. Peters to 3000m. Jaw dropping classic Italian villages clustered atop natural mesa fortresses, some with castles stoutly defending the fertile feudal fields below litter the approach from the north. Returning over Genoa, the Po Valley is icy all the way to the round wall of the Alps as they descend into the blue Mediterranean at Provence. Milano smog tries to obscure the view, but not even industrial humanity can blot the crystalline view of white peaks rising from glacial valleys of Lakes Maggiore and Como. Mt. Blanc downrange a bump of cloud as a front begins to move across the mountains from the ever grey north.

Then again, soaring over Garmisch, then Innsbruck with the glacial-blue Inns River running through it. The view east crystal clear, with the rocky Wilder Kaiser of our Tyrolian Christmas ski vacation clearly seen from directly over the sharp-ridged Zugspitze, the highest peak in Germany. highest in Austria, the Grossglockner, rises from a mass of peaks that make up the bulk of the Austrian Alps, before dropping a little in altitude toward Italy and the geologic wonder of the beautifully carved, granite-bare Dolomites. From the Dolomites Venice can be seen nestled in its lagoon, sheltered by the Lido strip from the northern curve of the Adriatic's rough seas. Beyond, towards Croatia, the Isstrian peninsula and good old Roman Pula visited twenty-one years ago during my first summer of hitchhiking and training travel. Rijeka and the quirky island of Rab visited on the same trip lost in the eastern haze as we glide down the Apennines once again. Shocking to go from the snowy peaks of central

Italy to the volcanoes of the south. Vesuvias the most fearsome volcano I have ever glimpsed. Its rust colored flanks and gaping, sharp beaked cone towering over poor little *Homo sapiens* settlements of Pompeii and Naples, surely puts nature's true might in perspective. Then cloud across the Mediterranean until unending waves of Libyan sands are lit orange by the setting sun on the way to Nairobi.

The cities and villages of Germany at night, clustered separately in the inky blackness, are connected by fine fibers of lit road: nerve clusters connected by tendrils. Nature repeats the same patterns on a multitude of levels and across a variety of cultures.

February '99: Standing in Michaeler Platz next to exposed 4th century Roman foundations with a touch of mural still on one wall, I gaze up at the enormous gate guarded by gold statues that leads into the heart of the Hofburg Palace in Vienna. Church bells from St. Michael's fill the square with wild ringing, and it dawns on me that a week from now I'll be in Washington D.C., another monumental city. I savor the moment, meditating on the ephemeral nature of empire, be it Rome, Austro-Hungarian, or American.

On the way back to the hotel, wandering through the narrow old streets, I escape into deserted Anneskirche, built in 1634. Its dark interior with gilded statues of angels reflecting what little light there is, is all mine. As I settle into a pew to absorb the silence, I hear low murmurings and realize one of the confession booths, faintly lit, is in use. The unintelligible confession sounds like a chant, thus sin becomes sanctity.

Back in Washington the sublime thoughts of empires waxing and waning is extinguished by the ridiculous Monica Lewinsky scandal and the country's obsession with presidential lies about sex in the White House: news as voyeurism! After a party in the old neighborhood that lasted until five a.m., I fell asleep at a friend's house. Awaking four hours later, extremely hung over, I showered, dressed, and walked up the hill for a strong coffee. Upon returning to their house, I picked the Washington

Post up off the stoop and brought it inside. Sitting in a rocker with my coffee and the paper, I pulled out a section and placed it on my lap. A gust from the open door blew the section open to the obituaries. It caught my attention because the Post never used to have pictures of the deceased in it before. As I looked over a few of the photos one leapt out at me: a childhood friend I took out to dinner last summer after not seeing him for twenty years. Dead at forty, with an amazing resume, but something terribly wrong with his psyche. Over dinner he had told me of his bipolar disorder. I didn't pay much attention until I belatedly realized it was a fancy word for manic depression. Donations were to be made to a mental health concern. In shock, I left my friends' house before they awoke and walked all the way into Georgetown, thinking of the great times we used to have running cross country, hopping trains through Europe. And then it's over…

"It's too bad that we grow old, too bad we prove less admirable than we thought, too bad that love fails, ambition peters out, friends die, dreams come to nothing." (Bernard DeVeto)

If it hadn't been for that gust of wind coming through the open door on a mild winter's day, I never would have known.

Then to Djibouti for three days of poolside reading due to the war between Ethiopia and Eritrea heating up and no flights coming in. The stark reality of planetary conflict coupled with the disgusting nature of the Sheraton Hotel is depressing. The hallway carpets looked and smelled as if twenty years of French Legionnaires had thrown up on them after bouts of drinking. The room wasn't much better. The smell of mildew and stale recycled air from the so called conditioner made the room almost uninhabitable. That's why poolside fresh air was the place to be! That and the interesting dynamic between the criminal Legionnaires and their hot girlfriends/whores flown in direct from Paris to keep them content.

Interesting old colonial town at the mouth of Red Sea completely contrived by the French for strategic reasons, yet with crumbling minarets soaring above decrepit buildings and dirt roads lined with shade trees. The market bleak with humanity: not much food and very few crafts. There are still 5,000 French Legionnaires stationed where the Rift Valley opens into the Indian Ocean, and the French money that maintains them is obviously what keeps this flea-bitten spot going. That and the seething numbers of Somali refugees who fill the camps in the barren desert just outside town.

On a run in Frankfurt just after receiving the news that my mother's lung cancer had spread to her lymph nodes, I came upon two nuns dressed in black on a trail beside the local cemetery. I took this as a rather inauspicious omen for my mother's future as I ran up alongside them, but as I passed, the chubby one next to me released a wrenching fart! The universe, and maybe even God, definitely chuckled! Humor *is* our only defense!

March '99: The beauty of the Balkans in winter! No small irony given the current problems of a massacre here, a massacre there, in Kosovo below. But from this height the snowy mountains and valleys crowded with villages is a stunning sight indeed. The sharp drop of snowy peaks into the bowl of Skopje is spectacular enough, but then the two lakes of Macedonia, Ohrid and Maliguit, their calm waters reflecting the surrounding mountains, really sends the head shaking in awe: nature doesn't pause for human slaughter. Then, just like that, the Greek coastline with its turquoise waters contrasting wonderfully with the snowy top and forested flanks of Mt. Olympus out the right side, while on the left the three fingers of Thessaloniki jut into the wine dark sea with the sharp snowy summit of Mt Athos gracing the tip of the third finger. On the way back up after a gorgeous spring day in Athens, the clarity as good as that city gets, Mt. Delphi at 5700' catches the eye not only because of its forested shape and snowy top, but also because its northern flank descends directly into the sea along a coastline that seems, except for a very few small villages, totally uninhabited. A whole swath of coast with forests and cliffs and sandy coves with what looks like a dirt road winding through it! Mt. Delphi and the island of Delphi?

Then back in the center of civilization: Vienna! Wandering through Josefsplatz, then through one of the many blind alleys leading to courtyards never glimpsed before and into the Treasury museum and the exquisite gilded crown jewels and staffs and filigree woven ware of the Hapsburg and Holy Roman Empire! And on to the Neu Hofburg and its half circle of marble columns and steps wide enough for the gods. An exhibit on the temple of Ephysus enthralls with its scale model of the sacred city on the coast of Turkey, with gorgeously carved columns and reliefs lining the walls with huge tapestries of 15th century Vienna hanging behind them. Again the theme of empires rising and falling echo through the vast, empty halls of the Hofburg. Having such places to oneself in the off season is a godsend.

In the military wing, knights line the walls on horseback and on foot in their fantastically elaborate armor, many works of the highest intricacy. I have the entire wing of the museum to myself and row after row of knights on horseback seem to move as I stand there meditating on the silence and the incredible complexity of each age that has inhabited the surface of this planet.

The following day at the Belvedere Palace I visit an exhibit entitled "America," showing the great western landscapes of Bierstadt, et alia. While perusing the paintings of my favorite place in the world, I occasionally glance out the palace windows over the rooftops and spires of Vienna with its woods rising up beyond and ponder the wonderful juxtaposition of one of the great cities of Europe and the paintings of the North American West. Then a casual stroll through the palace gardens full of purple crocuses into the labyrinthian streets of the alt stadt for an espresso under the spires of St. Stephans in winter sun, horse drawn carriages clip-clopping by…life doesn't get much better!

From the intense architecture of Belvedere Place and the Natural History Museum in Vienna, to the splendor of the Palacio in Madrid the following week, the tour of Europe's great cities continues unabated. Rushing off to the Prado to see the dark brilliance of Goya and Velasquez, before strolling through more narrow alleys in the old quarter on the way to the Plaza del Sol, then on to the good old Plaza Mayor. Then trying to find the curving street N. and I walked down in 1983 (ancient history), stumbling on a nice, clean pension where we spent a week, interrupted only by a trip to Toledo. Found the street just down from the Plaza Mayor toward the Magnificent Opera House, but the pension was no more.

Who would guess that exactly a week later I would be in Venice with the family after a leisurely drive over the Alps from Frankfurt! Or that in a short three weeks, I would go from the Belvedere Palace in Vienna, to the Palacio de Madrid, to the Palazzo Ducale, to the Belvedere fortress overlooking Florence from atop the Boboli gardens! Traveling rarely reaches such variety in such a short span of time (unless you're on a package tour, that is. If it's Monday it must be…)

The medieval walled city of Rothenburg on the Romantic Road south of Wurzburg, was our first call on a ten day European drive. The weather was overcast and grey which fit the heavy mood of the age in which the city overlooking the Tauber valley was constructed. Narrow cobblestone streets, gothic churches and massive fortress walls were a nice introductory first stop on our journey. Further down the road, in the foothills of the alps, we stopped at Füssen, and its famous Neuschwanstein fairy tale castle rising from a rocky promontory at the base of the Alps. A hike up behind it to a narrow suspension bridge spanning a gorge cut by glacial blue waterfalls gives a stunning view of the castle and its spires hovering over the flat landscape to the north. The last Bavarian King, Ludwig, who built this stunning castle, might have been mad, but there is genius in madness!

Then the next day through the snowy alps and over the Brenner Pass into Italy and the spectacular drive up the Val Gardena with granite Dolomites thrusting up out of the deep snow into a crystal clear blue sky. Hike up from a guest house in Pozza di Fasso along a forest path replete with stations of the cross to a village church quiet in its solemn views of the craggy peaks. Next day down the Val di Fassa and Val di Fiemme toward Trento with exquisite villages and spires perched on steep forested hillsides lining the empty road, then on into the Val Sugana which surprises with its lofty snow capped peaks to the north and south which drop in altitude to form a dry rocky gorge cut by the blue Brenta river which opens up into the plains just north of Venezia. A slow drive along country roads aflame in blossom brought us to sublime Castelfranco, ripe in spring budding and fine lunch in a restaurant buried in its fortress walls.

The drive into Venice a first as most take the train across. Actually a parking garage in which to store the vehicle for a few days so we can hop on the public ferry and ride around to St. Mark's the long way (not up the Grand Canal). It was Good Friday the next day so we wandered at leisure around the city fresh in spring air, with St. Mark's Basilica making the greatest impression with its detailed gold mosaic ceiling and wall set atop floors of multicolored marble wonder: a mix of Byzantine and Gothic. The Palazzo Ducale, home of the Doges, wasn't exactly uninspiring either, with ceilings as outrageous as those in Palacio de Madrid and frescoes of monstrous size and color lining the wood paneled walls. Planted on mud flats by Roman fugitives fleeing the invading Huns, Venice was born in the agonies of Rome's death, and died 13 centuries later, the oldest republic on earth. Only the French Revolution and Napoleon, which eventually brought about a modern Europe, could finally finish her.

Part of the reason for her success has to be laid at the feet of the official poisoner, whose office, over five hundred years, attempted to poison the Holy Roman emperor, the King of Hungary, the Sultan of Turkey, Charles III of France, Pope Pius IV and the Czar of Russia, amongst others. Venice also consolidated her power through the first recorded use of bacterial warfare. In 1649 she sent a physician with a flask containing powdered buboes to spread bubonic plague among the Turkish army in Crete. One French ambassador once called her " a very venomous and indestructible viper." In other words, nice countries finish last! And looking at the exquisite remnants of her wealth, all the subterfuge seems to have been worth it. Venus over Venice!

Sitting casually at outdoor cafes in the gorgeous weather for lunch and later for coffee, gazing up at the wonderful influence of Oriental architecture rising around us, is an absolute treasure. On departure the next morning, the public water taxi took us for the great tour down the Grand Canal and under the Rialto we'd climbed over countless times the previous two days. Definitely one of the greatest boat rides on the planet as it meanders along waters lined on each bank by monstrous homes built atop the mud. Said a prayer for my childhood friend, H., who committed suicide, and with whom I last visited this amazing city 22 years ago on a college backpacking tour of Europe.

The drive down to Firenze flat until we reach the forested Tuscan hills-dotted with villas of stucco with exposed stone at their corners adding aesthetic perfection. Hawthorne white in flower cover hillsides of mixed pine and spire cypress, while newly budded olive trees regimented in fields of vibrant green add a touch of domestication. Once we get off the highway northeast of Florence and wander leisurely through back roads to the top of the hills rising east of the Renaissance city, stone towers soar out of tree-tops for unobstructed views all the way down the valley past Fiesole to the Duomo in the clear spring air. Because it's Easter Eve, there are no rooms. But a hotel manager in Fiesole tells of a hotel back up in the hills under the Monastery which dominates this section of the Apennines: Monte Sereno.

In Bivigliano we find the Giotto Hotel, rough but perfect for us in its swaying pines and cool air and long hikes up to the Monastery to see snow capped peaks to the north and south rising above the rolling Tuscan landscape freshly awakened in flower. Exquisite!

Equally exquisite was the Uffizi and its striking Botticellis in their vibrant, hallucinogenic colors. The Easter celebration at the Duomo has a rocket dove shooting down the aisle from the altar and out the door to light a huge raft of fireworks before shooting back inside. A pagan ritual for sure! Later the Roman and Etruscan ruins set amidst fresh green grass of ancient Fiesole (where Boccaccio's *Decameron* stories were told by people whiling away the time fleeing the Black Death in Florence) contrast wonderfully with the medieval tower and town square under a deep blue sky. The museum holds one of the greatest collection of Greek, Etruscan and Roman ceramics I've ever seen. The unsurpassed views over Florence from Fiesole's monastery heights coupled with the clarity of the air make spring definitely the time to be in Tuscany.

Pisa, packed with tourists, and the leaning tower held up by a huge cable mechanism, has us doing the quickest tour ever of the site. We drive on up the coast through the stunning Ligurian coast with its village fortress towns perched high in the pine covered mountains, and fishing villages atop cliffs dropping into the Ligurian sea. We then flee across the flat, hot Lombardy plain with trees in rows and walled farm house compounds over the Po River flowing wide and deep toward the Adriatic, in order to get to the coolness of the Alps. Lake Como is our destination with its villages clinging to steep grades along the lake shore dropping from high snow capped peaks and shear cliffs. Monastery perched on isolated peninsula south of Colico my kind of place: clear lake water reflecting snowy heights. The next day driving up tiny mountain road through Italian Swiss villages where the road narrows so we have to squeeze through them. Up over the Julier Pass just down from St. Moritz in a snow storm at 7,500', then through rain at lower altitudes on a twisty road that never ends. Finally the valley at Chur and an easy drive through tiny Liechtenstein and the blast back to Frankfurt in gorgeous spring green with a mix of sun and showers gracing the way.

April '99: Tblisi, Georgia after an interesting flight on an Air Georgia Tupolev 154 from Frankfurt! Nothing like flying an airplane with a terrible safety record and design right out of 1954! The fuselage is so narrow you have to lean back to pee into the toilet with a wooden seat cover. Narikala mountain citadel lit across the river from my hotel quite impressive the evening I arrive. The next morning a hike up to the fortress with orthodox church inside for expansive views from its walls over the cypress and pine to the Mather-like gorge of the Mtkavari river with houses perched precariously on its palisade cliffs, and Metekhi orthodox church from the 13th century gracing the promontory across from the castle at its narrowest point. The old city below with its crumbling labyrinthian streets and sidewalks reminiscent of Thailand. The cobblestone is not however, and neither are the once graceful wrought iron balconies that now droop streetward, recalling some years of grandeur, most likely before the communist revolution? The potholed cobblestone streets are tree lined, but the buildings have not been painted this century. Peeking into the stairwells and inner courtyards of these once grand buildings, all one sees is squalor. This all contrasted by the many gorgeous churches with their smoky interiors, frescoes and icons of gold: hoping for a better life in the next world. On the fortress walls circling the old town, down along the river, are houses perched along its ramparts, nicely painted with balconies on several floors. This is close to the main square and street which could almost pass for First World with its shops and wide sidewalk and thronging masses enjoying the spring weather. From a bend in the road between many ugly communist government buildings and gorgeous buildings which must date from the time of the czars, one catches glimpses of the snow-capped Caucasus.

Venus over Tblisi: from Monte Sereno Monastery in the Apennines above Firenze, to the orthodox churches of Tblisi; Botticelli Angels to Ancient Georgian icons. In the basement vault of the Georgian State Museum is a collection of gold ornaments of stellar craftsmanship: Tiny animals of gold filigree from 1st century A.D., one lion minuscule but exquisitely wrought. Also headbands of gold with animal motifs, necklaces of gold filigree with pendants filled with diamonds or various gemstones of Agate, Amethyst and Turquoise. One mug of silver with raised animals on the outside is one of the most beautiful goblets I've ever seen. Greek cameo rings of the most delicate artistry, with tiny faces of fine styled hair and beards etched into colorful gemstones.

Twenty years of traveling since returning from the trip to Mexico at the beginning of '79! Hanging out in the cathedrals of San Cristobal and Oaxaca, then the leap to Australia and New Zealand: now, meditating in the smoky Zion orthodox church in Tblisi filled with icons shimmering in candlelight. Say what? Stone engravings adorning many of the outside walls of Georgian churches intriguingly similar to Celtic interwoven designs!

The crackling of candle wax the only sound in a church halfway up the pine forested mountainside above Tblisi, shafts of light falling from its lofty dome illuminate gold icons of Mary and the baby Jesus while frescoes of dark brilliance cover its walls and ceilings.

Walking back to the hotel through a crumbling neighborhood of dirt roads and blowing dust with just a few folks wandering aimlessly through it, I flash on the *Andromeda Strain* and realize this is what a *Homo sapiens* settlement would be like after a potent bug wiped it out.

On the way to Washington, ice sheet frozen wave patterns off the coast of Labrador, interspersed with mammoth bergs locked in the flow. Some kind of snowmobile track cuts across snowy wastes ashore, then heads across a frozen estuary to nowhere! Meditations on flight: hurtling through the upper atmosphere in a machine that wasn't even invented 100 years ago, passengers are glued to the windows trying to make sense of the vast, alien terrain that makes up their home. The track is the only sign of humanity for the next 45 minutes of flight, nothing but Canadian wilderness with just the slightest hint of spring thaw: a few lakes with a smidgen of dark open water forced from the ice by rivers that has gained momentum in rapids, and others with turquoise thin ice. Anticosti Island, in the mouth of the St. Lawrence, is covered with what look like logging roads deep in snow, but still with no sign of living, breathing *Homo sapiens* until the tip of the Gaspe Peninsula of New Brunswick. Then boom, roads, farms and bridges with the season further developed, the land retaining only a hint of winter.

The coastal isles of Maine are exactly like those of Southern Finland. Then the malls, interstates and golf courses of the U.S.A. make one cringe after that wonderful Canadian emptiness. What was it the Talking Heads sang on *More Songs About Buildings and Food?*: "I wouldn't live there if you paid me."

Flying into and then driving from Dulles into Washington, the suburban sprawl is almost overwhelming. The American landscape, which has always been commercial, used to have large swaths of rural country between its economic centers. But now, with unending suburbia spreading like a cancer across the farm lands of old, the economic centers are joined, creating a population density, in the east anyway, that rivals Europe. The traffic in Washington is now worse than Bangkok! The density is greater, but so is the alienation.

Howard Mansfield describes it best:

"American places are often but a rumor of community wrapped around the commerce of the moment. Tremendous forces are working against small communities. These have been well documented: the car, the TV, the video, the automatic teller machine, the entire growing electronic cocoon. We are more invisible to one another. Our inventions have atomizing effects and reinforce isolation."

We celebrate individualism and starve the commons. Yes, indeed! Then, as if an exclamation point was needed, I enter my hotel room and turn on the TV to hear two students have opened fire on their high school in Littleton, Colorado, killing thirteen fellow students before killing themselves. Welcome home!

Walking around Haine's Point in Washington, the contrived peninsula which juts out into the Potomac across from National Airport, I reflect back on similar Saturday morning strolls as a child. Nothing has changed in 35 years! The railings I used to suck on until my father scolded me are the same chipped puke green color, the trash comprised of fishing gear, beer cans and plastic bags, still litters the grass, and the sidewalk which graces the shoreline is still partially flooded, growing slimy algae at the point's tip. The only difference I can discern over all the time that's passed is the fresher smell of the once heavily polluted river. What has drastically changed is my mother is in the hospital with cancer.

And on to the Holy Land! Rent a car and drive up to Caesarea Maritima for a glimpse of the Roman and Byzantine ruins I didn't see when I lived and worked in the Negev with N. for several months fourteen years ago. The amphitheater is partially reconstructed but still is impressive. The promontory was actually first settled by the Phoenicians during Persian rule from 586-332 B.C., and was known as Straton's Tower, first mentioned in a document from 259 B.C. called the Zenon papyri. The amphitheater and city were built in the time of Herod who ruled from 37-4 B.C., and named after his patron Octavio Augustus Caesar. It became the seat of the Roman government in Judea in 6 AD. The artificial harbor that was built had an opening that was graced with three huge Roman statues standing guard. A Parthenon styled temple crowned the site, with broad steep stairs rising to it from the harbor's edge. Imagining the exquisite architecture of two thousand years ago with today's ugly Israeli buildings makes one wonder how far we've really come.

Then a drive along the sand dune coast up to Haifa with its old stone port buildings right out of the British mandate. Mt. Carmel rising up from the dunes, its forested ridge gracing the skyline as it tails off into the inland haze to the southeast. Then the drive through European-like farms with Kibbutzim harvest combines spitting out square bails of hay. Forested hills and farmed valleys give the entire region a comfortable feel. Then the view from the heights over the blue waters of Galilee, with Mt. Herman rising over 9,000' looming over the Golan and Syria to the north, snow still covering a bit of its summit. And then down along the water's edge, a lunch of St. Peter's fish and an ice cold Maccabi beer nourish the soul before the drive back through quaint farmland to the hustle and bustle of Tel Aviv.

Israeli mythology encompasses two phrases: " we made the desert bloom," implying there was no one else around when they arrived, and "Tel Aviv was built on sand dunes," implying an empty landscape. Both of these are as false as the American mythology of an unoccupied North America, or a new world occupied by savages. The manifest destiny spin of both civilizations are intriguingly similar. Palestinians, in fact, farmed oranges before they were driven out in their diaspora of 1948, and Jaffa was an Arab city famous for its oranges. It's interesting now to visit Jaffa, which for the most part has been cleansed of Palestinians, and see that there are three fine mosques still standing along the promenade at the base of the promontory. The problem is, I heard muted prayers inside, but never once heard a muezzin calling the faithful to prayer from the minarets. Freedom of religion? The archaeological remains displayed in the wonderful Jaffa museum prove without question that Jews buried their dead on the promontory 2,000 plus years ago. But if we're trying to build a multi-cultural world, you don't do it by muzzling places of worship under the guise of security!

May '99: Kazakhstan is the heart of the Asian continent, further from the sea than any place on the planet, with endless grass steppes trudging on for hour after hour at 500 mph! Then, at Almaty, the former capital, a northern spur of the Tien Shan Mountains rise up dramatically from the city to 12,000' plus. Spring at the meeting of the steppes and the high mountains is gorgeous, with gentle, warm breezes and trees newly in bud! Kind of a quiet, civilized little place on the surface with tree lined boulevards in the old part of town with nice old wooden Russian houses of light blue and green with lace borders. The beat Zentov Cathedral in a fine city park with trees freshly budded, built in 1904 without a nail is the city's pride and joy and one of the few truly historic structures to be found. Close to the cathedral is a striking W.W. II memorial with eternal flame and huge sculpture and children by the hundreds filing past leaving flowers. It seems during the battle of Stalingrad a handful of Kazak soldiers held off an entire Panzer Division to the last man. There certainly is much more focus on this monument than on a cathedral representing a still dead faith!

And then, one month short of the summer solstice, and five months after flying over the ice rimmed myriad islets, it's once again over the Finnish archipelago with a bit of green replacing the icy white of December. A crystal clear Copenhagen (with its new bridge to Malmo, Sweden under construction), jarred memories of backpacking through sixteen years ago, hanging out with Danish bums and sleeping in the park just up from the famous mermaid statue. Now, despite staying in fine hotels, I'm still on the road, perhaps no longer hanging with bums, but certainly with an eclectic mix world wide.

Red sun lingering over the Arctic Circle a month short of the solstice as our MD-11 soars over St. Petersburg and Lake Ladoga on the way to Beijing. Its rays bathe the interior of the cabin the color of an abattoir. The next morning, about two hours after it finally sets atop the almost mid-summer globe, it rises over the steppes of Mongolia already in a haze I recognize as being distinctly Asian. This haze, reminiscent of that found annually in S.E. Asia this time of year, persists on into Beijing, with the clear mountains and Great Wall of last December a distant memory. Out for a walk down to Tiananmen, the traffic and air remind me of Bangkok: the ugly modern architecture backed by brownish haze from gridlocked traffic is exactly the same. I'm the first back to China after NATO accidentally bombed the Chinese Embassy in Belgrade. In retaliation, the Chinese by the thousands trashed our mission in Beijing by breaking every window and covering the facade with paint bombs. It wasn't only the main building that was attacked, but also the consular and administrative buildings along the same road. But all was quiet and many of the Chinese laborers who work for the mission were laughing and joking about it to me upon arrival.

Off to Xi'an for the weekend for a change, but run into more of the same commercial shlock, only more concentrated within the fortress walls of this ancient capital where the silk road began.

In S.E. Asia, the constant haze was caused by burning rice fields for planting, so what is the root cause here? Industry! Xi'an, apparently, is one of the most polluted cities in the world, and the air quality doesn't make one question that statistic. But, blowing dust off the Gobi certainly must play a role in the pervasive haze which covered China on my flight from Beijing to Xi'an, as well as the flight from Helsinki. As we drive out to the terra-cotta warrior site, huge coal burning power plants rise from a tilled countryside filled with 2,000 year old, Western Zhou Dynasty burial mounds! If the air were clear, it would be quite a sight to take in all three hundred of these tumulus rising from fields green with winter wheat in a single glance. The terra-cotta warriors are actually a vast subterranean funeral vault army of over 7,000 soldiers and chariots and horses in formation east of the tumulus of China's first emperor: Qin Shi Huang. In 246 B.C. he inherited the Kingdom of Qin at 13 years of age, and spent the following ten years subduing all the other kingdoms of China.

The vault filled with life-sized ceramic warriors in battle formation was only discovered in 1974, when a farmer digging a well brought up fired clay hands and heads from the depths. It has to be the most outrageous archaeological excavation ever! The reglued figures (a rival general apparently entered the vault only a few years after it was sealed, smashing and setting fire to the subterranean army and stealing the authentic weapons they were armed with) are stunning in their individualistic detail. The life size horses that pulled now disintegrated wooden chariots are exquisitely wrought, with holes to keep them from exploding in the firing process. But even more intriguing are the jumbles of as yet unreconstructed warriors, lying cracked and broken under fallen roof beams, a jumble of hands, heads and ceramic armor: an archaeological nightmare to excavate on such a scale.

The congestion, shlock capitalism and pollution so common in Asia were enough to make even Beijing look good, but on the return we were diverted to Taiyung due to bad weather and spent some six hours on the ground in a place called the "Long Journey Lounge!"

With all the Bodhi trees in Beijing coupled with the White Pagoda looming atop a hillock isle in the middle of Bei Hai Park a stone's throw from the Forbidden City, it's intriguing to ponder where the spirituality of this powerful Asian philosophy is. Has it merely become a communist Confucianism? Not that different when you really think about it, both in their ideals attempting to alleviate humanity's suffering in this world through egalitarianism and cooperation. But, of course, ideals are one thing, reality another.

Back in Beijing, views from the Drum (oldest in Beijing at 700 years) and Bell Towers to the north of the Forbidden City out over leafy old quarter of the city with its congested one story brick and tile roofed abodes, gives the visitor a feel for what it must have been like before the modern age. In fact, looking north you can detect where the old city wall stood, for just where the leafy trees end, large apartment and commercial blocks begin, marking the beginning of the contemporary city. And if you drive or walk out that direction, you cross over the old moat that still holds water that formed the defensive perimeter of this ancient Ming capital formed in 1403.

But after a torrential night rain with the droplets slapping the wide leaves of the cottonwood outside my hotel balcony, any comparisons to Bangkok disappear with the crisp, clean air that moves in from the northwest. A cool fresh spring morning arrives the day I'm set to leave, with a blur of bicycles thronging tree-lined boulevards on the drive to the airport. It's amazing how a change in the weather and the clearing of pollution from the air can transform a place. In such weather Beijing feels comfortable and very civilized! What a change from the thick pollution and traffic upon arrival.

The flight out over the pristine Mutianyu section of the Great Wall and its twenty-two watch towers snaking along a ridge in the foothills of spring green with a quick glance back to see a crystal clear view of Beijing in a valley surrounded by farms, will be one of the great scenes not soon forgotten: but only because the normally polluted air was scrubbed for once!

Then, just like that, the green mountains northwest of Beijing become the sand bleak Gobi Desert the Mongols crossed in order to sack the Chinese capital. Flying over Mongolia and the endless steppes, I imagine Genghis Khan asking himself "There must be more to life than this endless sea of grass." Broaching his ideas to other fidgeting males intrigued with the idea of foreign conquest, with a little rape and pillage thrown in, the horde is quickly formed: anything but a meaningless existence in such a hardscrabble land. So, off they ride, as far south as Saigon and as far west as Europe! Kind of like the British driven to empire by their dreary weather.

A good sized river forms the border between Mongolia and Russia as it slices through hilly steppes forested on their northern flanks. Then, all of a sudden, fields of snow appear amidst an increasingly forested and well-watered landscape, with nary a sign of humanity…for a long time, in fact probably all the way down to Almaty of two weeks ago! But then, shockingly, a forest fire obscures the sky just east of a low snowy mountain range devoid of roads or other signs of *Homo sapiens*. Could this be nature at work, a lightning strike clearing out underbrush for more nutritious growth? It seems likely considering the remoteness of the land.

On the other side of the range flat grasslands return, and with them, bleak, isolated, regimented Soviet-era towns. Then many forest fires in the hills, one extremely large! Perhaps the one two hundred miles back wasn't natural after all. Below, more heartland Russia with dirt roads connecting scattered settlements and a big muddy running through it, followed by more forest yet even more fires. One huge blaze obscures an entire range and beyond with smoke, which makes me reconsider my previous doubts regarding the deleterious effects of concentrated humanity on the wider unpopulated regions of the planet. The smoke from the fires below has altered the air clarity for hundreds of miles downwind in a sparsely populated part of the world. I recall that 14 of the hottest years ever recorded have been in the last 20 years, as another plume covers a swath of Siberia below just short of Novosibersk, north of the Kazakhstan border. A pervasive haze in such a remote locale would certainly reinforce the perils of greenhouse gases and the resultant global warming. But, of course, if water covers 71% of the planet's surface, and say another 20% of land is basically uninhabited (the vast expanses of Canada and Russia), then how can 10% pollute the entirety to destruction?

The mighty Ob River at Novosibersk full of more depressing Soviet style apartment blocks is dammed south of town into a huge lake, then flows all the way to the Kara Sea above the Arctic Circle. If it is this wide way down here, imagine what it's like upriver!

June '99: Last time flying down to Athens over Belgrade and the snowy Balkans there was only scattered violence in Kosovo. Now, with a NATO air campaign pummeling the Serbs for their ethnic cleansing on a biblical scale (1,000,000 Kosovars fleeing across the Yugoslav border), we fly far outside Yugoslav airspace to avoid the hundreds of daily sorties. The clarity of Athens two months ago has vanished with the return of summer pollution. The window of opportunity for clean air in this ancient city gets smaller and smaller at the end of the millennium.

Back in Vienna exquisite in early summer warmth and lingering twilight making the architectural wonders of the once imperial city glow. Two cappuccinos the following morning while watching a Pentecostal procession wind past from Stephansdom to St. Michaeler Kirche. Black robed priests stroll solemnly past, followed by colorful religious banners carried by other priests cloaked in bright, intricate capes with lay people singing hymns in between. Then, a high priest heavily clothed in papal gear and pointed hat under a a four posted silk canopy passes by mid-procession, followed by beret clad soldiers in olive drab.

On the flight back to Frankfurt the sunset Alps show their severe northern faces high over spring green foothills and the pristine lakes Kammersee and Traunsee, glacier carved as they cut deep into gnarly peaks.

Interesting the symbiotic relationship between creatures of flight: man-made and natural that is. The vast fields of most airports are perfect for hawks hunting mice, as well as other varieties in pursuit of insects and crickets. At the Vienna airport there are always hawks circling or hovering midfield ready to strike a mouse, while human flying machines jet around and above them.

Ohhh, Budapest! Checked into the hotel and immediately set out across the famous Kettenbrucke suspension bridge connecting Pest with Buda over the muddy Danube swift with spring melt. Then up the trestle to the castle district and its immense palace, quaint pastel colored neighborhoods and sublime Matyas church found within and atop impressive fortress walls. Circumnavigated the walls under a fiercely hot sun in a clear sky, absorbing views of the wide Danube winding down through forested hills from the north, off to the south toward Yugoslavia where it sucks around fallen sections of myriad bridges demolished in the war. Across the river, the intricately wrought Parliament building, reminiscent of Westminster and designed by an English architect, heightens the wonder of this hilly setting for one of the great capital cities of the world.

Zagreb gorgeous in late spring/early summer, the pummeling of Serbian lands to the south ongoing. The flight back up over Ljubljana and Klagenfurt memorable for the great views of the green forested eastern alps, still with some snow. Far to the southeast, over the rocky range that leaps up from just outside Ljubljana, the Adriatic coast and Trieste and memories of a funky train ride down the Isstrian peninsula to Pula years ago with my friend who recently chose to end his life. The times we had together in Rijeka, and later on the island of Rab, then the ferry ride under a full moon through the coastal islands to Zadar, and the train through rough, spectacular mountains to Knin and on to Bihac with ancient caped and pantalooned shepherds in fields along the route reinforcing the magic of the planet. Why end it early when you know it will end naturally? And all too soon at that! A view out a jet window the catalyst for mind riffs. Then stunning Berchtesgaden and the Konigsee come into clear view below: how could such a spectacular glacial valley be associated with one of the most evil men of history?

Back in Vienna in what becomes a week spent dancing along the banks of the swift, wide Danube. Went for a long hike into the Wienerwald, starting at Nussdorf and hiking through vineyards up through thick forest to the classic brick tower, known as the Stefaniewarte, for a 360 degree view of Vienna and environs from atop the Kahlenberg. Then, for an even more spectacular view, a short walk around to the north, again through nicely forested footpaths, brings you to Leopoldsberg, perched wonderfully atop a promontory above the Danube full of barge traffic, and the quaint little town of Khalenbergdorf and its sublime vineyards. The views of the hilly, forested Wienerwald rising to the west of Vienna, along with the spires of the once fortified city and the gardens of Belvedere are fantastic indeed. This is the northeastern most reach of the mighty Alps, before being cut off at its knees by the equally mighty Danube.

The following day a train ride to Melk and its immense Benedictine monastery dominating the heights of the small village, before a classic boat trip down the Danube through the Wachau. The mountainous route lined with castles is reminiscent of the Rhine valley between Rudesheim and Koln, but is more pristine, with the mountains of the Dunkelstein Wald still thick and unpopulated. Spectacular Schloss Schonbuhel perched atop a rocky cliff, built in the twelfth century, begins the route, soon followed by infamous Burg Aggstein, airy home of the Kuenringer family, notorious robber barons who gave their prisoners the choice of either starving or jumping to their deaths from the cliffs the castle is perched upon.

Venus of Willendorf, the 26,000 B.P. earth mother figure was found in the Wachau, thus reinforcing the attraction the fertile soils, thick forest and river for fishing and transportation this region has had for *Homo sapiens* for millennia. The most stunning setting of any town in the Danube Valley has to be Durnstein, with its Kuenringerburg castle ruins which once imprisoned Richard the Lionheart on his return from the Crusades, looming high above the cliff top village (he was imprisoned for insulting Leopold V!). The baroque Chorherren stift abbey, founded in 1410 by the Augustinians, graces the forests and vineyards of the valley with its blue and white steeple rising colorfully above the river.

Krems, the end of the boat journey, lies just downstream and is itself an ancient village of multiple Renaissance and Baroque church domes, winding cobblestone streets, and great views of Stift Gottweig, a Benedictine monastery founded in 1083 impressively straddling a hill to the south. From the hilly beauty of Budapest's imperial architecture to the wonder of the Wachau, it's been a week exploring the two great cities and environs of the Danube.

But there's always more! A day dedicated to the Viennese dead, in fact. First, in the catacombs of Stephansdom, it's coffined Archbishops and internal organs of the Hapsburgs (viscera that is) in the oldest section of the burial chambers, followed by lumpen proletariat cast into huge vaults, some killed by the last Black Plague to hit this city in 1713. Initially the wooden coffins were stacked up in vaults, then when full, were sealed and another vault opened. The catacombs soon ran out of space due to the cellars of surrounding buildings, so prisoners were brought in to gather the bone and stack it in rooms, femurs here, tibia and fibula there. Peeking into one lit bone room, they actually made a design of sorts by aesthetically inserting smiling crania into a wall of stacked long bone! Nice design fellas!

Other vaults opened for public viewing had skeletons with tattered clothing clinging to bone lying atop wood all that was left of a coffin. Fascinating the reactions of living breathing beings in a dark labyrinth confronted with the reality of our bleak end. Some held their mouths in disgust, some groaned at the sight of bone mixed and broken so you couldn't tell where one body began and the other ended: one large, inter-mixed human family! The guide mentioned that at one point some two hundred years ago they couldn't hold services in the church due to the smells wafting from the vaults! Many seemed to be disconnected from the fact that we all will leave this world in a trail of anonymous bone. When we resurfaced from the crypt to the brightness of day, I recalled Khahil Gibran's great line: "the day blinds us with quantities and measures."

In contrast to anonymous death, over a few blocks from Stephansdom is the Kaisergruft, a series of imperial burial vaults underneath the Kapuzinekirche in the Neu Markt. Fantastic bronze coffins, some of mas-sive size and sculptured complexity, preserving the Hapsburg Kaisers, Kaiserin and their princes and princesses for as close to eternity as one can hope. My favorite elaborate coffin, and the one most realistic in portray-ing death honestly rather than as a heavenly fantasy, was Kaiser Josef (1678-1711), with bat winged skulls gracing either end of the casket, while grinning knight skulls incased in armor helmets support its base. Compared with the sixteen thousand poor souls whose remains are mixed and matched only a short walk away, royalty at least have the small honor of maintaining their bodily integrity, as well as being vaguely remembered, for a short time anyway. The historic dance of the Danube, from 26,000 B.P. to the present.

Continuing the same theme out at Schloss Schönbrunn, drinking a few beers at the Glorietta under huge, gold double-headed eagle (Hapsburg emblem) and O'Keefe-like cow skull motifs lining the inside walls with clear views out to Kahlenberg and Leopoldberg, I note the great number of very old people wandering around, absorbing the gorgeous late after-noon light on the palace and gardens. On the edge of the grave they are the rare *Homo sapiens* fully aware of the precarious beauty of existence, and therefore can truly live in the moment: in the black crows hopping across a green lawn filled with red flowers, the waning sun making the hedges and sculptures glow and the pastel yellow of Schönbrunn blaze like the sun itself. The dark catacombs of Stephansdom are just a heartbeat away.

The Abraxas is one of the few religions which captures the nature of reality, the dark and light side by side: summer flowers, scattered bones. The first instrumental off the classic album by Santana of the same name, *Singing Winds, Crying Beasts*, surges through my mind as I absorb the expansive view over steeple forested Vienna (especially the wind chime section), and seems to capture, as well as any classical piece, the intensity of our absurd lives on this planet. The weather and early summer gardens of the palace are what I call "silken": perfect seventy degree temperature, with fleecy clouds in a blue sky and a gentle flower-scented breeze.

July '99: Then gorgeous Budapest again and further explorations into the Museums of the city. The favorite being the Budapest History Museum in the Royal Palace, with its subterranean passages exploring the older parts of the citadel that were destroyed by the Turks in their sacking of the city in 1586. Also the Roman history of this locale, the founders of a great city at around the time of Christ on this same spot, which they named Aquincum. Then later, with the rain starting to fall, I sprint into the Matyas Church atop Castle Hill, and listen to a haunting service while meditating on the multicolored walls and pillars, not to mention stained glass and shining gold. Tired of the contrived worship I race out to the Fisherman's Bastion overlooking the entire city and watch the blackest clouds I have ever seen roll in over Gellert Hill. The leading section of this mass were like black fingers searching for some evil to do, and once over the Parliament building they began spinning. I thought the formation of a Tornado was afoot, but it never quite got enough speed up. But the rain soon poured down so ferociously I was stuck in one of the pointed, Turkish style guard houses atop the Fisherman's Bastion for over an hour, watching this great city and its tremendous river cutting through it, get pounded. I worship the natural world and *Homo sapiens* small place in it!

Next morning it's off to tour the outrageous Westminster-like Parliament building, the vast, pillared interior of the Ethnographic Museum (where there is an exhibit on, of all things, American Indian relics. The entire exhibit takes me back to the early years of this job, wandering through the Americas: there are Costa Rican animal grinding stone effigies, just like in San Jose, but the one thing which really makes an impression is the photograph of the "Earth God" gate at the Itzamna Palace in Mexico. It is the pattern connection I have been looking for, linking Mesoamerican Taotie patterns and those of the Shang Dynasty, China: 3000-1000 B.C.), and a stroll up Andrassy Boulevard, sneaking into gated driveways which open into great courtyards just off the sidewalk, before entering Heroe's Square. It is flanked by the Art Gallery (1895) and Museum of Fine Arts (1906) at the entrance to the grand city park and the curious Vajdahunyad Castle within that now serves as the Agricultural Museum. Fantastic walking city!

Winging homeward across the North Atlantic sealed by unending cloud. The greyness outside mirrors my own soul searching, as my mother has been diagnosed with terminal cancer. But when I focus on the very simple truth that most never seem to grasp, my heart feels a little lighter: everything in this universe eventually dies, everything! Or as the great Canadian rock and roller, Bruce Cockburn, wrote: "I think it's a sin to try and make things last forever, everything that exists in time, runs out of time some day…"

Only eventual clearing above Maine reveals a peak never glimpsed before: Mt. Katahdin (5267'), beginning/end of the Appalachian Trail, thrusting above the summer haze brought about by a severe heat wave. Once again I ponder: is this pollution from Ohio and Pennsylvania obscuring the vast forests of this northern state, or natural heat induced haze?

On the approach into D.C., we scoot right past Sugarloaf Mountain with its rocky top and cliffs glimpsed through thick summer foliage: a mountain with Civil War canon emplacements still intact, and great trails we hiked at all times of year, autumn being my favorite. The memory of driving out from Alexandria one winter day when we had an inch or two of snow, but Sugar Loaf had a foot! Sitting in the car sipping steaming hot chocolate from a thermos, staring out windows covered in condensation at the deepest snow I'd ever seen, was a treasure for a young mind indeed.

Still on the approach into Dulles, crossing the Potomac, one can see two different development philosophies at work. The Maryland side, upstream from Seneca, is still the rural landscape that I knew in my youth: thick trees obscure the C&O canal along the river bank, while inland forest and farms form a patchwork quilt of green and gold. Maryland has imposed strict development rules and is trying to preserve a greenbelt of sorts. Virginia on the other hand, home of conservative free marketeers, has a cancerous growth of subdivisions along the river, almost all the way to the Blue Ridge. The contrived communities below with their mandatory malls of incredible size, surrounded by parking lots of even greater dimensions, symbolize to me the emptiness of American life, a life based upon materialism run amok. A brand new school near the mall reinforces my train of thought: it has a bright green astro-turf football field, dwarfing the school. At least we Americans have our priorities straight!

Then taking the Metro into the District through Alexandria, where the mother who is dying bore me almost 41 years ago! Roots and decay! And speaking of roots, the following day I visit the old neighborhood in Alexandria where I was born, and the old house and neighborhood is almost exactly the same, but the trees which were large even then, are now three times as high, making the small houses of Old Dominion Boulevard seem even tinier.

Later in the afternoon, on a hike down to the Potomac (back on the Maryland side), the river is at an all time low. Talk about global weirdness! It has only rained one inch in month! In all my Washington years I have never seen it so barren. It looks like the surface of another planet with dry, granite peaks normally hidden by deep water jutting from the valley floor.

I make a connection in my mind's eye between the river's desiccation and my mother's cancer: they seem linked somehow. Welcome to the future?

The root theme continues as my mother, passing out farewell gifts, gives me a book entitled *Angell Genealogy*. Later, on the flight back to Frankfurt, the global positioning in-flight map marks Scituate Reservoir as we blast up the east coast. The reservoir flooded the old town of Scituate, where the Angell tribe lived, breathed and expired, their graves moved ahead of the advancing flood waters. Why would it be on such a map along with prominent cities like Providence and Boston?

We then pass over the very spot off Martha's Vineyard where JFK, Jr.'s plane went down exactly three days ago. The Icarus legend lives. The Greeks had it all figured out 2500 years ago. "Strange days have found us," Mr. Morrison of The Doors sang, "strange days have dragged us down."

Winging over to Tashkent from Frankfurt, Russia in high summer is much like heartland America (just less developed), with its patchwork quilt farms all the way to Samara. The huge dammed lake of the Volga River might as well be Lake McConaughy in western Nebraska. To reinforce the familiar feel of the landscape below, Springsteen's "The River" fills my earphones: "Those memories come back to haunt me, they haunt me like a curse…" Amen to that! Those memories of high school in America, and driving across the American heartland time and time again.

Big orange ball sunset, with Venus alight in twilight above and a few degrees to the south of the sun, while wonderfully juxtaposed in the east, a full moon rises grandly over the muddy brown fingers of the Tien Shan, crowned by two rounded snow-whitened peaks, as the range peters out into the tree-thick oasis of Tashkent, and the surrounding Kizyl-Kum Desert.

Tashkent not that interesting in its Soviet utilitarian square block architecture and forty-year-old street cars rumbling along tree lined boulevards, but its trees and fountains galore stave off the incredible 40 plus celsius heat of a Central Asian summer. Hidden away amongst the hideous architecture are a few old madrasas that are worth a visit, just to give the visitor a feel for the Islamic roots the Bolsheviks tried to completely erase.

Two of my favorites, Kukeldash Madrasa (1560), with its tiled facade of a repeated sun motif design over its entrance arch, and Barak-Khan Madrasa (15th century), buried in the labyrinthian backstreets of Zarkainar Street, whose houses are a direct link with that historic period, their adobe walls and wattle and daub roofing sealing their inhabitants off from a harsh world. This area of Tashkent acts as a time machine, capturing the authentic feel of pre-soviet Uzbekistan. The mosaic of tile and Arabic calligraphy on the brick facade of Barak-Khan as it rises three times higher than any of the primitive adobe hovels around it, and not a modern building in sight, will take you back four hundred years in a blink of the eye.

But Samarkand is the focus, of course. After a three hour drive south, over the Syr Darya River (that used to empty into the Aral Sea, but due to irrigation no longer does, which is why that so-called sea is evaporating into extinction) and through countless miles of cotton farms, the road finally rises through a defile in a finger of the Turkestan Range, dropping from snowy summits to be swallowed by the desert. Just south of this finger, and over the Zerafshin River which finds its headwaters in a range of the same name further south, rise the heaven-blue domes of Samarkand:

"Suddenly we caught a glimpse of painted minarets trembling in the blue astringent light and the great Madonna blue domes of mosques and tombs shouldering the full weight of the sky among bright green trees and gardens."
Laurens van der Post, *Journey Into Russia*, 1964

The Registan group of madrasas blows anything in Tashkent away. It is probably the most spectacular architectural ensemble in Central Asia, for that matter. Every square inch of the three structures is covered in a riot of mosaics. This spot historically was where Tamerlane stuck his victim's heads on spikes and where his people gathered to hear his grandiose plans for further invasions in what was a grand bazaar in 1404. It wasn't until 1417 to 1420 that the first madrasa, Ulug Bek, commissioned by and named after Tamerlane's belatedly famous astronomer son, was constructed. To think that this structure is nearing six hundred years of age in an earthquake prone part of the world, is incredible. Of course, it's been reconstructed several times in several sections, but still, huge swaths of original tile can be seen and touched:

"...crumbling sun-baked bricks, decorated with glazed tiles of deep blue and vivid turquoise that sparkle in the sun...a walled stairway with, on either side, a row of small mosques of the most exquisite beauty...wainscotted with alabaster and adorned with jasper...glimpses of courtyards and gardens...and in the open bazaars great heaps of fruit..."
Fitzroy Maclean, *Eastern Approaches*, 1949

One of the vendor women inside the Ulug Bek walls, with a stall actually in the old students' quarters, offered to take me up the leaning northern minaret for a small fee. With no light inside and brick chunks littering the steps, I felt carefully with my feet and hands in the pitch black for a way up the spiral stairs. Finally, toward the top a little light helped guide me up the increasingly claustrophobic stairwell (the thought of it leaning, ready to collapse, not exactly helping the psyche).

Once at the top, though, standing on a step up through some corrugated tin protecting the spire from rain damage, was one of the superb views, not only over the other two madrasas that make up the Registan, Sher Dor (1619-35) with its striped-lions-chasing-deer-tile-motif, and Tilla Kari (1646-1659) built from the ruins of a historic Silk Road caravanserai, but also of the massive turquoise dome of Bibi Khanym Mosque (1399-1404), built by Tamerlane's wife to welcome him home from his India Campaign of 1398-99, and towering above the adobe brown of the ancient oasis. An observer wrote of this mosque when it was finished: "Its dome would have been unique had it not been for the heavens, and unique would have been its portal had it not been for the Milky Way." Say no more.

The view from the towering minaret of this extraordinary architectural group reminded me of the minaret view over Old Delhi and the Red Fort from the spires of Jama Masjid Mosque, yet was even more primitive then Old Delhi (if that's possible), due to the small size of the old Silk Route city of Samarkand as it hunkers down under the monstrous Tien Shan and Pamir mountains rising to well over 6000m not far to the east. Six hundred years really hasn't changed a thing. From Xi'an, the beginning of the Silk Route, to Samarkand, its major link with the west, in two months of travel, certainly gives one historic perspective.

And speaking of which, when Tamerlane died on the eve of his invasion of China in 1405, he was buried in the mausoleum he had built for his grandson who had died fighting in Turkey in 1403. Inside, under a towering ribbed, cantaloupe dome 32m high, lies his death wish: "only a stone with my name upon it"!

Only, the stone with his name upon it is one of the biggest chunks of jade in the world. A Persian invader tried to carry the piece away in 1740, but dropped it, splitting it in half. Rather than endure the bad luck such an accident would surely bring, he returned the stone immediately to its place in one of the greatest decorated mausoleums anywhere (except for the Taj Mahal itself, which was built by one of Tamerlane's Mughal descendants). High corners with that distinctive stalactite ornamentation which graces so much of the Islamic world to this day, combines with blue and gold geometric patterns and gold leaf inside the dome to create a stunning architectural achievement for the resting place of one of the last of the great conquerors of history.

His grandson Ulug Bek was more interested in studying the stars than conquering the planet. He built an observatory enclosing a giant sextant on Kukhak Hill, the highest point above Samarkand, making it the best equipped observatory in the medieval world. Because of its progressive scientific analyses, this observatory was filled with what many fundamentalists (yes, nothing has changed) felt was heretical thought. The motto of Ulug's teacher, Kazi Rumi, was "Where knowledge starts religion ends," so they obviously had something to fear, and still do!

Ulug's astronomical calculations put him on a par with Copernicus and Kepler, even thought they didn't become known to the world until 1648, when a copy of his *Catalog of Stars* was discovered at Oxford. He plotted the position of the solar system and 1,018 stars, and calculated the length of the year to within 58 seconds. He paid for such insights with his life. His own son decapitated him for these heretical discoveries in 1449.

One of the crowning achievements of architecture in its time has to be the Sha-i-Zinda Ensemble, a long street of exquisite mausoleums housing the remains of most of Tamerlane's intimates from the late 1300s and early 1400s. The various structures and their remaining panels of tile mosaics has to be the greatest collection of such antiquity in the world. There are Silk Road Chinese influences in one, with landscape mosaics of foliage with birds, rivers and clouds, while others are more traditionally Islamic with their faience panels sculpted with flowers, calligraphy, and abstract designs bordered by bands of further mosaic and terra-cotta of raised complexity. All that remains is in near perfect condition after six hundred years! What this walk must have been like when all the walls were still completely covered with blue and white-tiled intensity, must have been as close to heaven as anyone in that time could come.

August '99: Too many tourists in Vienna force me out into the countryside. After an hour train ride south to Payerbach, a trailhead close to the station is discovered, followed by a hike up through Heidi-like fields full of cattle with clanging bells. After a couple of hours picking up various trails, not really knowing which to take (but catching some fine views of the valley below and the Raxalpe in the distance), I stumble across the exquisite white limestone outcrop of Jubilaumaussiche, graced with gnarly zen-like pines, with a bench and a view to die for. Far from the madding crowd indeed! Then galloping straight down on the return, through fine fir and pine forests, but not a creek in sight! Incredible thirst drives me to a little outdoor cafe just across from the train station where a draught beer is sucked down in record time just as the train back to Vienna pulls up. What a quenching spot, in all aspects!

Then that evening, under the lofty spires of the Ratshaus, is an outdoor film festival of opera and symphony. Appropriately enough, Richard Strauss's *Alpensymphonie* is screened, and while it is playing a shooting star, the likes of which I haven't seen since the final days in San Francisco before taking this job, blazes as large as a firework through twilight to the left of one of the smaller spires. The Big Dipper is then glimpsed over the soaring spires on the opposite side of the 1883 neo-gothic structure, juxtaposed beautifully with the Burgtheater (1888) and its busts of the three great German language writers observing the epiphinal moment in eternal solemnity: Goethe, Schiller and Lessing.

Then to continue the space motif, the next day is the greatest solar eclipse to strike Europe in decades, and more importantly, the last of the millennium. I depart for Damascus just before the initial phases of the eclipse, and follow it in varying stages of sun coverage the whole way down to Damascus. As we are making our approach just outside the green oasis, in the desert wastes east of the city, is when it reaches its peak in the Middle East. The lifeless desert littered with ancient volcanic cones rimmed with fleecy clouds darkened by the eclipse makes an alien landscape even more so. Damascus is under curfew until the eclipse is over, giving the city an eerie feel. Paganism is alive and well. But apocalypse? Hardly. As Jesus said so poetically: "I will come like a thief in the night." In other words, when people *least* expect it!

As a birthday present I'm off to Malta for the first time, home of the knights of the Order of St. John after being thrown out of both Jerusalem and off Rhodes by the Ottoman Turks. Trying to get my bearings after arriving in the dark, I meet an old fellow in the hotel lobby named Constantine who offers to show me a place where I can get a cold beer in an outdoor cafe overlooking the harbor ringed with massive bastions. We venture off over a fixed bridge (used to be a drawbridge) spanning a deep moat cut from limestone and through a hideously remodeled gate into the labyrinthian streets of the city begun in 1530 by the homeless knights. Charles V of Spain ceded the island to them for the fee of one Maltese falcon per year. Sound familiar? He thought the knights stationed so strategically could only help keep southern Europe safe from the encroachments of the Turks.

Constantine gave me a running guided tour of the historical buildings as he walked me to the cafe on his way home. He came from a shipping family that made its fortune transporting oil from Philadelphia to Malta in the mid-nineteenth century. He is the last in the family line and has no children. So, a lonely old guy can take a half hour out of his life and show a visitor around. A clean, well lighted place, no? For that's exactly what he took me to, perched under a tree next to the gate to the Lower Barraka gardens above the Grand Harbor just up from Fort St. Elmo. He refused a beer, taking only iced water, before answering thoroughly every question I threw at him. He spoke of the Phoenician arrival in Malta in 790 B.C., the Roman arrival in the second century B.C., the Arabs capture of it in 870, the Normans, the knights of St. John, Napoleon's navy and the British, who in 1798, destroyed it and took the tiny island, just 17 miles long. The naval power that secured Malta's two deep natural harbors ruled the Mediterranean.

In 1565 the sultan sent 30,000 warriors in 200 ships to take the island from the Order's 641 knights and their 8,500 soldiers. Fort St. Elmo bore the brunt of the first attack, falling after 31 days with the loss of 1,300 defenders. The Turks then turned their attentions on Fort St. Angelo, across the Grand Harbor, but fled in disarray three months later after failing to breach the ramparts at a cost of 20,000 dead. Only 600 defenders were able to bear arms at the end of the Turkish siege. Then, of course in World War II, the Germans destroyed a good part of the British Fleet here through aerial bombardment, to say nothing of the town.

Constantine told me to look for his family name on the floor of the massive cathedral which dominates the walled city. And sure enough, the next morning, while marveling at the multicolored tombstones of 375 knights which cover the St. John's Cathedral floor, I found his family coat of arms tucked up near the front. Talk about living history! The tombstones as paving stones contrasted by the Mattia Preti painting of the life of John the Baptist on the length of ceiling above demands several hours of meditation, if you are lucky enough to have the time. But as I was scheduled to fly out that afternoon I sped out of the nave and clambered along the ramparts looking over the Grand Harbor and Fort St. Angelo on the opposite side. A Libyan ferry, the Benghazi, smoked into the harbor from Tripoli with what looked like twelve people on board. I found out later Malta is only 180 miles from the North African coast. I continued my morning hike around the peninsula capped by massive limestone structures, passed Fort St. Elmo and ended up at a harbor side cafe on the Marsamxett side of town for an ice cold coke. I mulled the history this strategic isle while the locals swum beneath me off limestone outcrops covered with seaweed.

Two days later it's the North African coast of Tunisia, with the desolate promontory of Punta Farina thrusting northward, an ancient piece of it sharply eroded offshore in the shape of a ship under full sail. But despite the desolate look of the land, there are several lakes just inland from the sea, and as we approach Tunis one of the shallowest lakes is bright red with an algae that must thrive in the 45 celsius temperatures outside. Out of the hotel and into the heart of the modern city, (this is not Africa!) its shaded souk seething with humanity provides shelter but no coolness. Then into the narrow white washed streets of the old medina under the towering Ez-Zitouna mosque, founded in the 7th century, when the city itself was founded.

Then a dash out to Carthage, founded in 814 B.C., to see the ancient Phoenician ruins underneath those of the conquering Romans. The sun is setting upon reaching the gate to the site, and one can feel the air cool drastically as it drops toward the horizon. The entire archaeological site is to close at sun down, but a few extra dollars helps grease my way in for a private viewing of the complex.

From the Romanesque statuary lined up across the topmost layer of the site, including a carved legless elephant evoking Hannibal's march across the Alps in 218 B.C., to the flanks of exposed pillars from first (in descending order) Roman and then Phoenician construction, one can view bits of mosaic and painted friezes still visible if you're brave enough to jump fences and ignore the no trespassing signs. Carthage was finally sacked by the Romans in 201, thus becoming a bustling provincial capital exporting corn to the empire.

The site is stunning for its grand vista across the Gulf of Tunisia; and just after sunset a full moon rose big and bright over the stark desert mountains of the Maouin Peninsula across the bay, setting the smooth ocean water shimmering magically in a spot rich in human history. As the twilight was replaced by moonlight I stopped by the amphitheater for a quick walk around the tumbled down stadium with its sunken pathways and rooms for caged animals carved from the rock below.

Then up to the gorgeous village of Sidi Bou Said perched on a hilltop overlooking the bay. What a place, with whitewashed adobe houses with blue trim, just like in Greece! Does this date back to the close links between the Greeks and Phoenicians? The crowning jewel after a walk through the narrow streets of this village is to come out atop a sheer cliff and seat yourself in one of the three terraced cafes overlooking the Gulf of Tunisia and have a tea and a few tokes on a tasty houka.

September '99: "Life is suffering, tee hee, ha, ha…" Soaring over Izmit, Turkey, where a month ago some 14,000 people perished in an earth-quake, followed by a quake in Athens that killed hundreds, which was followed by further aftershocks in Turkey killing even more, while at the same time Indonesian Militias were butchering the population of East Timor after the independence vote there, which was just before a huge 7.6

earthquake in Taiwan killed another 5,000 people, but synchronous with Dagestani terrorist bombings of apartment buildings in Moscow, slaughtering some 250 innocent people: this is good old planet earth near the end of the second millennium! Two thousand years of contrived time keeping by *Homo sapiens*, all so we can measure, fairly precisely, the unending tragedies of life on the planet. "…Smile on little buddha, smile on, it's only illusion then you're gone," as Toad the Wet Sprocket sings on *Mortal Coil.*

Pervasive haze, not unlike S.E. Asia, form Vienna to Ankara. This was the hottest, most beautiful summer in German memory. These two observations coupled with the two hurricanes in the Atlantic heading for North America seem to reinforce the pessimistic outlook that things just might be heating up.

Heading down to Tirana, Albania a few days later, the islands off Split are like blossoms with their undulating turquoise inlets of shallow sand pinched between petals of land. Then the huge dry mountains of Albania, east of Tirana, where just last spring refugees by the hundreds of thousands were fleeing the bloodbath of ethnic cleansing in Kosovo. Now, they're all at what's left of home, not safe, but home.

As I said at the beginning of this journal: These are trips down memory lane; so flying over the isles of the Croatian coast, the memories of 1977 at eighteen years of age, ferrying among those very Jugoslavian islands from Rijeka to Rab to Zadar with my friend H., dead for eight months now from suicide, is a bittersweet thing indeed. Yet the scintillating setting sunlight on the Adriatic, between the elongated islands, jolts one to recognize the miracle of this fecund planet, which raises the question: why would anyone want to leave it early?

Not a new thought I imagine, but just as cancer cells devolve from normal cells, so *Homo sapiens* have left their natural arrangement with the planet behind to begin altering the ecosystem in dramatic ways, becoming cancerous in their own right: killing the very earth which gives us life.

Something incredibly aesthetic about razor sharp ridge lines of snow thrusting above low cloud in the Alps. Himal (snow) Alaya (home): I wonder if there is a sanskrit connection with the Hebraic word "aliya", which translates as making a pilgrimage of sorts to the home land, to Israel, and the Nepalese word "alaya", the high mountains being the abode of the gods.

A view of Mt. Blanc from over the isle of Elba, with the gnarly isle of Corsica silhouetted by a setting sun, counters the view of two days ago of that very peak from the civilized lakeshore of Geneva.

That city is a high-water mark of Civilization! Climbed the towers of St. Pierre's cathedral in the heart of the old town for views of the Perl du Lac and surrounding Jura and Alpine peaks. Then after descending, visited the subterranean archaeological excavations underneath the church. The Cathedral has a faux-floor, due to the excavations which have unearthed pre-Roman remnants. There are Roman mosaics, statuary, wells, etc., all dating back at least 2,000 years, and all beautifully presented and lit in situ. Not to mention the great stratigraphic profiling, with accompanying dates for each clearly defined human layer, to remind the visitor that over time our own century will be just another layer chronicled in soil.

October '99: Turkey vultures circling over the Potomac River now filled to the brim from Hurricane Floyd as I cross the American Legion Bridge to Dulles and the return to Frankfurt. They seem to circle in wait for my dying mother, slowly being hollowed out from the inside by cancer as she reclines on the living room couch, trying to escape through television. Forty-one years ago I was a new-born nursing at the breast of her once vibrant body, now on the edge of the grave.

From stone-carved churches of Lalibela, Ethiopia, to the towering carved facades of Petra, Jordan. On takeoff from Ben Gurion we fly up over the dry, rounded hills of the West Bank and immediately get a great perspective of the situation on the ground that doesn't appear on many maps. A myriad of Palestinian villages nestled in small valleys and on hill-tops are contrasted by huge, new Israeli apartment complexes scattered across the countryside, connected by modern roads, fresh scars purpose-fully cutting off one small Palestinian village from another. Then we pass to the north of Jerusalem, and amidst the tightly packed humanity of the old walled city glints the gold of the Dome of the Rock, the most domi-nant structure in the entire area. No wonder the Israelis are scared. It gleams all the way over to the caves of Qumran, home of the Dead Sea Scrolls, where we turn due south, following the western edge of the Dead Sea and its quickly retreating shoreline past the historic Masada mesa and its eastern flank trail I hiked fifteen years ago in what had to be record time. Then down over the Ha'Arava valley itself and the desert wilderness N. and I explored during days off while working on the moshav at Tsofar. From that moshav it was always frustrating knowing that Petra was just a stone's throw east across the border, in the towering gnarly-red Esh Shara Mountains. We couldn't get to it due to the political situation, but that has recently changed, even though it still takes some two hours to pass through the Arava border crossing.

The old camel trading routes carrying frankincense and myrrh passed through Petra, winding through the narrow Siq with camel train motifs lining its walls, before dropping down through other wadis into the Arava and Tsofar on their way to Gaza and ancient Jaffa. This is the reason we found so many interesting structures in the stark desert canyons west of the moshav (a well, base stones of columns, building foundations, bits of ancient coin, etc.).

After clearing immigration we visited the fortress in Aqaba that T.E. Lawrence surprise-attacked from the rear, then drove through the razor sharp mountains that run north and south along the Jordanian border and came upon the stunning desert monoliths of Wadi Rum, where Lawrence hid with his band of Arabs, avoiding Turkish troops between attacks on the rail line linking Damascus with Aqaba. The stunning cinematography from David Lean's film *Lawrence of Arabia* was shot in those red rock valleys, and there is still a spring there called Lawrence spring.

Petra was the capital or necropolis of the Nabataean kingdom, which at its height controlled a swath of territory from the Sinai to Syria. It is still debated what purpose it served. A trading center possibly as early as the fifth century B.C., its era of greatest prosperity was most likely between 100 B.C. and 150 A.D., when most of the exquisite facades were carved into the red sandstone cliffs. The approach to the valley of carved facades is the most spectacular approach of any archaeological site in the world. The Siq, as this eastern approach is called, is a narrow ravine carved from the sandstone by flash floods over the millennium. It is lined with a channel cut from rock a meter off the floor of the ravine, to bring the waters of Wadi Musa (Moses' spring) into the city. The steep cliffs which form the Siq are lined with monuments and niches, as well as the aforementioned camel train led by Bedouin. As one nears the end of the Siq, a slice of the most photogenic of the monumental tombs cut into the cliffs is framed by the end of the narrow ravine. The classical facade of the 1st century B.C. Treasury (as it is called due to the huge urn said to be filled with gold coins that graces its apex), contrasted by the wavy water worn walls of the wadi, is one of the greatest scenes in the world. The classical facade of this and other 2,000 year old tombs in the valley of Petra, show the Nabataeans close trading links with the Hellenistic world. The rock-hewn motif found at Petra is also reminiscent of Lalibela.

The capitals of the pillars "holding up" the 40 meter high edifice are delicately carved, shielded from the elements by an overhang formed by the carving of the structure from the sandstone. The other finely carved Greek-like reliefs haven't been so fortunate, including the huge urn atop the tomb: centuries of Bedouins have unfortunately taken potshots at these figures, wearing them down to a faint trace of their former glory.

The views from the heights above the rugged sandstone labyrinth and out over the Arava and the border with Israel, was indeed breathtaking, and completed the frustrating circle of not being able to visit the ancient site from the moshav below all those years ago. Mt. Aron, with a mosque atop its slender peak where Moses buried his brother, the first priest, during the Jews wandering in the wilderness, must have the greatest view of the entire region ,and is a place I'd like to get to someday.

On return to Frankfurt, a weekend drive through brisk air and vineyards up the Rhine Valley under towering castles to the Lorelei cliffs. The 433' high prow looms over the dangerous narrows, where in German legend a fairy similar to the Greek Sirens lived and sang on the exposed rocks forming rapids, luring sailors to their deaths. Hikes up through autumnal oak forests with acorns covering the ground to Castle Maus, and expansive views out over rolling farmlands to the east, while below barges crowd the river, carrying coal, sand and other heavy cargoes in their deep bellies.

Another autumnal drive up to Berlin through old East Germany is a treat: first up the Fulda Gap through which the Russians were to pore on their invasion of Western Europe, then into the Thuringian Wald and its thick, dark misty forests, graced first by the ruins of ancient Brandenburg castle on a distant ridge, followed by the fine fortress palace of Wartburg perched atop the wooded hills above Eisenach. After dropping down into the flatlands, two distant hilltops topped by sentinel castles guard the main route to Berlin, giving the passage the feel of a Tolkien land. These two castles, Muhlburg on the south and Burg Gleichen to the north, loom darkly above the narrow pass below and must have been a formidable barrier in medieval times.

The fachwerk villages passed on the journey really aren't much different from those in the west, although I imagine the collective farming that was practiced up until ten years ago is now privatised. The west has poured so much money into the east over the past decade that it nearly bankrupted the country. The road construction alone, upgrading what were quaint potholed roads into superhighways, is ongoing the whole way to Berlin, and must be costing billions annually.

Arriving in Berlin from the south, I am shocked by how gorgeous the countryside around the new/old capital is: lakes, forests of mixed fir and deciduous trees growing from what looks like sandy loam. It is all very similar to the ecosystem around the Chesapeake with its watery forests. The city itself is a historical and architectural wonder, except for the myriad cranes crowding the skyline of what was the east, just across where the Berlin Wall once zig-zagged through labyrinthian streets. There are bits of it still standing in some obscure parts of town. One section I followed was in a bleak street with ugly Soviet style apartments on one side, and equally ugly Western bauhaus style ones on the other. This was on the way to the Check Point Charlie Museum, which has a vast collection of historic photos of when the wall was first erected in 1961, demonstrations, a gyrocopter used in an escape, a bulletproof car used for same, tunneling equipment, ladders, and of course great photos of when the wall finally came down in November of 1989. It is in the very block where Check Point Charlie existed, and has photos of the many tense standoffs that occurred between Soviet and American troops there, as well as descriptions of the many spy exchanges that took place. Departing the Check Point Charlie block, a huge historic sign still proclaims: YOU ARE LEAVING THE AMERICAN SECTOR.

On my way north I detect the back of what looks like a cathedral down a side street to the east and proceed to check it out. My discovery reinforces the marvel of serendipitous discovery, for the cathedral turns out to be the impressive Berlin Konzerthaus bookended on the Gendarmenmarkplatz by two fantastic structures, the Franzosich and Deutscher Domes. I hike up the spiraling steps of the former and get great views over the entire once divided city. I also plan my next move over to the monstrous Berlin Cathedral and a cluster of old buildings nearby it that seem intriguing. The cathedral actually sits on a man-made island in the Spree River, and on its banks just before the cathedral is a large square, appropriately named Lust Park, or enjoyment park. Trees lining the river bank are bright yellow with black trunks. A few people lounge on benches amidst the fallen leaves of this brilliant autumnal scene. What a photograph that would have made.

Inside the cathedral someone is playing the massive organ, so I collapse in a pew and meditate on the serenity of the paintings on the underside of the massive dome, and recall that at the same hour a week earlier I was in another cathedral nestled in labyrinthian red rock, called Petra.

It turns out the group of buildings I had spied from the Franzosich Dome were none other than the Inseln Museums, still pock marked with bullet holes from W.W. II. The Bode Museum on the prow of the island begins a string of national museums that will be unparalleled when their reconstruction is finished. The world famous Pergamon is open for business in the middle of this cluster, with an Asian collection which could very well be the finest in the world.

I continue upstream along the banks of the Spree, through rough areas and other sections being completely reconstructed, past the Frederichstrasse Bahnhoff, to the Reichstag and its new glass dome, an architectural attempt at lighting a building rife with Nazi darkness. Constructed in 1894, the building was actually torched by Hitler and his Nazi cronies in 1933, in order to symbolically destroy the German post W.W. I experiment with a parliamentary democracy. The views of the Brandenburg Gate, Victory Monument (Siegarsaule)and Tiergarten forest from the glass cupola and its interior spiral walkway as it winds up to a vantage point just under the top, is something to behold: dark history fused with hope for a more responsible Deutschland.

Back in Washington a few days later to spend time with the person who gave me life before she is gone forever. Hiking the gnarly Billy Goat Trail pinched between the C&O canal and spectacular Mather Gorge of the Potomac below Great Falls: lofty cherry-red maples cling to cracks in patchy, lichen covered grey schist above swirling white water under sheer cliffs cut by eternal Shenandoah runoff:

perched atop a cliff sculptured by the age-old hands of the murky Potomac, i am absorbed in the moment, memories and tree limbs float swiftly by...

There is more wilderness along this two mile hike eight miles upstream from Washington D.C., than in all of domesticated Germany, except for the Alps.

November '99: "I never wanted to concentrate my energies in one narrow channel." Kenneth Galbraith on BBC Hardtalk 11/1/99

There are now 6 billion people on the planet, and ironically enough, I'm headed for one of the bleakest examples of overpopulation: Africa. As if any more evidence of the quickening destruction of the environment were necessary, flying north from Dar es Salam through the choking haze of the Serengeti, an elongated mountain rises. The thick forest which obviously once covered the massif has been logged to such an extent that only a very thick remnant remains atop it like a buzz cut, smoldering fires victoriously gnawing at its boundaries. Synchronously, a Time Magazine article on board titled "Greenhouse Effects" lists Kenya under a spreading disease column due to the fact that malaria has killed hundreds of people in its highlands, where the illness didn't previously exist.

On approach to land at Jomo Kenyatta International in Nairobi, the hemmed in wildlife of Nairobi National Park can be seen dashing around below, a high fence separating the animals from the burgeoning, and increasingly desperate *Homo sapiens* population surrounding them. After touchdown we taxi off the runway and along the fence line to see a group of six giraffes under towering acacia watching planes takeoff and land.

Off to Rwanda the following day across the stark Rift Valley, its escarpments plunging primordially into the topographic crack which exposes our ancient origins, the bulk of Kilimanjaro dominating the south. Then into Kigali, home of the greatest genocide (800,000 killed) humanity has known this decade, but only this decade, what with the poor Cambodians still reeling from the previous highwater mark of mass killing. The slaughter that occurred in this tiny landlocked country is a disturbing bookend to the bloodiest century in human history. But the century isn't over yet, and the same sort of trouble is brewing again in Burundi, next door.

Crossing the southern reaches of Lake Victoria on the return, myriad isles inhabited by thatched roof villages clustered around scalloped bays crowded with pirogues. Yet each isle is totally denuded, the deforestation changing the ecosystem in subtle and not so subtle ways: a 30,000' high classic anvil-shaped thunderhead hovers nearby, ready to drop torrential rains that will wash away valuable soils to the bottom of the great lake, making a hard life even harder.

The savannah which surrounds the lake to the east has a slight shade of green, but as we soar back across the Rift, this quickly gives way to an inhospitable terrain that becomes more so as a La Nina drought deepens. This in turn creates degrees of famine which pressures a society with increasing levels of crime: car jackings, rapes, murders, muggings, you name it, as desperate people leave the lands which no longer support them to flee to the city in false hope. Robert Kaplan's *The Coming Anarchy* is here! The ancient Rift Valley and environs can be viewed metaphorically as a fracture which continually unleashes our primitive natures: genocide, anarchy, corruption. From the *Australopithicines* and *Homo habilis* to two thousand years after Christ, nothing really has changed. In an age drowning in information we have lost perspective.

I had heard Nairobi was an increasingly dangerous city, but nothing brings reality home like a walk through its streets at night. Just before the sun set one evening I walked out of my hotel to search for an Indian restaurant. Strolling down Kenyatta and Moi Avenues, I was the only white face in a thronging sea of black, but was oblivious to the fact until I got the sense someone was following me. I got off the congested sidewalk and began strolling through the parking lots which border the shop fronts, when I glanced behind and detected four young males dressed in tattered clothes following me. Thinking back to a Lufthansa crew member who just a few weeks before had his ear chopped off in broad daylight on these very streets for not giving his assailants enough money, I suddenly felt vulnerable. With adrenaline surging, I cut between diagonally parked cars, found a split-second opening between the heavy traffic, and lost them. I should have turned around then and headed back to the hotel, but I was starving for samosas.

When I finally found an Indian place, the sun had set, darkness was falling. Departing the restaurant about an hour later, the streets were deserted. The thronging commute was over. Little did I know that the local population lives in fear of the streets of Nairobi after dark too. That's is why they were in a rush to leave before sundown. As I walked along the nearly empty sidewalks, "taxi drivers" in beat up old jalopies beckoned for me to ride with them, but I figured I was safer walking. At least I could run like the wind if need be, and not be trapped inside a cab, taken to the edge of town, beaten, robbed and possibly killed. It was tempting to hop in one of these cabs, because the desperation of those remaining on the streets was palpable. Groups of impoverished males hanging in decrepit street corners along unlit streets drove me to walk in the middle of the road, dodging traffic, as I fearfully navigated a way back to my hotel through the dark labyrinth. I thought colleagues were exaggerating the dangers of Nairobi, until I found out first hand they weren't. From metropolis to necropolis!

In contrast to the concentrated humanity, a drive with a colleague the next day through the Great Rift full of zebra, giraffe, baboons and Masai pastoralists tending their cattle was refreshing. The Rift Valley escarpment flanks covered in massive euphorbia candalabrum cactus trees under cedar forests atop the ridge where Kikuyu maize farms begin is a geologic sight to behold. The entire tectonic gash reminds me of the gnarly dry range of Jordan and Petra rising out of Israel's Ha'Arava, part of this same earthly fracture 2,000 miles to the north.

Talk about the theater of the absurd! Bo Diddly, Little Richard, Elvis and the Supremes blare from my colleague's jeep stereo as we bounce along washed out dirt roads to a Masai encampment while zebra and giraffe flee into the acacia. The thin, tall Masai brightly colored come to greet us with staffs in hand as we pull up to their manyatta (a collection of cattle dung walled huts with acacia thorn fencing forming a circle to keep their cattle in and hyenas out at night). My colleague has been coming out to meet them regularly after almost being killed in the bombing of the U. S. mission. He began collecting the bones of African wildlife after his brush with death (osteology as therapy), when some Masai he met along the only paved road in the area showed him what they had. He now has a complete elephant skeleton in his driveway, not to mention hundreds of other animal remains, ranging from lion heads, eland, water buffalo to gazelle scattered around his property. One of the Masai took me out into the bush to track four giraffe that had been lurking nearby. We snuck up quite close to them before they spotted us and dashed deeper into the acacia under Suswa volcano. Later we drove into what looked like a ghost town, with buildings of rough stone and others of adobe. This was the cosmopolitan city of Ewasu, with such fine hotels as the Inter Continental and Hilton, scrawled over the doorless doorways of two decrepit structures. Catering to your every need. We stopped for a warm beer in the First Class Bar, as there is no electricity. As international aid money pours into the pockets of corrupt leaders, this is how the other half lives.

The following day down to Karen Blixen's stately colonial home of *Out of Africa* fame in the trees under the Ngong Hills. The romantic notions of Kenya can still be felt far out of Nairobi, but the security systems and private guards patrolling this now fancy neighborhood of large homes, brings one back to the present. She had a coffee plantation in the old days, and the huge industrial roaster and grinder lay down a thickly forested path behind her home in great condition. I wonder what that coffee would have tasted like? Then up the road under the green Ngong Hills before dropping over the precipice into the southern reaches of the dessicated Rift. Towering giraffes nibble at acacia under a huge volcano in what looks like an intermittent lake bed. They then gallop off magically in slow motion as we stop to have a closer look. Further on, past a river with a little water in it crowded with baboons, we see a massive dust devil approaching the road. As it nears I jump out to stand in its path. It is stronger than I thought and rips the hat from my head and spirals off with it while almost knocking me over. Ahh, primitive encounters in the Rift.

Burundi: The Mitumba Mountains of Congo across Lake Tanganyka covered in the perpetual haze from fires billowing smoke high atop ridges is a standard of densely populated Third World countries at the end of the millennium. Then flying up to Kigali again, I see that the ranges on either side of the valley up to Rwanda are almost completely denuded, and the villages and farms so numerous and so packed together, that the stress on the land translates into stress between Hutu and Tutsi tribes, which has led to genocide in the recent past and could do so again in the near future. "Primitive" societies destroy the natural state just as much if not more than industrial ones, not to mention each other. And speaking of primitive, or primeval, on the flight back to Nairobi a series of volcanoes lurch from the Tanzanian end of the Rift, in the direction of Olduvai Gorge, thus cementing the perspective this crack in the Earth gives us at the fin de millénaire. Where will it all go from here? I can't wait to see.

Just across from the Nairobi Natural History Museum, where I went to meditate on the archaeological remnants of our evolution, is the snake and reptile house. As I was observing two very active cobras I heard this consistent grunting and thought that surely two folks were having passionate sex behind a nearby closed door. As I observed the cobras perform an active dance of their own while watching me through the plate glass, the panting continued in a persistent, almost embarrassing manner. I glanced around, but no one else seemed to notice. I couldn't see where the nearby sound could possibly be coming from. As I turned to leave, I saw behind me a large concrete pen that I thought had been empty. As I peered over the low wall toward its base I found the source of passion. A large leopard turtle had mounted the rear of another, his turkey neck fully extended from his shell with mouth gasping as he banged away at his consort in all too human sound and form.

And speaking of Robert Kaplan's treatise on Africa at the edge of the abyss, which was presciently published just seven weeks before the Rwandan genocide of 1994, and in which he paints a depressing picture of the continent's overpopulation, resource scarcity, drug-infested slums, rampant crime and thug-like leaders, one has to wonder just what the future holds. Given the recent democratic success in South Africa and Nigeria, hope is not lost, but given the overall scenario, the odds seemed to be stacked against the continent. Nairobi, apparently once a civil city, has now come to embody exactly what Kaplan predicts for all of Africa: a place where demographic, environmental and social stress lead to the emergence of criminal anarchy. One of the local newspapers, the *East African Standard*, captured the daily carnage on 11/02/99:

CARJACKERS UNLEASH TERROR

One person was killed and several others injured in Nyandarua District on Sunday when armed carjackers commandeered five vehicles and committed a series of robberies.

SCHOOL THREATENED

Nyali -The manager of Rise and Shine Primary school in Nyali has been threatened with death unless she sacks a teacher at her school…

FAMINE BITES

Moyale -Acute food and water shortages continued to ravage the district…The two-kilo food ration of maize per household given to residents monthly falls far short of the needs of the people who are already starving.

PASTORALISTS ADVISED

Isiolo -Insecurity and inter-clan conflicts are to blame for the slow pace of development among pastoralist communities in East and North East Provinces. Assistant minister Mokku said pastoralists waste a lot of time and resources in endless conflict.

APPEAL ON FAMINE

Minister of Planning, Gideon Ndambuki, has said in Makveni that the drought and famine gripping the country has accelerated poverty.

WATER SHORTAGE HITS MUMIAS

Mumias town has been hit by an acute water shortage for the past one week. Residents have resorted to using untreated water from nearby streams and rivers at the risk of contracting water borne diseases.

GANGSTERS KILLED

Bungoma -An irate group of villagers burnt to death two suspected gangsters who allegedly robbed a bread distribution van crew.

LEOPARD MENACE ROCKS GEM

A rogue leopard is on the loose and is terrorizing residents of Omindo village in Gem, Siaya District. The villagers expressed fears that the leopard, which attacks its victims in broad daylight, could soon prey on their school-going children.

RUSTLERS KILL TWO PEOPLE IN GARISSA

Two people were shot dead and three others seriously injured when at least 80 heavily armed cattle rustlers raided Manyattas in Garissa District. The rustlers made away with hundreds of head of cattle, donkeys and goats before escaping towards Isiolo District.

Of course, a daily culling of the *Washington Post* would reveal many a shocking story of violence, but these snippets give an idea of the criminal anarchy brought about by the very social and environmental stresses which Kaplan mentions. To say nothing of AIDS, which the *International Herald Tribune* writes has "…metastasized into a disease whose progression is no longer measured solely by the depletion of a patient's T-cells but increasingly by every percentage point that is shaved from a nation's gross domestic product. More than 5,000 people with AIDS die each day in Africa, and epidemiologists expect that figure to climb to almost 13,000 by 2005. By that time, health experts say, more people in sub-Saharan Africa will have died from AIDS than in both world wars combined or from the bubonic plague, which killed 20 million people in 14th-century Europe. In Africa's most industrialized states, including South Africa, Zimbabwe and Kenya the gross domestic product could be 20 percent lower by 2005 than it otherwise would have been."

From Rift Valley *Homo habilis* to staring at the beautiful in-flight flex of a monstrous Boeing 777 wing above the myriad lakes of Labrador. The evolution of *Homo habilis* (toolmaking man) is a wondrous thing indeed. Those who say the creations of *Homo sapiens* are unnatural and therefore destructive, forget that these creations are forged by an imagination secreted by an organ created by Mother Nature. It follows then that humanity's ability to produce things out of thin air and alter the world is quite natural. A Boeing 777, then, is not only highly functional but as natural as a bird's wing; for Mother Nature has destroyed more of her own creations on this planet than all of humanity combined, to say nothing of altering ecosystems. Now, if we could only get those radiation eating Deinococcus bacteria up and chomping on the mounds of radioactive refuse!

Petra-Lorelei-Berlin-Mather Gorge-Rift Valley-Death!

And speaking of destroying ecosystems, Mother Nature's very own creation, cancer, has just ended the life of my not quite 72 year-old mother. In fact, she sat on the couch reading quite normally as I composed the previous section on Africa's travails. May she rest in peace after a psychologically challenging life: so much loss and pain that surely death is a welcome thing indeed. As Jonathan Raban writes in his recent book *A Passage to Juneau,* "death is a wilderness in which everyone is at a loss for words." Amen to that, but the planet keeps spinning and the grass keeps growing.

Then recalling a few days before my mother's death the afternoon spent in unseasonably warm weather along the Potomac, below Mather Gorge, on Sherwin Island. A turkey vulture rookery on both sides of the river, with hundreds in the trees above me and covering a massive chunk of schist thrusting from bedrock across the deep, primal flow, surely presaged my mother's death within the week: the sinking warm sun, huge, black ugly-necked vultures swooping from the tree tops, spooked by my passing, as if I was toying with the grim reaper himself. Then a passage from Terrence Malick's *Thin Red Line* fluttered in from somewhere, spoken, I think, by the character appropriately named Witt: "One man looks at a dying bird and thinks there's nothing but unanswered pain…but death's got the final word…it's laughing at him. Another man sees that same bird, feels the glory, feels something smiling through it!" Like the Buddha? This planet and all its miraculous life forms is indeed the glory, and the horror which coexists with that glory and gives it its healthy edge makes the entire package possibly the greatest thing that has ever existed, anywhere in time.

Rising from Athens with the Parthenon out the right window, we climb steeply to see Mt. Olympus, soaring snow-crowned far to the north, dominating the Macedonian origins of the Greek peninsula, with the capital's suburbs stretching endlessly below. This is the home of our "civilization!" We've progressed materially and medically, but to what end?

January '00: I ponder on millennium eve what it was that Joyce's Stephen Dedalus said: "History is the nightmare from which I am trying to awake." After the bloodiest century in recorded history, it's difficult not to agree. Or as Kurtz in the movie *Apocalypse Now* keeps chanting, "The horror, the horror!" The heart of darkness always seems to lurk around the next corner. So what lies in wait for us at the beginning of the new millennium?

Then the clouds part, exposing the east coast of Greenland: knife-sharp peaks hold back the ice cap, but it breaches them and pours ice flows into myriad fjords. The same western headwind which buffets us into an hour longer flight, whips snow across the fissured glacier and drives spindrift across razor ridges. On the western side, the setting sun sets monoliths rising from open ocean aflame. A twenty mile fjord littered with ice bergs aglow in the same orange sheen, when, just up an inlet on the southwest corner, a little red ship heads towards…where? There's nothing but a massive glacier at the head of the fjord where that ship is heading. How could anything humanity produce affect this monstrous landscape?

Then home again, where my mom has returned, in a sense, too. Her cremated remains sit in a beautiful box in her bedroom. I open it and take out the thick plastic bag full of ash and bits of bone, give it a double kiss the way I kissed both her cheeks when saying my final good-bye six weeks ago, then return the remains to the box. Ashes to ashes, dust to dust…the ultimate story of everything on the planet. Just add water and stir!

Winging into Almaty with a full moon bathing the spectacular Tien Shan to the south and a mighty Big Dipper hanging in a clear cold night sky to the north and the white-washed steppes going on and on and on. The drive down to Bishkek, Kirgyztan the following day felt like a return to the American Rocky Mountains. Yurts off in the vast steppes under towering peaks and lone shepherds tending flocks of sheep on horseback, brought flashbacks of the Navajo in the four corners. The Mongol looking Kazakhs look like the Navajo too, their mobile Yurts finding solid form in the adobe Hogans of the Southwestern U.S. after crossing the Bering land bridge. Red fox, huge eagles atop telephone polls and the faint smell of sage in the air combine to make it all very familiar, half a world away, in a land where Russian is the lingua franca.

Bishkek a beat little city under towering peaks, the roads terribly potholed and lined with the destitute warming themselves over pathetic fires. An old trash dump just off the road is being meticulously unearthed by the local citizenry, a sure sign of desperate times. On the way back to Almaty we race along an icy, tree-lined stretch of road which reminds me of a similar drive back from Peshawar to Islamabad, 500 miles due south over one of the greatest collections of peaks on the planet: Tien Shan, Pamir, Hindu Kush.

February '00: You know life is good when you fly into a great city like Budapest on a dreary Monday afternoon, fling the suitcase in the hotel room after removing a swim suit, and head immediately out the door for a brisk walk along and over the Danube to the Gellert Baths, where you submerge yourself in a soothing Turkish bath. The mosaic walls with nymphs hanging over doorways coupled with the ancient men shuffling through herb-scented steam in loin cloth, takes one back to the days of the Ottoman Empire. The perfect medicine for a cold day in Central Europe!

The following week it's over the ice cap of Greenland again, this time even further north to avoid the vicious headwinds. The immensity of the glacier forming the heart of that huge island ringed by sharp, towering peaks evoked memories of Jack London's existential agonies, caught beautifully in the beginning of *White Fang*: "A vast silence reigned over the land. The land itself was desolation, lifeless, without movement, so lone and cold that the spirit of it was not even that of sadness." His adventures in the Klondike forced him to confront the stark realities of existence in a way few do, surrounded as they are by the trappings of civilization. I too see London's "noseless one" in the bleak, lifeless terrain below, where the ice goes on and on and on and on, only to tumble in deep crevasses into fjords cluttered with icebergs leading to a frozen sea: "I am aware that within this disintegrating body which has been dying since I was born I carry a skeleton, that under the rind of flesh which is my face is a bony, noseless death's head. All of which does not shudder me. To be afraid is to be healthy. Fear of death makes for life...The world-sickness of the White Logic makes one grin jocosely into the face of the Noseless One and to sneer at all the phantasmagoria of living. (*John Barleycorn*, 194)

March '00: During a spring blizzard in Vienna, on a stroll under the immense domes of the Hofburg, I reach into my pockets for warmth but feel something crumbly in one. Pinching the matter between thumb and forefinger I withdraw it for a look. It's a dry orange blossom picked the week before on a walk through Carthage in Tunis. I bring it to my nose and inhale the incense of North Africa as I stroll through thick flakes towards the opera house, and ponder the inexorable march of history as the Chinese threaten to invade Taiwan.

Almost exactly twenty months after leaving Bangkok, I'm winging south from Dhaka just like old times. Huge columns of smoke, larger than any I remember, billow from separate clear-cut scarred valleys in extreme S.E. Bangladesh. The old smoke and haze and heat of S.E. Asia is still building, but to what climax?

On the flight from Frankfurt to Dhaka, just as the sun peeked around the horizon, we were over a landscape (Makran Desert ?) of dry craggy mountains, desert and wind whipped sand dunes, without a green thing in sight. Parts of this planet, that everyone claims is getting smaller, continually reinforce the fact that this globe is still as alien as any planet surface in our solar system.

Then into Burma! Every valley so clogged with smoke you can only see the ridge tops. And on the descent into Bangkok, soaring in over the rice basket of S.E. Asia, every third rice field is being burned to make way for the new crop and monsoons of summer. The resultant haze that hovers over the Thai capital leaves me depressed. The congestion and traffic hasn't improved even with the construction of an elevated train system along Sukhumvit, adding to the hollow feeling inside, and the amazement that we lived here for three years! Surely it was the amazing variety and quality of travel one can experience out of Bangkok that was the initial attraction of living there. But once everything of interest in S.E Asia and beyond has been seen, it would be a tough place to live in again. Re-acclimatization is definitely a must.

April '00: Incredible taking off from Dulles on a clear, translucent April evening, launching out over the Potomac just above Seneca, heading toward Sugarloaf Mountain. Then the sharp turn northeast follows River Road and the memories of youth that fill the downriver route: rowing across the broad waters at Seneca to the Virginia side in a little orange sport yak in my early teens, towing my older brother behind in an even flimsier white plastic boat meant for backyard baby splashes, Dad anxiously watching from the Maryland shore; the sprawling Allnut farm on Sugarland Road and the beer and sex coming of age hayride parties of high school; after one such party wiping out in a jalopy of a car with girlfriend riding shotgun into chest-high wheat when taking a sharp corner too fast; not to mention senior prom dinner at that very farm left in our jet wake; then the omphalos of teen years, Winston Churchill High, passes by to starboard, with all its attendant joys and sorrows; C&O Canal meandering past Great Falls through Wide Water with its always memorable hikes along the Billy Goat Trail; then over Carderock and the house where Pops now eats alone, and Northwest D.C. with more recent history with the good folks along leafy Sherier Place, before the Lincoln Memorial, Washington Monument, Mall, Capitol and distant views of the Shriners Temple in Alexandria signifying my entry into this wild world…A takeoff down memory lane!

Palm Sunday afternoon in deserted Dominikan Kirche, Wien. There is still incense wafting through the huge, ornate inner sanctum, shafts of light defined by smoke left over from morning services. Meditative silence as I sit in a pew inhaling the fine scent and the baroque ceiling.

Slovenia, the land of pine-forested mountains crowned with onion domed churches under towering Julian Alps.

As if I don't travel enough through work, over Easter the family piles into the van for what turns out to be a 1,400 mile, nine-day circle tour of the Alps. First stop after the drive down along the Rhine to Basel then up to Bern, is the medieval hilltop fortress village of Gruyeres. The region famous for its cheese is surrounded on two sides by peaks still white with winter snow, and on the third by green spring grass and cattle. The citadel of Gruyeres rises aesthetically amidst the already stunning scenery, and best of all for us, the streets of this tourist destination which must be packed in summer, are deserted. The following morning we drop onto the shores of Lake Geneva at Montreux, then up the Rhone valley to the back door route into Chamonix from Martigny. The clarity is stunning, just as I left it two months earlier on my first ski journey to this most spectacular of European valleys. The flanks of the Grand Montets, still deep in powder, are first glimpsed as we reach the top of the pass at Le Tour, just east of that immense and highest peak in the Alps, Mt. Blanc. Since it's so clear, we head for the gondola which ascends precipitously to the Aiguille du Midi (3842m), the sharpened tooth just east of Mont Blanc's massive glaciers. After the kids are scared quite nicely on the second half of the gondola ride, where it seems the cab is going to smash into the hanging rock and ice just below the peak station, we clamber through the thin air to the viewing platform for unobstructed views of the entire range, the Matterhorn rising most prominently to the east. The Vallée Blanche glacier which begins on the backside of the Aiguille du Midi, is still scattered with skiers making the twenty-four km. descent back to Chamonix. A few more days under blazing sun and cool nights and hikes up to glaciers, and we're off along the Arly river route to Albertville, down past Grenoble and into Provence, where we finally confront soaking rains and increasing Easter weekend crowds. Into gorgeous Sisteron perched along the Durance River slicing through a geologic wonder of tilted sedimentary rock under a Citadel for lunch, then down through further geologic wildness of Provence to Castellane, astride the translucent Verdon under a towering mesa crowned with a church, where we find a fantastic evening meal but nowhere to stay. Forced on through driving rain over the gorgeous Haut Provence by lack of vacancies at each hotel, pension and road house, we arrive in Grasse to more "complet" signs and push on to Antibes, in hope of a break in the hotel room department. We stop at several more hotels as we follow the signs to the end of the tiny peninsula Antibes is perched upon, but in vain. Then we find ourselves on the ramparts of the walled city in the middle of a huge party crowd thronging the restaurants and bars lining the narrow streets of historic Antibes. A parking place miraculously appears, but little did we know when we pulled in that we would spend the night in it. The kids first experience of roughing it! But it turned out to be advantageous for visiting Antibes, for after awakening and watching the gorgeous sun rise over blue Mediterranean waters framed by snowy peaks of the Maritime Alps behind Nice, we strolled through the empty city to the marché provençal devoid of tourists for a coffee and croissant. After watching the fresh fruits and flowers and fish stands being set up we headed for a little beach just the other side of Port Vauban and had it all to ourselves for a quick swim under the fortress walls and church towers founded by Greeks in the 5th century B.C.

After our swim we ventured back into the medieval city to find it choked with tourists, at ten o'clock! Then, as we attempted to flee the crowds and drive off the ramparts, the increase in traffic was appalling. If we hadn't slept on the fortress walls of Antibes, we probably would never have seen the historic city and 16th century Fort Carré, let alone experience the intimacy of its early morning hours.

Finally clear of traffic and back on the highway east towards Italy, we blew past the spectacular setting of Monaco and Monte Carlo in an attempt to leave the crush of tourists behind. But that was impossible, we came to discover, as every Italian seaside ville was equally overrun by folks flocking to the shore. We finally found a motel room in St. Bartolome on the Ligurian coast, just a short hike from the classic medieval Italian walled village of Cervo, descending along a ridge to the sea. Cervo was beautiful despite huge crowds, and the Big Sur-like weather coupled with the spring green of the olive groves outside its walls made it worth the fight for a room. Not to mention the huge lunch devoured at one of the best sea food restaurants along the entire Ligurian coast. Italian families celebrating Easter, sitting for hours with babies and grandparents, eating plate after plate of marine delicacies with pounding surf just outside.

In order to get away from the crowds we figured the Alps was where they were not, the locals having had their fill of snow and high peaks after another long winter. So we drove through myriad tunnels along the coast to Genoa, where we turned north, hooking up with the same route as last year. The highway towards Milan was totally empty. And Milan itself must have been empty, for the normally foul air was crystal clear. So clear in fact that the distinctive shape of the Matterhorn could be seen rising above the foothills of the Alps to the northwest! That has to be a first, in the last half century anyway. Then through exquisite foothills of the Alps, bursting with soft spring foliage under deep blue skies with quick glimpses of the distant snowy ranges we were headed towards. All blissful until we hit a nasty traffic jam at the St. Goddard pass, caused by stop lights pulsing traffic through the ten mile long tunnel. The Mont Blanc tunnel is still closed after a fire inside of it killed some seventy people a year and a half ago, a reality my children are aware of and fear. After two nervous hours we were finally through the nightmare and speed down the northern slope of the range, toward Lucerne. After another endless tunnel around the shores of Lake Lucerne we'd had enough and stopped in a little non-descript village on the lake to search for a place to stay. Eureka! Beckenried! An ice-cold Hefe Weisse bier on the shores of gorgeous Lake Lucerne: peaks in all directions and an old paddle steamer flying a huge Swiss flag off its stern picks up passengers at the dock next to the hotel. Civilization! The next morning we're off up the Stanserhorn, first in a historic old tramway, then by modern gondola. Again, the weather is stellar, and the unobstructed views of a huge swath of the Alps impressive. The dark north face of the Eiger looms to the southwest amidst the Jungfrau cluster with not a cloud in the sky, just blinding snow pack.

The village of Engelberg sits in a valley far below, and with it memories of the summer of 1977. At eighteen years of age, with pal H. now dead by his own hand, we traveled there to hike the Alps. And hike we did, over passes, through meadows, camping under a simple tarp in the middle of nowhere, drinking wine at night and talking, talking, talking. If some figure had approached as we sat staring at the dying rays bronze the last snowfields, and told H. he would kill himself in exactly twenty-one and a half years, we would've laughed uproariously. Sweet bird of youth, flown. Atop the Stanserhorn a mixture of wonder and sadness, an old, old story, I know.

After snow fights with kids and climbing snow drifts still deep atop the summit, we descend back to our lakeside hotel and catch a meditative paddle steamer for a cruise to picturesque Lucerne, gazing at other cute villages under high peaks along the way, then return to our hotel's waterside restaurant for fresh fish and more ice-cold wheat beer. Suicide?

May '00: A day after returning to Frankfurt it's off to East Africa and further evidence of its rapid decline. The only white wandering the streets of Nairobi after a morning arrival, I pay a visit to the still grand edifice of the National Library (its entrance still graced by two reclining lion) while being harassed for money by a multitude of the impoverished. But the structure's surface belies the stark reality of the contemporary scene. More apropos, in the yard surrounding the main library for the entire country of Kenya, the grass grows wild amidst piles of burning trash. Inside, every table is packed with what must be university students, so intent in their studies you could hear a pin drop. But one look at the ratty collection of books filling the shelves makes one wonder what they could possibly be studying that has any relevance to their country's current predicament. After closer inspection, not one book was less than thirty years old, which made me look even closer for rare first editions, ratty or not. After discovering a mysterious stone staircase sweeping aesthetically up a back wall, I ascend it to find an even more decrepit reference room filled with classic colonial tales of life in once romantic East Africa. A portrait of a young Queen Elizabeth II, which once must have hung prominently in this room is now stashed in a musty corner, a roof leak buckling the once beautiful flooring under it. As I gaze at the fallen Queen, the muezzin in the central mosque next door starts up, its spires framed perfectly by a window open to the smoking fires in the library's yard. The sun is setting, so I head back to the safety of my hotel. Whites and Asians, I notice, do not leave the safety of their automobiles, even in daylight.

Flying to Dar es Salaam the next day, the top of Kilimanjaro with only scattered snow fields reveals the fact that a prolonged drought has severely hit this area of the planet. Of course the same thing is happening in Glacier National Park in Montana: glaciers retreating from positions consistent for over a hundred years. Then on the news later that night, a report on Lake Eyre in central Australia flooding to a depth of few feet for only the third time this century. The bird life this event has attracted brings seething life to a normally desolate environment. Flying out of Dar, Zanzibar a white-washed ville perched on a verdant isle just off the African mainland, the channel separating the chunks of Earth filled with Bahama-like turquoise sandbanks.

To escape the wilds of Nairobi, I hop a Cessna for a flight across the rugged Rift Valley dappled with fleecy cloud to the green glory of Masai Mara National Park on the Tanzanian border. There are several small tented camps with dirt air strips at which we drop off a passenger or two and pick a few up. Taking off from these strips and hopping to the next camp was worth the money paid for a two day safari in the bush, because it was the classic low-level flying one sees on film clips of Africa: Zebra, Eland, Cape Buffalo and Wildebeest by the thousands scatter as we skim overhead at two hundred feet, the pilot banking sharply to avoid this hill and that, giving the passengers even better views of the wealth of wildlife below. Upon arrival at the camp, we toss our bags in the five star tents and head out on a game drive. Just across the airstrip a herd of Elephant chomp on some bushes, a couple of babies staying close to their moms. In a river bed full of stagnant water, further evidence of the drought despite the green grass, three giraffe nibble at aesthetically elegant acacia, while upstream several hippo snort and yawn in a deeper pool.

Big Sky country, as I've said before, is what East Africa reminds me of. Wonderful escarpments, grasslands, unobstructed vistas, and myriad wildlife make it all a refreshing change from the increasingly troubled *Homo sapiens* settlement at Nairobi. In two days of safari I saw: Bat-Eared Fox, Cheetah, Leopard, Lion, Elephant, Hippo, Zebra, Eland, Topi, Wildebeest, Cape Buffalo, Thompson's Gazelle, Baboon, Bush Babies, Impala, Sacred Ibis, Egyptian Goose, Giraffe, Crocodile, Eagles, Hyena,

Jackals, Ostrich and fowl and vultures of endless variety. Everything except white and black Rhino. The second morning we went out at sunrise, past a huge herd of Elephant, and found a pride of Lion lounging over a Wildebeest kill. There were two males, four females and some ten cubs and adolescents. A male and one of the females were sleeping a short distance from the pride, apparently mating. As we watched the entire family group go about their daily routine, the lyrics from a popular song coursed through my brain, "You and me baby we're nothing but mammals so let's do it like they do on the Discovery Channel."

And speaking of wildlife, the day after returning to the anarchy of Nairobi from bucolic Masai Mara, it's off to the epicenter of genocide, Kigali. From 30,000' I ponder the disconnect of twenty-four hours earlier cruising around the very terrain passing below. I follow the Mara River to below the hillock where we saw at least five hundred Hippo in the river water bubbling with methane from their feces. Completely natural! On the way to Lake Victoria we pass over the gorgeous light green Oloololo Escarpment, seen yesterday morning on the drive out to the Hippo pools past a herd of twenty Elephants on the move in the Masai Mara.

The descent in over the banana plantations tended by orderly houses with red dirt roads clogged with people speaks normalcy in a land recently rocked by holocaust. The Kajera River winds peacefully through hills nearby, but six years ago it was clogged with bodies flowing toward Lake Victoria. Just before touchdown I spy the presidential palace where the plane carrying the presidents of Rwanda and Burundi crashed after being blown out of the sky by (?). The Hutus who were in control of the country claimed it was the rebel Tutsis from their camps in Uganda who shot down the plane. The Tutsis claimed it was hard-line Hutus in the president's own administration, who killed him for agreeing to allow moderate Hutus and Tutsis to join in a power sharing arrangement at peace talks in Arusha, Tanzania. What followed supports the latter argument, as Hutus went on a genocidal killing spree, killing Hutu moderates and all the Tutsis they could get their hands on. In one hundred days they killed one million people. As I stepped from the plane in Kigali I glanced at the tarmac and saw the unmistakable starburst patterns of mortar rounds every four to five feet.

Flying back to Nairobi, Mt. Meru and Kilimanjaro can both be seen from over Lake Victoria. How is that for clarity! Then, coming in over the Rift Valley once again, Mt. Suswa, an extinct volcano, intrigues me. Inside its cone is another smaller cone with what must be a magma plug inside of it forming a steep mesa; so steep in fact that it forms a moat of thick vegetation or forest around the mesa. What lurks in that deep, dark moat? It doesn't look like anyone has ever been in there, too steep! Too scary? Just before landing in Nairobi, we wing over the fractured contemporary scene: a herd of Wildebeest in Nairobi National Park crowd the fence line, the other side of which are various industrial parks interspersed with classic, circular Masai manyattas, their cattle nibbling on the drought-brown grass.

On the flight to Bujumbura I notice the only forested section on the southern end of Lake Victoria, are two national park islands, forming Rubondo National Park in Tanzania. But a quarter section of one of the islands is completely denuded, obviously lying just outside the park boundary. Otherwise the deforestation on the mainland is complete. How long can the national park hold out? Desperation is a powerful force. I don't know about Tanzania, but in Kenya desperation for land and food could spell the end of protected areas, as this report in the *East African Standard* described the situation 120 miles southeast of Nairobi:

Meanwhile, Administration Police officers and game wardens under siege from a group of squatters were forced to open fire, killing one person and injuring at least three others in a confrontation at Mikululo Ranch, Kibwezi, Makueni District, on Saturday. Two game wardens were shot with poisoned arrows and sustained serious injuries. They were flown to the Forces Memorial Hospital, Nairobi, in a Kenyan Wildlife Service plane. The skirmishes occurred when security personnel tried to evict about 900 squatters from KWS land.

This is the future. It's unavoidable. In Zimbabwe, President for life Mugabe is allowing squatters to seize white owned farms, so national parks elsewhere in the region cannot be too far behind.

Then the spiraling descent into poor Bujumbura, Burundi, perched wonderfully on the northern tip of spectacular Lake Tanganyka, but anxiously awaiting a repeat of Rwanda's genocide inside its own borders in an ongoing conflict that has already killed some 200,000 people. In order to control rebel Hutus from Congo fomenting dissent amongst the majority population, the minority Tutsi government places them in camps (concentration?) in order to *protect* them. All this just a stone's throw from the huge mountains of the laughably named Democratic Republic of Congo rising majestically from the opposite shore, hiding an ongoing world war amongst five nations (Angola, Zimbabwe, Rwanda, Uganda & Congo) taking place inside its borders. And for what? Mineral wealth!

As Agence France Press editorialized in Nairobi's *The Monitor* on May 13th: With violence erupting in Sierra Leone, Zimbabwe and the Democratic Republic of the Congo, Africa has entered the new century much as it ended the last one: at war, in extreme poverty and neglected by a world apparently unwilling to help remedy the continent's ills...For U.N. Secretary General Kofi Annan, Africa's post-colonial political leaders bear most of the blame for the relentless slaughter. 'The quality of the leaders, the misery they have brought to their people and my inability to work with them to turn the situation around are very depressing,' he told the BBC in a stinging attack in April."

Then, in stark contrast to Africa, the family drives to Holland for a long weekend. The civility, cleanliness and orderliness of the countryside is exquisite after the squalor of Nairobi. Walks through pleasant villages with small and large canals running through neighborhoods of modest houses with no curtains drawn in fear or paranoia is a refreshing reality indeed. A perfect mix of urban and rural lands of dark green grass covered with healthy cattle, goats and horses soothes the soul with its simplicity. Touring a working windmill exhilarating in its similarity with sailing: the massive sails circulating round at great speed with slots of wood that can be taken off in order to reef it when the wind is too strong! Amsterdam is wonderful too with its concentric canals lined by ancient townhouses, Rijksmuseum and Van Gogh Museum, but it's still a big city. The Dutch countryside is the place to be!

June '00: A Washington D.C. trip demands a visit to the Holocaust Museum, especially after exploring the Ann Frank house in Amsterdam last week. The building's concentration camp watch tower architecture and displays are powerful indeed, but what of the other other holocausts past and present? There is no Rwanda memorial, where the feverish pace of killing dwarfed even the Nazi's butchery, nor mention of poor Cambodia, to name two recent holocausts. A Holocaust Museum that excludes other holocausts, not to mention those ongoing, such as in southern Sudan, is a travesty.

Spain's patchwork quilt farms interspersed with ragged dry hills, much like the area along the Nebraska/Wyoming border. Granada off the left wing tip under Sierra Nevada still scattered with snow, and memories of the Alhambra seventeen years ago with N. after hitchhiking all the way down from Glasgow. Wow! Then Gibraltar with a cap of white cotton a la Table Mountain in Cape Town, before heading down the Moroccan coast and the hundreds, thousands of miles of deserted beach down Nouackchott and Dakar way. The countryside between Casablanca and Rabat more Europe than Africa, with tidy farms of gold and green. Rabat as wonderful as ever during an evening stroll down through the thronging medina to watch the sun sink in the Atlantic from a pier at the harbor mouth, its golden rays turning the ancient walls and minarets of this capital city a golden hue.

July '00: As if traveling the globe through work wasn't enough, a great summer of travel with the family on home leave follows. From the swamp of Washington D.C. in late June, to the coolness of Northern Michigan in early July, to the thick fog and sun of San Francisco later in the month, a whirlwind tour of the States is both invigorating and depressing. The natural beauty of the country the source of the former: its wide open spaces, even in congested urban areas, is refreshing after the concentration of humanity in Europe. In D.C., for example, I went for a run along the C&O Canal and saw several five-foot tall heron fishing in the canal, hundreds of turtles, a six foot long back snake crossing the towpath, a poisonous copperhead nestled in leaves beside a deer path awaiting its prey, and a bambi galloping down the towpath ahead of me. You would never see that variety of wildlife in Europe, because it simply doesn't exist.

Touching base with the wildness of the States is an important reason for returning, right up there with seeing family and friends. The birch and cedar forests carpeted with ferns and moss along the sand dune shores of Michigan's shining big sea water, coupled with flying into San Francisco over the Sierras and catching an unobstructed view of Half Dome, El Capitan, Vernal and Nevada Falls cascading white with runoff from the Little Yosemite Valley after crossing the Rockies and vast basin and range, reinforces that it's all still there and as wild as it's always been. Thank god for the North American West.

The depression sets in when the newspapers are read, the television watched, the radio listened to, the insularity of the world's sole remaining super power fully grasped: a spoiled nation consumed with business and competitive consumption and little else. As Calvin Coolidge said, "The business of America is business," but at the dawn of a new millennium it has become such an obsession that it crushes all in its path, including civility. As Garrison Keillor so brilliantly writes, "The Media wandered, lost in narcissism and fear of death and a slavish servility toward the rich and a knee-jerk contempt for leaders. If ever an era needed bucking up, it was this one—but academics had given up. You asked for a vision, they gave you dissenting opinions."

The once great *Washington Post* now a mediocrity, the *Detroit Free Press* and *San Francisco Chronicle/Examiner* failing to reach even that level, the grating local news in every market opening with the slaughter of the day, followed by perky sports and weather personalities, the endless blather and constant advertisements on radio when all you want to hear is some music, all reinforce Mr. Keillor's critique: "Talk radio was part of the tide of dreariness slopping across America. Franchise architecture, generic shopping malls, popular music as ugly and empty as it was possible to be." I never thought it would happen, but I started yearning for a return to Europe and its vibrant multiparty democracies after becoming nauseous watching the contrived orderliness of the Republican convention. For a second I thought I was in Singapore, where fascism with a smiling face drives the free market machine and dissent is not tolerated. Ultimately, not even wilderness is enough.

August '00: An article in *National Wildlife* magazine concludes that cities can create their own micro-climates, thus reinforcing my suggestion that doomsday scenarios of an environmental calamity in the future seem at present to be based on local phenomenon, with the Earth as a whole going through normal climate fluctuations (the global average temperature has risen six tenths of a degree Celsius over the past century). Using satellite images of urban and suburban sprawl, NASA researchers found that these areas are heat islands with longer growing seasons. The heat island of Atlanta, for example, where it is often 5 to 8 degrees F. hotter than the surrounding rural areas, suggests that the record setting heat days in American cities in the 1990's, which most of the global warming arguments are based upon, are localized. Not to say these islands of heat don't have an affect on the environment as a whole, for researchers say Atlanta creates its own low pressure system that produces storms. The perspective I've acquired from crisscrossing the globe so frequently is that the areas of human concentration on the planet are so small, relatively speaking, that their global affect cannot be planet threatening, not yet anyway.

Then, as a counter to my argument in the same article, an Israeli scientist says that air pollution prevents rainfall. He found that tiny airborne pollution particles can prevent water in clouds from developing into raindrops or snowflakes. "Human activity may be altering clouds and natural precipitation on a global scale." And I do recall monsoon clouds in Bangkok coming in black and menacing, but never unleashing the expected torrent.

The debate continues in the July *Atlantic*, with an article by Daniel Sarewitz and Roger Pelke Jr. One paragraph in particular captures the current state of the planet beautifully: "…human beings have been changing the surface of the earth for millennia. Scientists increasingly realize that deforestation, agriculture, irrigation, urbanization, and other human activities can lead to major changes in climate on a regional or perhaps even a global scale. Thomas Stohlgren, of the U.S. Geological Survey, has written, 'The effects of land use practices on regional climate may overshadow larger-scale temperature changes commonly associated with observed increases in carbon dioxide. The idea that climate may constantly be changing for a variety of reasons does not itself undercut the possibility that anthropogenic carbon dioxide could seriously affect the global climate, but it does confound scientific efforts to predict the consequences of carbon dioxide emissions.'"

This argument makes such sense because it points to a number of reasons why global warming is occurring, while at the same time leaving the carbon dioxide question open for further study: for wild temperature fluctuations occurred on this planet long before the industrial revolution came along, to say nothing of one large meteor wiping out the dinosaurs: an all natural extinction!

As if to drive the point home over the summer of 2000, *Harper's* had an equally enlightening article on the state of fresh water at the dawn of the new century. Jacques Leslie states in *Running Dry*: "In the developing world the crisis has already arrived. As many as 1.2 billion people—one out of five on the globe—lack access to clean drinking water. Nearly 3 billion live without sanitation: no underground sewage, toilets or even latrines More than 5 million people a year die of easily preventable waterborne diseases such as diarrhea, dysentery, and cholera; in fact, most disease in the developing world is water related. As Peter Gleick writes in *The World's Water 1998-1999*, "For nearly three billion people, access to a sanitation system comparable to that of ancient Rome would be a significant improvement in their quality of life. And as if making a direct link with the *Atlantic* article's mention of irrigation as a prime concern, Leslie quotes Sandra Postel on her survey of the global water crisis, *Pillar of Sand: Can The Irrigation Miracle Last?* "The overriding lesson from history is that most irrigation-based civilizations fail. As we enter the third millennium A.D., the question is: Will ours be any different." So it looks like increasing heat from a variety of sources (not just carbon dioxide emissions) and a lack of fresh water will bring on the Four Horsemen of the Apocalypse (The West Nile virus in New York city a foreshadowing?)!

And on the geopolitical water front the prescient words of World Bank vice president Ismail Serageldin, spoken in 1995, have to be remembered, "The wars of the next century will be over water."

September '00: Then the media grows frantic over a report from tourists visiting the North Pole that they saw open water from a Russian ice breaker. Scientists typically take various positions, some seeing it as further evidence of the world's overheating while others say open water occurs at the pole every summer, only in the past there were no tourists to see and hype the fact.

Transiting Cairo, my Lufthansa plane parks next to the Gulf Air flight to Bahrain that crashed exactly one week before on its approach to Manama. My courier colleague was killed along with 142 passengers and crew. I meditate while on the tarmac that he last touched earth here, breathed and smelled the hot air off the desert, and watched the planes taxiing to and from their positions while chatting with his escort. On board he probably was thinking of dinner with his wife of two months and the fact that he'd been fortunate to land one of the greatest jobs in the world. His tragedy certainly makes the rest of us think about the dangers of our profession, and how it could happen to any of us at any time.

Lifting off, Giza lost in thick pollution, but Saqqara, Dahshur, Maidum and Seila downriver on the green edge of the fecund Nile valley are stunning as pyramid time capsules. Five thousand years now? Yawn, another millennium. Then we leave the narrow fertile strip lining the banks where *Homo sapiens* are able to survive surrounded by desert and head out over the vast desolate expanse of which so much of the Earth is composed.

Over Lake Tana on a turbulent twilight descent into Addis, a glance back to the northwest reveals a cluster of mushroom thunderheads with lightning exploding in their stems set against a burnt orange sky with Venus burning brightly above.

A week later in Madrid, on a warm twilit night, the sharp juxtaposition of the 4th century B.C. Egyptian Templo Debod on its hilltop with the Palacio Real next door: remnants of two great empires now expired, with bright Venus hanging in the western gloaming as an exclamation point to the transient nature of all. Heironymous Bosch's "Death's Victory" perused in the Prado earlier in the afternoon captures that bleak reality faced by both individuals and nations.

The Pergamon Altar in the eponymous museum in Berlin is perhaps the most stunning museum presentation in the world. The Roman, Lucius Ampelius, described it best when it was in situ on the west coast of Turkey after 170 B.C.: "In Pergamon there is a great marble altar 40 feet high, with remarkable statues—- the entirety is surrounded by a battle of giants." To say nothing of the Telephos frieze within, Telephos being the legendary founder of the city of Pergamon. Then in another part of the museum is the monstrous remnants of Babylon, the spectacular Ishtar gate and Processional Way from the 6th century B.C., with its blue glazed facade of countless lions towering above the visitor. All this inside huge halls, a slice of ancient history stashed in a museum in central Europe.

On the return from Berlin the crumbling towers of the Ruin Brandenburg nestled in the forested Thuringian hills are wonderfully juxtaposed by ugly East German cement guard towers keeping an anachronistic watch across the border between East and West.

October '00: Then, with a snap of the fingers, you and the family are in a rent-a-car driving the narrow roads of verdant Ireland, leaving Shannon toward the cliffs of Moher. With Bed and Breakfast signs littering the roadsides you know finding a place to stay for the evening won't be difficult, so after a stunning hike with views of the cliffs in sun, a short drive up along the Burren coast with its striated carboniferous mountains leads us to a cute place with a view of the sea and alien landscape. The next morning, a pilgrimage to a megalithic dolmen crafted by ancient minds on a windswept plateau, before a descent into more fecund lands graced by lakes and monasteries with narrow towers for the protection of Book of Kells-like manuscripts from marauding Vikings. This followed by a scholarly pilgrimage to the poet Yeats' tower rising from a chattering river into fleecy clouds ahead of an approaching storm, a descendant of that monastical literary heritage. I never realized the widening gyre image was taken from the spiral stairs winding up the tower to its crenelated rooftop. And what a view from that tower: the Burren glimpsed off to the west with green rounded hills framing the east, and rushing river below with autumnal colors in the forest around its base filling out picture perfection. This followed by a fairly uninteresting yet challenging drive along the narrow lanes up to Sligo, the only point of interest being the extensive megalithic burial site of Carrowmore crowning a low hill under the more lofty table mountain holding the tumulus of Queen Maeve. Then a continuation of the literary tour as we "cast a cold eye on life and death, horseman pass by," at Yeats' grave under massive Ben Bulben in the pouring rain. Just as we arrived to pay homage, a tour bus pulled up and dispensed some fifty tourists, thus ruining the ambience of our visit: cast a cold eye on tourists, tour buses pass by!

Then a hike up stunning Mt. Erigal in Donegal after slogging across bog at its base that would never end. The view from the summit of the coast and dunes and islands dotted with little white cottages contrasted by bleak surrounding mountains with lakes nestled in their folds magic before a squall line blasts us off the top. Then N.'s brother's wedding in the North of Ireland with a band from the south. The Protestant guests going wild when they break into Irish jigs! How is that for diplomacy!

Lifting off from old Zagreb into clarity over the alps never glimpsed before: from the Julian Alps, Klagenfurt and the glacial silt colored Drava River in the southeast corner of the range to Berchtesgaden and the Salzkammergut in the north, looking west I could see all the way to Mt. Blanc, with the Grand Combin, Jungfrau, Dolomiti, Gross Glockner, Kitzbuhlerhorn, Zugsptize and Wilder Kaiser all laid out beneath my port hole. Musing after this visual feast that since the stateside summer I have visited more foreign lands than most do in a lifetime: Zurich, Rabat, Budapest, Addis, Djibouti, Vienna, Washington, Madrid, Paris, Berlin, Ireland and Zagreb.

November '00: Coral reefs are also under threat. Whether it's rising sea temperatures or fishermen in Indonesia and the Philippines using cyanide and dynamite to kill fish on the reefs, nature on the planet is certainly under threat in a way it has never been before. Like the previous analysis of global warming, *Newsweek* writes "Incomplete scientific data and the fuzzy nature of climate models provide easy ammunition for skeptics, but many scientists are convinced that the crisis is real. 'It's all too easy to get lost in a maelstrom of ambiguity,' says University of California, Northridge, marine biologist Peter Edmunds. 'We need a strong statement to motivate politicians to do something about global warming.'" If politicians won't, then nature will! A fresh outbreak of the Ebola virus in Uganda has infected some two hundred people and killed at least eighty with no end of the plague in sight. Is this mother nature fighting off the human onslaught? As Thomas Homer-Dixon states, "But nature is coming back with a vengeance, tied to resource scarcity and population growth."

On the flight to Tashkent the classic movie "Network" is shown. With the 2000 presidential elections still undecided and the media's bizarre behavior always part of the mix, Peter Finch's ravings seem all the more rational: the "I'm as mad as hell and I'm not going to take it anymore," and "democracy is a dying giant" speeches seem like they should be replayed nightly in America to give citizens an honest critique of the corporate controlled culture we inhabit. Which reminded me of a scene I absorbed over the summer in the heart of the media empire. An image of the American Death Machine (as Henry Miller famously called it) on a short visit to New York: after arriving from upriver on the Hudson line I grabbed a coffee and headed for the mezzanine above the floor of Grand Central Station, both to admire the gorgeous architecture and observe the frantic daily pace of *Homo sapiens* arriving for work. Amidst the hectic movement across the floor below I spotted a shuffling figure, barely managing to progress through the maelstrom. But he did, and as he neared the grand staircase up to street level I could see clearly he was an elderly gentleman of means (at least eighty), dressed in a three piece suit. The stairs gave him problems however, each step a chore as people whizzed past. Habit keeps most of us lashed to the wheel, but this fellow, despite the admirable quality of wanting to work at such an advanced age, physically couldn't pull it off anymore. He should be somewhere meditative, admiring the wonder of life rather than flirting with death in the very rut which was his life here on earth. Then again, the machine demands allegiance.

Then out to Uzbekistan, that holiday destination at the top of everyone's list. With several days to fill I hop a scary flight out to one of the three major Silk Road cites, Bukhara (Samarkand and Khiva the others), on a lovely Yak 40, flying in true communist style. Bukhara reached its zenith some one thousand years after Christ, with a population of

300,000, 250 madrasas, a multitude of caravanserai, a library holding 45,000 titles, and a Samanid empire covering present day Uzbekistan and Tajikistan and large portions of Afghanistan and Iran. When Genghis Khan rode into town with his thundering horde, he reportedly entered the Kalyan mosque, brushed the Koran from its wood holder onto the ground and cried out, "The hay is cut, give your horses fodder," which his troops interpreted to mean slaughter all and raze the city, which they promptly accomplished. This left only the Kalyan minaret, built in 1127 to a height of 47m sitting on a ten meter foundation, still standing with its 14 bands of kufic calligraphy and at least as many bands of intriguing brickwork gracing its slender majesty. The reason it still stands is because Genghis himself was impressed, gazing upon it with 'a finger to his mouth in a curious token of amazement.' In retrospect it is obvious that he was thinking of the good use he could put it to, mainly throwing people off of it, which he and later rulers did for centuries, earning for this beacon of the Kizyl-Kum the moniker, "death tower." The tallest structure in the world when it was built, the Kalyan tower with its turquoise necklace of glazed brick gives the visitor the greatest perspective of this ancient crossroads of the Silk Route, particularly of the famous ensemble it rises from: The Kalyan mosque (built in the 12 century but destroyed by the Mongols, then rebuilt 1514-15) and the Mir-i-Arab (1535) madrasa.

The Kalyan mosque is huge, its size on the same monstrous scale as the Bibi Khanym in Samarkand, visited a year ago or so. The Mir-i-Arab across the courtyard was one of only two working madrasas in the entire Soviet Union to remain open. It is still open, and some 120-130 students study Islamic law and literature and Arabic, and it is because of this that it cannot be visited. From the top of the minaret the blue dome towers of this ensemble below, coupled with the broad mosaic facades of other mosques and madrasas rising from the mud streets and adobe houses across this ancient oasis town, can take you back eight hundred years easily. Off in the northwest corner of town, and not far from this group of religious monuments, lies the Ark, a 2,000 year old fortress that is having its walls reconstructed after too many years of neglect and erosion. Who first built on this spot isn't known, but the Arabs first destroyed it in the eighth century, the Samanids rebuilt in the 10th, Genghis and company destroyed it in the 13th, the Sheibanids rebuilt it in the 16th when it became a city within a city for the emirs that came and went. The Bolsheviks finally destroyed it in 1920 in their successful attempt to drive the last emir, Alim Khan, from its protection. It is most infamous in the west for its jail, the Zindan, also known as the bug pit, just outside its towering walls.

In 1839 a Lieutenant-Colonel arrived in Bukhara on a mission to make the Emir Nasrullah an ally of the British and not the Russians (an early chess move that would evolve into the Great Game). But things went wrong from the start: Charles Stoddart rode into the Ark when only the Emir is allowed to do so, he walked toward Nasrullah when he should have crawled, then presented a letter not from the Queen, but from the Governor General of India. Incensed by all of this, the Emir tossed him into the Bug Pit, a six meter deep brick well crawling with rats, scorpions, cockroaches and ticks. Stoddart was in the depths for six months, facing execution if he did not convert to Islam. Guess what? He converted! receiving clean clothes, housing, and freedom to wander the labyrinthian streets, not to mention circumcision.

A few years later a colleague, a Captain Arthur Conolly of the Bengal light Infantry, came to rescue Stoddart. Unfortunately for them both the East India Company had just been defeated in Afghanistan. Nasrullah got word of this sign of British mortality and promptly sent both the Brits to the Bug Pit. The Emir then offered Conolly mercy if he converted to Islam, but seeing that his colleague was no better off for having done so, refused. They were both executed in the large square in front of the Ark's magnificent gatehouse, and apparently buried near by. The days of empire indeed!

Old Bukhara on the whole is a rather washed out brown color, but the great multicolored facades of the myriad mosques and madrasas, their robin egg blue domes, the ceilings of neighborhood mosques hidden along muddy lanes, the intricately carved wooden columns holding up those roofs and the traditional interior painting of vased flowers and alabaster molds of Islamic reliefs, reveal an artistry of the highest order amidst the bleak Kizyl-Kum desert.

My personal favorite is also the oldest structure in Central Asia, dating from 907 A.D.: the Ismail Samani Mausoleum. What makes this mausoleum unique, despite the fact that three generations of Samani's were buried there over a thousand years ago, is that it is composed of pre-Islamic brick techniques, pushing creativity of that most utilitarian of building materials to outrageous extremes. Built from clay bricks made of egg yolks and camel milk, they are arranged in a basket weave of varying textures at different squares of the structure. The mausoleum rises from an ancient soil level depression in Samani Park, while off in the distance are the crumbling remains of the 13 km. fortress wall that has encircled the oasis town since the 9th century, having been continuously rebuilt after all the many invasions. Eleven meters high and made of adobe blocks, there is not much left, but from the Samanid Park you can see the last of one of the eleven massive gates still standing. So, in one meditative glance you can transport yourself back a thousand years, back to when one of the few centers of world civilization was in the middle of the Central Asian desert.

From an ancient capital of civilization to a more contemporary one the next week: Wien. A weekend there brings visits to exhibitions and museums of some of the greatest artists and thinkers to walk the planet, Klimt and his wild women at the always majestic Schloss Belvedere, a variety of Picasso's sketches and paintings at the utilitarian Kunst Forum across from the Palais Freyung, and a visit to the Freud museum, housed in his office used before fleeing the Nazi advance to London. These cultural meditations taken in between lengthy visits to the great cafes of Vienna, the Ottoman arches of Cafe Central being a favorite, not to mention the Christmas markets picturesquely scattered around the imperial city.

"Our real illiteracy is our inability to create. To paint is a religious activity." Thus began a revelatory visit to Hundertwasser Haus and Kunst Haus Wien buried in the back streets of uninspiring apartment architecture down along the Danube Canal. Which was just the point of Hundertwasser's artistic and architectural philosophy: "Kunst Haus Wien would be a bastion against the dictatorship of the straight line, the ruler and the T-square, a bridgehead against the grid system and the chaos of the absurd." The dictatorship of the straight line is nowhere in sight in either structure, even the gallery floors exhibiting the wild hallucinogenic colors of Hundertwasser's paintings in Kunst Haus Wien are uneven: "The flat floor is an invention of the architects. It fits engines—not human beings. If modern man is forced to walk on flat asphalt and concrete floors as they were planned thoughtlessly in designer's offices, estranged from man's age-old relationship and contact to earth, a crucial part of man withers and dies. This has catastrophic consequences for the soul, the equilibrium, the well-being and the health of man. Man forgets how to experience things and becomes emotionally ill. An uneven and animated floor is the recovery of man's mental equilibrium, of the dignity of man which has been violated in our leveling, unnatural and hostile urban grid system." To say nothing of the outside of the buildings, with their refreshing askew checkerboard window designs and whimsical trees growing out of niches. "The tree tenant symbolizes a turn in human history because he regains his rank as an important partner of man. The relationship man-tree must again take on religious dimensions. We are suffocating in our cities from poison and lack of oxygen. We systematically destroy the vegetation which gives us life and lets us breathe. We walk alongside grey and sterile facades of houses. It is our duty to reinstate the rights of nature by all means." With Hundertwasser, not only does Vienna contain some of histories past greats, but also some of the world's contemporary visionaries.

Over Belgrade and the confluence of the Sava and Danube, a glance to the west captures a sunset-orange slip of Adriatic framing peaks of the rugged Balkans: earthly magic amidst the mundane.

Mad cow disease, having started in Britain is now sweeping Europe. Panic covers the front pages of all German language papers. This disease is a direct result of free market capitalism standing the natural order on its head. By feeding herbivores chopped up meat in order to squeeze more profit from them, then saving even more by not heating the meal to the prescribed temperatures, the perpetrators have unleashed another plague upon the planet. The British halted this meat meal composed of scrapie infected sheep being fed to its animals in 1988, but allowed companies to continue exporting it abroad. The direct consequence of this short-sighted policy is now among us. Humanity's tampering with the natural order is all it takes to bring on the four horseman of the apocalypse, and it seems several of the horses are just outside the gates. Will genetically modified foods be next?

Bleak, snowy, Minsk, Belarus. Seven Tupolev 154's out of commission parked end to end along one taxiway to impress a conference of the Commonwealth of Independent States' dignitaries on their arrival to this last bastion of communist dictatorship in Europe. President Lukeshenko is such a loser my kids have a school food drive in Frankfurt to take care of his people.

Flying into Vienna on a dark November evening: Ramadan moon with Venus perched off its lower sickle hangs over Schönbrunn Palace in dazzling Christmas lights with a huge decorated tree in its courtyard, the Glorietta aglow atop its hilltop home.

December '00: A room with a view of misty Lac Leman in Geneva above which Mt. Blanc and the serrated ridge above Chamonix are bathed in gold by the setting sun.

Then a trip to Ankara and a pilgrimage to Ataturk's massive memorial on a hilltop overlooking the city surrounded by shanty towns. As Robert

Kaplan perceptively writes: "A gigantic Hellenistic temple, the great tomb is architecturally pagan, with sculptured torches on the walls, wolf tracks carved into the floor, and relief etchings of soldiers embracing mother goddesses. It is a ferocious place. As I walked around this temple precinct, guarded by white-helmeted troops, I felt had Adolf Hitler died a natural death, this is the type of tomb he would have had." The pagan motif is so strong because it was the revolutionary Ataturk who set Turkey on the path to secularism and away from the Islamic courts that had run the country for centuries. The greatest example of Ataturk's secular philosophy undermining the ancient faith of the country is in one the largest mosques in the world, Kocatepe. In the mosque itself prayer services are ongoing in a massive great hall, but underneath this sacred place is one of the most modern shopping malls in Ankara, on multi-levels. Not even in America have I seen such a crass combination of faith and commercialism.

But to get to the heart of Anatolia, one must visit the Museum of Ancient Anatolian Civilizations, housed in a fifteenth century Byzantine bazaar on the flanks of the highest mountain in town, crowned by a Roman citadel. The oldest surviving paintings known hang there. They're from the settlement of Catal Hayuk to the south and picture the village underneath a spouting volcano, leopards and other wildlife, including vultures in flight, symbolizing the way in which flesh of the dead was removed before burial underneath the floors of their adobe apartments. They are all nine thousand years old. The first city plan in history! More recent history can be found scattered around the bleak architecture of Ankara: Julian's column from 360 A.D., Roman Baths from around the same time, as well as the Temple of Augustus, intriguingly attached to one of the city's oldest mosques, Hacibayram, its dervish namesake entombed in a special shrine visited by thousands daily.

Then yet another departure with the family for a week of skiing in the Austrian Alps. Frankfurt is so dreary in the winter, but just five hours away by car is one of the prettiest landscapes in Europe. The gondola ride up to Steinplatte, in Waidring, through towering snow-encrusted pines and over granite boulders peeking from fresh powder, to the endless views of a good portion of the eastern Alps, with Austria's highest, the Gross Glockner, and the gnarly beauty of the Wilder Kaiser dominating the scene from the terminus at 1800m, is medicinal! The fresh air and sun and snow make for an exhausting yet revitalizing week in the land of quaint onion-domed churches rising from small villages gracing quiet white valleys.

January '01: Honor the new millennium with a viewing with the kids of 2001: A Space Odyssey. H.A.L. the 9000 series computer is as relevant as ever as the world becomes more wired and therefore more precarious. As California's recent energy crisis has revealed, all the cutting edge technology in the world is only plastic, metal and silicon without the juice to power it. The kids are confused by the hallucinative ending, but seem to understand the cyclical death and rebirth of the astronaut (and therefore us all) at the end.

Then off to Nairobi on an MD-11 cargo plane with friendly pilots who invite me into the cockpit for takeoff and landing. The huge side windows up front make for excellent viewing from the jumpseat. Taking off from Frankfurt with a monster load in the double-decker bays always amazes me: modern flight is a magical thing indeed. The Big Dipper out the window bright in the abyss, coupled with Saturn and Jupiter still making the rounds, takes the mind back to H.A.L. and the monolith that sparked the chimps to pick up water buffalo bones and use them as weapons to control the waterhole. The vast mysteries of existence are written in the sky nightly, but most never bother to raise their eyes, let alone turn off the tube.

I read in the January 1, 2001 Newsweek magazine a fine analysis of the troubled U.S. election from a mysterious overseas source: "Imagine that we read of an extremely close election in the Third World in which the self-declared winner was the son of the former prime minister, a former spymaster seeking revenge and still highly active behind the scenes. Imagine that the lightly experienced son lost the popular vote by nearly a half a million votes but won based on some old colonial holdover (the Electoral College) from the nation's pre-democracy past. Imagine that the victory turned on disputed votes cast in a province governed by his brother.

"Imagine that the poorly drafted ballots of one district led thousands of voters to vote for the wrong candidate. Imagine that the members of that nation's most despised caste turned out in record numbers to vote against the son, who had executed more of them than had any other provincial official. Imagine that some members of that most despised caste were intercepted on the way to the polls at roadblocks...Imagine that certain votes cannot be counted in this province unless the candidate requesting the count can somehow prove beforehand that he would win if the votes were recounted.

This e-mail made the rounds before 'the son of the prime minister' was installed by the country's highest court, which stopped the vote counting on a pretext involving the calendar and vague warnings of a 'cloud' hanging over the son. We can also imagine the response of the U.S. government to such an election abroad: 'grave concern and threats to cut off aid.'" Laurent Kabila, the rebel leader who wrested control of Zaire from the three decade long dictatorial rule of Mobutu Sese Seku in 1998, was recently assassinated in Kinshasa by one of his guards. The inner circle of Kabila's government chose his son to succeed him as president of the Democratic Republic of Congo. The Supreme Court of the United States selected George W. Bush in the very same way. India is now the world's greatest democracy!

Paleoanthropologists in Kenya have just reported they have found hominid remains dated to six million years before the present, some 2.5 million years earlier than good old Lucy's torso from Ethiopia. His jaw is surprisingly similar to that of *Homo sapiens*, which only deepens the mystery. "We are the miracles that God made To taste the bitter fruit of Time," Ben Okri wrote. These lines mulled as I stare out the window at

Lake Turkana in the desperately dry region of Northern Kenya, then down at my black shirt, on which has fallen the grayest of hairs.

The famous archaeological site of Koobi Forsa where Richard Leakey unearthed the 1.8 million year old *Homo habilis* skull is on the distant shore of the lake dotted with three desolate isles, with Mt. Kenya seen clearly off to the south, its pinnacle summit poking through thick cloud. Then Kilimanjaro and its rounded bulk can be seen past Mt. Kenya, the volcanic line to the east of the Rift Valley clearly defined. Descending over the Rift, Lake Nakuru with its ring of pink Flamingos a stunning blend of geography and wildlife, followed by Lake Naivasha bordered by plant nurseries and on over Longonot Volcano, striking with its crinkled lava flows cascading from one of the most classically shaped cones I think I've ever seen (with a smaller cone aesthetically rising from the flanks of the larger one!). As with the more enigmatic Suswa Volcano to the south, the crater floor is forested and looks completely untouched.

When the weekend rolls around it's off to the magical island of the Al Busaid Sultans of Oman, Zanzibar. When I board the flight in Nairobi my ticket is for Zanzibar and my baggage is tagged for Zanzibar, but we don't land in Zanzibar; on the pilots' whim we go to Dar es Salaam. What should have been an hour journey ends up taking fifteen, but that's Africa at the dawn of the new millennium. When I finally arrive I head up to a rooftop restaurant for breakfast. The expansive view over the old Arab settlement of Stonetown to the many forested islands and shimmering white sandbanks in the turquoise water, makes the hassle worth it.

It's amazing to think it was the United States that first opened diplomatic relations with Zanzibar in 1837 with a consulate, and signed the first commercial treaty with the Sultanate in 1833! The first Zanzibar embassy was sent to New York in 1840. But the Arabs from Oman had already been reaping the rich East Africa trade from this strategic spot for almost two hundred years, after throwing the Portuguese out of their old stone fort on the harbor. Slaves, gold, spices, ebony and ivory came through Zanzibar on its way to the Arab and Indian worlds via those classic schooners of the Indian ocean, the Dhow, which still quietly ply the clean, warm waters around the island.

The ragged, deteriorating Third World city of Stonetown, with its narrow market streets, exquisitely carved wooden doors and reverberations of muezzin calling the faithful to prayer, is really an Arab medina and reminiscent of the souks of Rabat and even Bukhara. The waterfront is especially picturesque with the aforementioned Portuguese turreted fort from the late 1600s, next to the government Beit al Ajaib (House of Wonders), a huge multi-leveled columned structure with wrap around porches of immense size and fantastic views, which sits next to the Beit al Sahel palace. This Palace by the Shore, as it was called, was built by Seyyid Said bin Sultan, ruler of Zanzibar and Oman (1806-1856) during his first visit to Zanzibar in 1828. The British with their mighty fleet took the island in 1890, crushed a rebellion in 1896 by one of the sultans in the shortest war in history, taking 45 minutes of bombardment, and had their puppet sultans run the lucrative trade until the Zanzibar revolution of 1963, which brought the sultanate role in the island's history to an end.

The natural beauty is really what attracts most visitors, as the squalor of the island's villages is really no different from that found in the rest of Africa. I went for a journey to Kizimkazi along the southern coast to swim with dolphin in gorgeous water crashing onto bone white sand under rock cliffs topped with palms swaying in warm breezes. Quite a change from dreary Frankfurt in winter, but that's what this job is all about.

Interpol says the smuggling of wild animal parts for use as medicine, their fur, as well as horn for dagger handles worldwide, now rates second behind narcotics and ahead of gun running and gold smuggling.

Kenya's landscape, including the normally parched Rift Valley, is as green as Ireland, except for blood-red soil showing through. Rivers are overflowing to such an extent that several drownings in the Nairobi area have occurred since last night. But that doesn't stop the poor from begging in the streets of Nairobi, many missing limbs drag themselves through the muck to beg from passing cars: saints in slime! as Jack London would say.

But in its cold indifference, the universe can still be quite spectacular, as the lunar eclipse the night of my departure from Nairobi revealed. The one hundred percent coverage of the moon by Earth's shadow in Kenya colored the moon a deep orange due to the sun's rays being bent around and through our planet's atmosphere. Beautiful void!

Then off to Addis where they have finally exhumed Haile Selasie's body from the latrine into which he was unceremoniously dumped twenty six years ago. Two months earlier there was a ceremony reinterring his remains in a sarcophagus matching his queen's in Trinity Cathedral. Their throne chairs sit nearby, and when I made my pilgrimage a group of white robed mystics chanted eerily nearby, celebrating the three thousand years of Solomonic rule he represented?

Down to Djibouti again, when over the Hadar region of Ethiopia where Lucy was exhumed and rivers of lava run black through salt pans and cracked earth, memories of Thomas Carlyle's "Everlasting No" chapter of *Sartor Resartus* (1834) came to mind:

"To me the universe was all void of life, of Purpose, of Volition, even of Hostility: it was one huge, dead, immeasurable Steam-engine, rolling on in its dead indifference, to grind me limb from limb. O, the vast, gloomy, solitary Golgotha, and Mill of Death!" (198-205)

February '01: In order to battle the "immeasurable Steam-engine, rolling on in its dead indifference," I head to Victoria Falls, Zimbabwe rather than stay in the confines of Pretoria for a weekend. Flying in over the scrub-green Kalahari, the only hint that something unusual moves through the unspectacular land is a massive line of mist wafting heavenward in the distance. Unless directly overhead the narrow gorge the Zambezi plummets into is too narrow to see even from altitude, so after I dump my belongings in the hotel and begin to hike a stone's throw from the falls, I have felt its mighty rumble, but have yet to catch a glimpse of it.

The view from Livingstone's statue (humorously claiming that he discovered the falls in 1855) over the Devil's Cataract and down the length of the chasm formed by the incessant pounding of a river that drains a huge portion of south-central Africa, is overwhelming; also refreshing, as the mist unleashed by the turbulent crash of such volume sweeps back and forth whimsically with the breeze to either drench or sprinkle one. When I strolled through the rainforest ecosystem created by the mist on the Zimbabwean end of the 1676m long chasm, a thunderhead moved in overhead, and though it never started raining (the mist being enough anyway), the lightning strikes slashing through cloud billowing skyward followed by thunder booming in symphony with the constant rumble of falling water, created a dynamic ambiance I'll never forget. Then hiking to Devil's Point where the Zambezi regroups to cut a path through 110m high cliffs under the famous railroad bridge where passengers can view a small part of the falls from mid-span, I sit for an hour and meditate on how the vapor rises to form the very cloud passing overhead, which in turn creates lightning. Water *is* an animal! The falls' African name is Mosi-oa-tunya—"the smoke that thunders," a similar name given to the second most massive fall in Africa, Tis Abay Falls in Ethiopia, which I visited on the way to the magical stone churches of Lalibela over two years ago. From the birthplace of the Blue Nile to the Zambezi, heart of Africa.

On a river cruise above the falls that evening we float past elephant, water buffalo, hippo and crocodiles resting on sand banks: with distant plunge shaking the ecosystem, its haze perpetually rising. Then the next day it's an early departure for a raft trip down the Zambezi below the falls, where it is pinched between 220m high grand canyon-like multicolored cliffs graced with cactus trees. Being forced through narrows by the Zambia and Zimbabwe sides of the canyon angers the river, and the resultant class five rapids we plow through and almost flip in turn out to be the hairiest whitewater I've ever rafted. You have to watch it when you fall from the raft into the maelstrom, as I did: there are crocodiles along the riverbank just waiting to help. The jet black metamorphic rock aesthetically topped with sporadic tufts of green grass along the shore add to the primal feel of the gorge's depths.

In *The Frankfurter Allgemeine Zeitung* (2/13/2001) an interview with German astronaut Ulf Merbold on what it's like to gaze on Earth from on high: "The sphere of the earth is enchantingly beautiful, the stars shine out of a pitch-black heaven. Below, the sky is bright, because the air disperses the light. In space, even the sun shines onto the day-side of the earth from an unbelievably dark, black heaven. That's the most extreme contrast I've ever seen in my life." Imagine if we saw the sun in that "dark, black heaven" during the day, without the sugar coated blue diffusion of light. Seeing our sun as just another star burning in the abyss would shift our consciousness, or would it?

Two weeks to the afternoon after rafting the primal flow of the Zambezi, I am skiing down the glacial Vallée Blanche behind Mt. Blanc in Chamonix, dodging crevasses instead of crocodiles. A dark blue dome over sharp-toothed ridges carved by Glacier du Géant brought back memories of Henry Adams' existential dilemma in the *Education* early last century: "For the first time in his life, Mt. Blanc for a moment looked to him what it was—a chaos of anarchic and purposeless forces—and he needed days of repose to see it clothe itself again with the illusions of his senses, the white purity of its snows, the splendor of its light, and the infinity of its heavenly peace. Nature was kind, Lake Geneva was beautiful beyond itself, the Alps put on charms real as terrors; but man became chaotic, and before the illusions of nature were wholly restored, the illusions of Europe suddenly vanished, leaving a new world to learn. On July 4, all Europe had been at peace; on July 14, Europe was in full chaos of war" (289).

The following Sunday afternoon, three weeks from the anarchic roar of Victoria Falls, a stroll with N. through the detritus of ancient Rome's Forum serves to drive Adams' perspective home: marble pillars toppled by time and invasions tell the ongoing story of the world. What of our own concerns and cities will remain in two thousand years?

www.ingramcontent.com/pod-product-compliance
Lightning Source LLC
Chambersburg PA
CBHW061342280526
45784CB00001B/105